To Teach Well

To Teach Well
An Early Childhood Practicum Guide

Kathryn Williams Browne
Skyline College

Ann Miles Gordon
Consultant

Merrill
is an imprint of

Upper Saddle River, New Jersey
Columbus, Ohio

Library of Congress Cataloging-in-Publication Data
Browne, Kathryn Williams.
  To teach well : an early childhood practicum guide / Kathryn Williams
Browne, Ann Miles Gordon.—1st ed.
    p. cm.
  Includes bibliographical references and index.
  ISBN-13: 978-0-13-199502-4 (pbk.)
  ISBN-10: 0-13-199502-2 (pbk.)
    1. Early childhood teachers—Training of.   2. Student teaching.   I. Gordon,
Ann Miles. II.   Title.

  LB1775.6.B76 2009
  371.1—dc22

                                          2008015702

Vice President and Executive Publisher: Jeffery W. Johnston
Acquisitions Editor: Julie Peters
Editorial Assistant: Tiffany Bitzel
Senior Managing Editor: Pamela D. Bennett
Senior Project Manager: Linda Hillis Bayma
Production Coordinator: Carol Singer, GGS Book Services PMG
Design Coordinator: Diane C. Lorenzo
Photo Coordinator: Sandy Schaefer
Cover Designer: Candace Rowley
Cover images: Kate Browne
Operations Specialist: Laura Messerly
Director of Marketing: Quinn Perkson
Marketing Manager: Erica DeLuca
Marketing Coordinator: Brian Mounts

This book was set in Times New Roman by GGS Book Services PMG. It was printed and bound by The P. A. Hutchison Company. The cover was printed by Phoenix Color Corp.

Photo Credits: Kate Browne, pp. 3, 6, 13, 25, 39, 41, 50, 55, 62, 66, 73, 80, 84, 92, 103, 105, 118, 122, 127, 132, 140, 145, 152, 156, 172, 182 (top left, bottom left, bottom right, center), 183, 186, 194; Mary Jennings, pp. 10, 34, 70, 113, 168, 175, 182 (top right), 198; Anthony Magnacca/Merrill, p. 93.

Pearson® is a registered trademark of Pearson plc
Merrill® is a registered trademark of Pearson Education, Inc.

Pearson Education Ltd., London
Pearson Education Singapore, Pte. Ltd.
Pearson Education Canada, Inc.
Pearson Education–Japan
Pearson Education Australia PTY, Limited

Pearson Education North Asia, Ltd., Hong Kong
Pearson Educación de Mexico, S.A. de C.V.
Pearson Education Malaysia, Pte. Ltd.
Pearson Education Upper Saddle River, New Jersey

Merrill
is an imprint of

10 9 8 7 6 5 4 3 2 1
ISBN-13: 978-0-13-199502-4
ISBN-10:   0-13-199502-2

To mentor teachers everywhere, including those who mentored us, but especially to the Mentor Teachers of the San Mateo, California, region. They are true professionals in their dedication and generosity of spirit.

Kate Browne and Ann Gordon

preface

D o you remember how you felt the first time you walked into a classroom as a child? It was an exciting time, filled with expectations and aspirations of success. Yet it was also a time of uneasiness and uncertainty. Now you are a student teacher. Here comes the surprise and the anxiety again! How do we learn to be a teacher of young children? Too often the real world of teaching seems overwhelming.

To Teach Well: An Early Childhood Practicum Guide gives students an accessible, lively introduction to student teaching. Chapters with real-life situations and features that illustrate teaching practices will help you connect your fieldwork experiences with the knowledge and theory you've learned in your coursework. This text is appropriate for student teaching, practicum, or other fieldwork placement for students getting hands-on experience in an early childhood classroom.

Features of To Teach Well

A successful student practicum is one that presents a realistic view of what it takes to be a teacher in today's educational settings and helps student teachers come to know their own capacities and attitudes. *To Teach Well* is an informational text with a workbook component that encourages student self-reflection. It allows instructors to use the book in many different ways to stimulate the students' fieldwork experience. Throughout the book, contributions from student teachers and mentor supervisors give the text relevance and authenticity. Developmentally and culturally appropriate practices are woven throughout the text to ensure that students become aware of national standards for programs and practices.

To Teach Well introduces student teachers to the fundamental principles of teaching and professionalism so that they have a strong base on which to build the knowledge and skills they learn through their practicum. The text guides students from the first days of getting started in their fieldwork through the many areas of responsibility they will encounter as they teach. Each chapter stresses thoughtful consideration—both in the chapter content and throughout multiple activities—that helps students gain insight into their teaching experiences. A "top 10" list in the first nine chapters either highlights basic principles or offers the student concise and relevant tips for teaching.

Teachers' self-awareness is one of the most important elements in effective teaching; it keeps them grounded and present for their children, thus helping them gain a healthy attitude toward their own self-understanding. In a way, the subtitle of the text could be "It Begins with Me." The book promotes the process of reflective teaching from the beginning of a student's classroom experience in each chapter through these features:

Reflective Incident: The reader responds to a real student teacher's classroom incident or a chapter topic by answering the following questions: How would I feel? What would I do? What might the results be?

My Reaction: This feature gives specific examples of situations that other student teachers have experienced and how they felt and responded, offering students a realistic and sympathetic look at other new teacher–student struggles and triumphs.

Journaling Assignment: This activity serves as a prompt for student's journals, or an online discussion board, or a talk with the supervising teacher, again bringing home the point that reflection equals growth.

Practicum Activity: Students apply their on-site learning to questions that encourage critical thinking and problem solving. Their responses then can be discussed in their student teaching seminars.

Lessons from the Field: An experienced teacher describes an area of teaching from the point of "what I know now that I wish I'd known then," suggesting that teaching is a lifelong learning process as well as echoing the need for self-reflection.

Format and Chapter Focus

Each chapter has a specific focus and offers basic information and strategies for making the student teaching experience as productive and valuable as possible. Theory evolves into practice through the enhancements noted previously that are woven throughout the chapter. Instructors are given multiple ways to interact with students, reinforcing the chapter content. Relevant photographs and charts further illuminate theory and implementations of key concepts.

Chapter 1, "Getting Started," starts with an overview of the top 10 fundamentals of teaching and the roles and responsibilities of teaching. Fieldwork guidelines include preparing students for a successful start and some of the situations they may encounter.

Chapter 2, "Becoming a Professional Teacher," focuses on professionalism. Professional standards and goal setting are discussed along with assessment and evaluation. The top 10 reasons for teacher assessment and evaluation help students understand the value of assessments as avenues for growth and give them specific examples of teacher assessment tools. This chapter also introduces students to a professional code of ethics with exercises by using the National Association of the Education of Young Children (NAEYC) Code of Ethical Conduct to problem solve real scenarios faced by student teachers. Students also explore career options and learn to create their own professional portfolio.

Chapter 3, "Understanding and Guiding Behavior," reviews the important concepts of guidance, which can be a source of confusion and insecurity for new teachers. Basic guidance beliefs and the differences among guidance, discipline, and punishment are clearly defined, as are developmentally and culturally appropriate guidance. The top 10 guidance techniques offer students an overview of strategies, ranging from the least intrusive to those requiring the most teacher intervention.

Chapter 4, "Observing and Assessing Children," covers the critical areas of observation and assessment of children with attention to NAEYC standards and school readiness. The top 10 characteristics of quality child assessment along with sample assessment tools help the beginning student learn the value of observing children and using authentic assessment to create positive interactions, learning environments, and curriculum.

Chapter 5, "Environments and Schedules," demonstrates ways to consider children's needs through the use of appropriate environments and schedules. The top 10 tips for building developmentally appropriate schedules and basic space-planning considerations give student teachers insights into behavior management as well.

Chapter 6, "Curriculum," explains how children learn and how play as the learning medium provides the basis for developmentally appropriate curriculum. The top 10 questions when creating curriculum serve as guidelines for developing age-appropriate, culturally responsive, integrated, emergent, and inclusive curriculum. The how-to of written lesson plans and planning and leading group times give student teachers the necessary tools to master these important tasks.

Chapter 7, "Team Teaching in Early Childhood Settings," explores the common practice of sharing teaching responsibilities with other adults. The chapter offers specific examples of the challenges of team teaching along with top 10 tips for team teaching to help beginning teachers learn to work well with other adults.

Chapter 8, "Collaborating with Families," explores family–school connections and discusses why they are important. The diversity and definition of today's family sets the tone for understanding the parent–school relationship. The top 10 tips for positive family–school relationships help students begin to make the important links to the families of the children in their classroom.

Chapter 9, "The Dynamics of Diversity," addresses equity, inclusion, early intervention, accommodations for disabilities, and the antibias approach. Students are asked to reflect on the many facets of diversity. The top 10 strategies for addressing diversity contain practical suggestions and reflective exercises that help students employ what they have learned and encourage student teachers to examine their own feelings and responses to the meaning and expressions of diversity today.

Chapter 10, "Teaching in Various Settings: My Reflections," is in a workbook format that personalizes students' teaching experiences and expands their reflective abilities. Eight types of early childhood programs are described, and the student uses the form for the specific type of program in which they taught. Students are asked to describe their experience and identify challenges. The My Reflections section offers a place for students to respond to questions such as the following: How do I feel? What can I do? Whom can I talk to? What do I bring to the current situation? How does my experience in ECE so far help me? What professional standards can I use as resources? This helps the students move from divergent thinking to problem solving while summing up their journey to become a teacher.

Acknowledgments

A theme of this text is that good teachers continue to learn throughout their careers. We have appreciated that concept as we have had the support and response from many who opened our eyes and minds to new thoughts and ideas. From Anita to Yuji and everyone in between, whose Practicum voices are heard in the Reflective Incidents, My Reactions, and throughout the text: gracias por todo. The comments, reflections, reactions, and questions from the students in early childhood courses at Skyline College in San Bruno, California, gave us insights that can only come from new and fresh minds. The San Mateo mentor teachers of the California Mentor Program added their expertise through their Lessons from the Field articles and reminded us of some basic truths about teaching. Julia Browne organized our resources and writing approach to show us how today's students learn best. Sue Warford of the Child Development Center at the University of Rhode Island shared her teaching resources and wisdom on providing the best experiences for student teachers. Stanlee Garriott of Skyline College made sure we had quiet space in which to do our writing and cheered us up with amusing stories and photo opportunities.

The Pearson staff has been extraordinary in their support and encouragement. Julie Peters, whose knowledge of the field is exceptional and whose gentle encouragement and feedback pushed us forward, is an author's best friend. She and her assistant, Tiffany Bitzel, asked and answered questions, sent appropriate resources, and were always there for us. We appreciate your efforts.

Sometimes authors are too close to the subject matter to see what is missing or what needs to be changed. We thank the team of reviewers who pointed out the errors of our ways with kind and encouraging comments: Susan Anton, Hostos Community College of the City University of New York; Joan Campbell, Santa Fe Community College; Kathleen DeVries, Red Rocks Community College; Patricia

A. Dickmann, Ivy Tech Community College; Jennifer M. Johnson, Vance-Granville Community College, Patricia Luken, Broward Community College; Cathy Mogharreban, Southern Illinois University; Cecilia Pittman, Oklahoma City Community College; ReJean A. Schulte, Cuyahoga Community College; Terrie L. Thompson, Madison Area Technical College; Susan VanNess, Manchester Community College; and Kathleen P. Watkins, Community College of Philadelphia. This book is by far a better text thanks to their efforts.

brief contents

contents

chapter 3   Understanding and Guiding Behavior   45

chapter 4   Observing and Assessing Children   70

chapter 5   Environments and Schedules   91

chapter 6   Curriculum   112

chapter 7   **Team Teaching in Early Childhood Settings**   **138**

chapter 8   Collaborating with Families   161

chapter 9   The Dynamics of Diversity   181

Note: Every effort has been made to provide accurate and current Internet information in this book. However, the Internet information posted on it are constantly changing, so it is inevitable that some of the Internet addresses listed in this textbook will change.

Getting Started

Why Become a Teacher?

Winona became a Head Start teacher's aide when her children were enrolled in the program on their reservation. As she taught, she realized how much of the children's learning was based on her own Native American values, especially the ability to connect with others through storytelling. This inspired her to take classes, further her education, and continue to teach. For Winona, it was important to give back to her community by passing on their culture to her students.

Olga is a 23-year-old working as an assistant in a child care center sponsored by her church, where she also teaches Sunday school. She likes to feel useful to families, so she babysits regularly within her church community. Olga is challenged by the opportunity to learn how to care for and educate children in a group setting and has already adapted some of her insights to her Sunday school class. She likes being a member of a teaching team.

LeAnne's mother ran a family child care home while she and her brother were growing up. They often helped out their mother after school. Now that LeAnne has children, she too has started a family child care home. This work gives her an opportunity to stay at home with her own young children, help out with the family finances, and do work that she enjoys. LeAnne has been taking some courses at the local community college as time permits and will continue to work toward an associate degree in early childhood.

Sam comes from a long line of teachers. His father and grandmothers taught and it seemed natural to Sam to go into teaching. He got a degree in early childhood education (ECE) and has been teaching first grade for 6 years. He has become a mentor teacher in a local program and enjoys working with people who are just beginning their teaching careers. For Sam, teaching is part of the commitment he takes on as a citizen of this country. He cares deeply about the kind of future his students will have and their ability to work with people of other backgrounds, religions, and races. The school where he teaches does not have the kind of diversity he would like to see, and he hopes that in the near future he will be able to transfer to a school where changing neighborhoods are creating greater diversity.

These four teachers have different reasons for the different paths they followed to the classroom. They are motivated by any number of issues and interests.

What they have in common, however, is that each of them *wants* to be a teacher. Not all adults are able to work with young children. Good teachers, like Winona, LeAnne, Olga, and Sam, understand the positive effect they can have on children and their learning. They feel that the work they do is important and that they have something to offer the field of early education. Their talent may be a desire to work with children with special needs, or a unique ability to communicate with parents, or an artistic talent that enhances the curriculum. This inner motivation gives these four people the confidence they need to become effective teachers.

As you embark on your own personal journey toward early childhood teaching, you will find yourself with countless questions, such as "Hmmm—why do I want to do this work?" or "Yikes—what am I doing here?" In preparing yourself to be a teacher in the future, take time now to think about your own *disposition* for teaching.

Lilian Katz has been writing for decades about how our personal tendencies and general habits of mind shape how we teach (Katz, 1995). More recently, the National Council for Accreditation of Teacher Education (NCATE, 2006) defines dispositions as

> the values, commitments, and professional ethics that influence students, families, colleagues, and communities and affect student learning, motivation, and development as well as the educator's own personal growth. Dispositions are guided by beliefs and attitudes related to values such as caring, fairness, honesty, responsibility, and social justice.

The work of an early childhood teacher is complex, and often intense and sensitive. Consider your own dispositions of teaching as you read this introductory chapter.

Fundamentals of Teaching

There are a number of factors that help create an effective teacher. In combination, they can be guidelines for personal and professional growth throughout a lifetime. Individually, each defines an aspect of the role and responsibility of teaching young children, and outlines a critical function in becoming an effective teacher. Together, they form the essential elements in preparing to become a teacher. The 10 fundamentals enhance your ability to practice reflective teaching, so that you learn as much about yourself as you do about children, environments, and curriculum. You will find these guiding principles in the chapters that follow. Figure 1.1 lists the top 10 fundamentals of teaching.

Have a Passion for the Work. Do you remember some really good teachers you had? Surely one of the factors that made them memorable is that they had a passion for teaching and were able to communicate the excitement of the subject matter to you. It was clear they loved their job and couldn't imagine doing anything else.

1. Have a passion for the work.
2. Master knowledge of development and learning.
3. Adhere to professional and ethical standards of teaching.
4. Engage in reflective teaching.
5. Create positive relationships.
6. Respect family individuality and diversity.
7. Be an effective communicator.
8. Observe and assess children's development and behavior.
9. Manage the classroom and guide children's behavior.
10. Plan and execute appropriate curriculum and environments.

Figure 1.1
Top 10 Fundamentals of Teaching
As you read the top 10 list, make a note of which ones are already on your list and which you will work on during your student teaching.

That teacher would never say "I drag myself to work every day just to pay the bills" or "My job is so boring." The teachers you remember knew the demands of their work in the classroom as well as the deep satisfaction it provided them, renewing their enthusiasm.

Teachers who are passionate about teaching have a strong, persistent interest in the way children grow and develop. The subject of human growth and development is very exciting to them. They enjoy watching children change throughout the school year and how their life circumstances affect them. They are challenged by how their own teaching may enhance or diminish what and how children learn.

Someone who loves to teach has a disposition for wanting to communicate the joy of learning. Teachers are in an exciting position as they watch the world unfold before the eyes of their students. Awe and wonder, curiosity and imagination are evident in the many teachable moments in a child's life.

Master Knowledge of Development and Learning. An indispensable part of any early childhood teacher's background is to have a working knowledge and understanding of child development and early education. What can be expected developmentally from the particular age group with which you are working? What are the teachers' goals for the group? How do these children learn best? What is each child's preferred learning style based on what you have observed? A teacher's knowledge of these questions and their answers leads to good judgment and wisdom about teaching in the early childhood classroom.

Each classroom is filled with children who are at various levels in their overall development. When teachers are aware of the cycles within human development, they see that children's growth and maturity

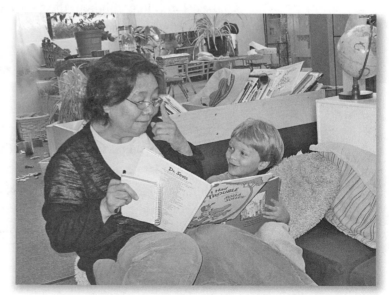

The joys of teaching are communicated in many ways.

follow an uneven path; therefore, teachers are prepared for a diverse mix of abilities. Through developmentally appropriate methods and techniques, the teacher helps children consolidate their gains through rehearsal, practice, and repetition until they gain mastery over a skill, whether it be pouring juice, buttoning a sweater, or doing double-digit addition. They have faith in the knowledge that children will learn and grow at their own pace and according to their own time.

Adhere to Professional and Ethical Standards of Teaching. Through the National Association for the Education of Young Children (NAEYC), the early childhood profession has a set of professional guidelines and a code of conduct that express the values and beliefs of those who teach in the field. The standards for early childhood professional preparation include promoting child development and learning; building family and community relationships; observing, documenting, and assessing children; teaching and learning; and becoming a professional. The code describes a teacher's responsibilities to children, to families, to their colleagues, and to the community at large. Both Professional Preparation Standards and the Code of Ethical Conduct will be elaborated in Chapter 2.

Why have professional standards or a code of ethical conduct? Standards outline what it means to be a professional teacher, describing the components of the work. In addition, each day teachers are faced with conflicts that range from the use of punitive discipline with children, to teacher misbehavior, to parent pressure. Beginning teachers need to know the importance of making decisions based on a code of ethics. A specific set of values is not just about what one teacher would do in a situation; it is about what *all* teachers should do.

Through experience and insights over the first few years in the classroom, teachers gain confidence to formulate their own philosophy of learning. Teachers' educational philosophies are based on their own values and beliefs about what is best for young children, their own experiences with groups of children, and the code of ethical conduct.

Engage in Reflective Teaching. Reflect on the four teachers described at the beginning of the chapter. In one way or another each of them made the connection between wanting to teach and finding personal meaning in what they do. They were able to make that link because they engaged in *reflective teaching*.

When you participate in reflective teaching, you set aside the lesson plans and guidance strategies to look at the broader meaning of teaching. You take time to think about your role, your attitude, and your behavior. You look at the classroom as a community of learners—and realize that you are one of them. This goes to the very core of teaching: the relationship between self-understanding and its impact on educational practices.

Working with young children challenges teachers to look at and consider changing their own attitudes and behaviors. Because teachers spend a great deal of time observing children's growth and development, they understand that changes

- Am I aware of my own identity and its influences on my beliefs and behaviors?
- Are any of my beliefs about child-rearing different from the way I was raised? Which ones? How have I changed that?
- Am I comfortable working with parents whose child-rearing values are different from mine? How do I show it?
- Do I truly foster a respect for the value of those who are somewhat different from me? How?
- Do I examine my biases and look at ways I can change my own attitudes? When? How?
- Do I show a preference for children who most closely fit my own ethnic, cultural, and religious background? When? How?
- Do I sometimes pass along my biases to the children I teach? When? How? With whom?
- Do I learn from other teachers? Do I learn from children?
- Do I see children as capable and able to use each other as resources? How do I show that?
- What are my feelings about people with disabilities? Do I want to teach children with special needs? What influences my beliefs?
- Do I truly enjoy differences in human beings? In my classmates, friends, and children? When? With whom?

Figure 1.2
On Reflective Teaching: Questions to Ask Myself
Reflective teaching involves forming questions to ask yourself as you experience your teaching practice.

Source: From Gordon/Browne. *Beginnings and Beyond*, 7e. © 2008 Wadsworth, a part of Cengage Learning, Inc. Reproduced by permission. www.cengage.com/permissions.

continue throughout the life cycle and that learning is a lifelong process. Adults grow, learn, and change as well. Those who view themselves as learners become successful teachers whose lives are meaningful and who have confidence in themselves and their teaching.

Each chapter of this text will encourage you to practice reflective teaching throughout your student practicum experience. Figure 1.2 begins this process. The questions will stimulate you to watch yourself grow, learn, and change. Also, each chapter features a Reflective Incident to prompt the process of self-knowledge. The longer you teach, the more you will be confronted with questions about your attitudes, biases, beliefs, knowledge, and understanding of the world in which children live.

Create Positive Relationships. To work effectively in an early childhood setting, you need to develop positive relationships with other adults as well as with the children. These relationships, based on trust and respect, begin when you and your supervisor set goals together for your teaching experience and he or she becomes a guide for your growth and development as a teacher. Maintaining a positive attitude throughout the process is key.

One way to maintain a positive attitude and a positive relationship with those you work with is to become a good team member. Take responsibility for learning the guidelines you are given as a student teacher. Be on time, dress appropriately, do your assignments in a timely manner, listen respectfully, and ask questions as needed. These simple but necessary tasks will give you the confidence you need and will win you the respect of your coworkers.

You may already have a good feeling about working with young children from babysitting, coaching, or taking care of your own siblings or children. Some student teachers have had previous work experience in educational settings. This should certainly help you in your initial approach to children in the class where you are student teaching. At some point, perhaps even on your first day, children will begin to test you. They want to know if your boundaries are different from the rest of the teaching staff and they may sense your insecurity or nervousness. Your knowledge of the school's philosophy and procedures will be a critical factor in your ability to relate positively to the children from the beginning.

Flexibility, acceptance, patience, encouragement, dependability, and a non-judgmental attitude are key elements in creating positive relationships wherever you are. Chapters 3, 6, and 7 will demonstrate these elements in detail.

Respect Family Individuality and Diversity. Three of the core values in the NAEYC's (1998) Code of Ethical Conduct are to (1) recognize that children are best understood and supported in the context of family, culture, community, and society; (2) respect the dignity, worth, and uniqueness of each individual (child, family member, and colleague; and (3) respect diversity in children, families, and colleagues. These values form the foundation on which we build relationships with children and their families.

You may have already experienced living in a community with great diversity. Many student teachers have family or friends who come from ethnic, social, or economic cultures other than your own. Some may have worked or lived with people who have disabilities. If so, you are fortunate, because understanding and respecting individual differences is an important concept for any teacher.

Cultural awareness and sensitivity affects the way you interact with children and their families. When a teacher has knowledge of the social and cultural context in which a child lives, the program and curriculum can be more meaningful, relevant, and respectful of the families enrolled in that setting. Insight into the family gives teachers the ability to respond positively to the individual child's unique learning style, growth, language skills, and communication style. Chapters 7 and 8 explore these issues in depth.

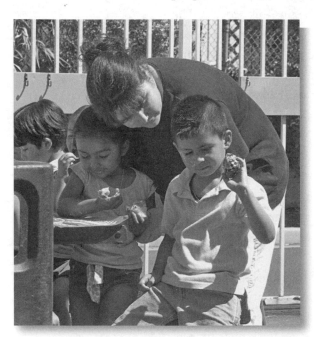

Student teachers learn about the contexts of family and culture to better teach the children in their program.

Be an Effective Communicator. Early childhood teachers work not only with children but also with adults. At your job site, you may meet other professionals (consultants, physicians, child psychiatrists, specialists), support staff (secretaries, janitors, cooks, bus drivers, maintenance workers), coworkers (teachers, directors, aides, volunteers), and family members (parents, grandparents, nannies). Good communication skills will help you become more effective with all of them.

The skills needed for good communication apply to working with children or adults. Your goal is to create a mutually trusting and respectful relationship within the classroom and the workplace. To do that, you need to be clear in what you want to say and to understand fully what is being said to you. Here are some ways to begin:

- *Listen carefully to what is said.* This means that you listen more than you talk so that you can get at the meaning and feelings of what you are hearing. This skill, called "active listening," is discussed in Chapter 3.

- *Ask a lot of questions.* Get as much clarification as you can on how best to do your job. Keep a notepad with you to jot down your questions so that you can ask them at the appropriate time, not while everyone is busy with children.

- *Respond to the questions, comments, and observations you hear.* Be interested, don't just *act* interested. Keep the focus on the adult or child who is talking to you, not on your next response.

- *Use body language.* With children, get down to their eye level and make clear, simple statements. For all, use facial expressions that indicate interest, concern, and understanding. The person you are talking with will likely use nonverbal clues, such as facial or hand gestures and body stance. Look for them.

- *Be culturally sensitive in your communication with others.* Remember that each person comes from a set of values fostered over a lifetime by family, culture, religion, and socioeconomic background, and it may be different from yours.

- *Learn to deal with conflict through effective problem-solving skills.* These are discussed in Chapter 3.

Observe and Assess Children's Development and Behavior. Your eyes and mind need to be wide open when you teach. Good observation skills are fundamental tools in understanding children. When you observe how children play, how they behave, and how they interact with others, you become more aware of their needs, abilities, and concerns (Jones, 1993). You gain a picture of where the child is today. As you assess the information you observe, you can then plan for growth and learning opportunities for the future.

Learning to observe and record behavior effectively takes time and practice. We assess children's growth and abilities to establish a baseline that helps us plan curriculum, guidance measures, communication with families, and program decisions.

You will learn some techniques in Chapter 4 that will help you enhance your knowledge of individual children, the group, and child growth and development.

Manage the Classroom and Guide Children's Behavior. Class management is one of the most challenging aspects of teaching. Effective classroom management is based on the expectations you have for children's behavior, use of the space, interactions among people and materials, and time frames that make up the daily schedule. The routines, rules, and procedures also help determine how well the classroom is managed. Children need to know that what happens in class is predictable and consistent

The goal of effective classroom management is to maximize learning through a well-organized system that supports productive and positive behaviors. Children's behavior will be more positive when expectations are clearly communicated and supported by appropriate room arrangements.

A good guidance philosophy goes hand-in-hand with classroom management. The most effective methods of guiding children are clear, consistent, and fair rules that are enforced in consistent and humane ways. Successful guidance strategies emphasize the positive aspects of a child's behavior, not just the problem behavior. Guidance measures have greater meaning to children if they are encouraged to take responsibility for their own actions and are part of the problem-solving process. In Chapter 3 you will learn a number of successful methods for guiding young children.

Plan and Execute Appropriate Curriculum and Environments. A sound curriculum is the hallmark of a quality program for children. Today's teachers ensure that young children are exposed to developmentally and culturally appropriate curriculum that reflects their needs and is meaningful in its content. A key element to understanding curriculum in the early years is the premise that *play* is the primary medium that forms the foundation for learning (Erikson, 1963; Piaget, 1954).

There are many curriculum models available, notably the Reggio Emilia approach, High/Scope, Montessori, and Bank Street (see Chapter 5). However, many teachers develop their own curriculum using an eclectic, or blended, approach that encompasses some of these models.

To develop curriculum, you must first set goals and establish priorities. What do you want children to learn? When do they need to learn it? What is the best way to teach the material? You take into consideration the wide range of abilities evident in a single classroom and the skills that are appropriate to learn at this age. Emergent curriculum (see Chapter 6) is built on the interests of the children in the class where the teacher helps them explore their ideas in greater depth. This often leads to a project that will engross children for week or even months. Curriculum building is also based on the knowledge of how individual children learn best. Multiple intelligence theory (Gardner, 1993) helps teachers understand how to create curriculum that appeals to a broad range of interests and abilities.

The curriculum mirrors the goals and philosophy of the program, and so does the environment. With the intentional placement of furniture, plan for where and how adults are deployed, and the scheduled amount of time for each portion of the day, teachers demonstrate program priorities. For example, in early childhood settings where children's self-reliance is valued, the environment is created to support independent behavior. An antibias curriculum (Derman-Sparks and the ABC Task Force, 1989) values differences in race, culture, ability, and gender, so those environments reflect that belief in the choice of curriculum, books, materials, toys, and equipment. Inclusive environments foster the participation of children with varying abilities and disabilities and adapt the facility to create a safe and challenging environment for all. Chapters 5 and 6 will explore all of these issues in greater depth.

Roles and Responsibilities

What do teachers do all day? In most of early childhood education, the backbone of the program is the teacher. The teacher is a model for the children, and so teachers must focus on the quality of the child's relationship with them. Nearly 60 years ago, Katherine Read Baker (1950) outlined the teacher's role in her classic foundations book, *The Nursery School: A Human Relationships Laboratory:*

> She needs to have an understanding of what the child has learned, what his parents want for him and themselves, and what the child himself seems to want. For all children the goal of the teacher is to provide a curriculum that will promote the development of the individual who enjoys learning and can make good use of the available resources for learning (p. 59).

Indeed, a teacher must be a consummate and welcoming host, storyteller, traffic cop, conflict mediator, medical examiner, psychological and academic assessor, kind but firm disciplinarian, and file clerk. Not to mention plumber, therapist, poet, musician, and janitor!

Although it is true that the teacher wears many hats, the first is interacting with children in the classroom and managing the environment. This will be your initial focus as a student teacher. Setting the tone provides an emotional framework for the children, both as a group and as individuals, and handling the children's behavior is often as compelling as organizing the room and yard or assessing the children's growth and learning. You will work with adults as well, including other teachers, aides, volunteers, and administrators, and develop relationships with parents and other family members.

Outside the classroom, teachers have a role beyond working with children. They keep records, attend staff meetings, connect with families in conferences, make home visits, hold parent education meetings, attend school social functions, participate in workshops or other professional development opportunities, and hold student–teacher conferences. They also plan and evaluate the curriculum, often purchasing and preparing materials for the program.

This student teacher is experiencing one of the roles he will take on as a teacher.

As a student teacher, you will have a role in your practicum site that is unique to your position (see Figure 1.3). At the same time, you will be acclimating yourself to the world of a children's program, to the culture and rhythm of the group. Over the course of time, you will move toward being part of the educational team. In short, you will become a teacher!

Figure 1.3
Teachers' Versus
Student Teachers'
Responsibilities

Teachers...	Student Teachers...
Interact with children	Get acquainted with children
Observe and assess growth and learning	Practice observing children
Manage the classroom	Watch how the team deals with children; alert children to dangers; model themselves after the teachers
Create and maintain the environment	Clean up after themselves; ask where they can help with routine tasks
Plan and evaluate curriculum	Start implementing the ongoing activities of the program; ask when and how they can try to do some on their own
Attend meetings	Find out when they can meet with the supervising teacher outside class; see when the staff meetings, conferences, and class events take place and how they can get involved

---

My Reaction

"How Did I Begin?"

How did I get started? I tried getting my goals and objectives together in my journal before seeing Sarah yesterday: talking to myself out loud, in writing—a thought here and a thought there. The most persistent thought was the sense of lack of confidence; I have not worked in any preschool situation before. In spite of having two amazing semesters of coursework and being a full-time mother with two wonderful grown-up sons, I'm nervous! Sarah smiled and said, "That's how I started." She made me think we're sharing a secret. She put me at ease right then and there. This is my mentor.

—ICHUN

Supervision is a delicate and important matter, both to you and your supervising teacher. Meetings are probably the most time-consuming of all out-of-class jobs, and you will want to be sensitive to the demands on your teacher's time as well as clear about getting the one-on-one time you need to improve your work. Read how Ichun felt in the My Reaction feature as she began student teaching. Making a plan for when and how long you can meet, and having an agenda (or at least a question and comment) for those times will be helpful.

Your role and that of your supervisor can take on many forms. You might see yourself as a kind of *apprentice* who is learning from an experienced teacher how to become proficient in the child care and education profession, much as merchants in the Middle Ages took on young people to teach their trade. Supervising teachers often see themselves as *mentors*, which has a history of its own.

> The first record of mentoring comes from Homer's classic work, the *Odyssey*. In this tale, the adventurer Odysseus is about to depart on a 10-year journey and he leaves his son Telemachus with a servant/friend named Mentor. In the father's absence, Mentor's role was to guide and inspire Telemachus as the youngster prepared himself for his future task as the ruler of Ithaca. This first story about a Mentor has a strong feminine aspect also. In the *Odyssey*, Athena (also known as the goddess of wisdom) disguises herself as Mentor and comes to Telemachus several times to guide and counsel him. (Sherk & Perry, 2005, p. 2–1)

At the same time, you might be thinking that you'd better hurry up and practice all the teaching experiences you can, because soon you'll be in charge yourself. Such an attitude can add tension and urgency into your work, spurring panic or withdrawal. This hat, more like the one in Disney's "Sorcerer's Apprentice," may not fit you or sit well with your supervising teacher, either. Your supervisor may be dealing

Table 1.1 Key Terms for Student Teachers

Term	Definition
Mentor	A mentor provides vital day-to-day instruction that allows a student teacher to become a successful professional educator.
Field placement	The goal of a student teaching course is to find the best match of setting or supervisor with student teachers. This process involves the faculty, supervisors, and student teachers.
Student teacher, intern, practicum student, or practicing teacher	Students who are learning to become teachers often have different titles; they may be called student teachers, interns, practicum students, or practicing teachers. All will spend substantial time in program settings, learning to teach by doing the work of professional educators, with guidance from both the program supervisor and the college-based teacher educators. An intern often gets a stipend and is a professional-in-training.
Partner school	Partner schools work closely to provide interns the best learning experiences. Partner schools and colleges or universities share responsibility for preparing interns to be successful professional educators.
Master or supervising teacher	The master or supervising teacher observes, guides, and evaluates the student teacher during practicum/student teaching experience.
Faculty instructor	The facutly instructor is a college instructor who will observe and evaluate the student teacher, in addition to the mentor/supervising teacher, during the student teaching experience.

with competing demands, not so sensitive to your needs, or may see you as an extra pair of hands more than a learner. These expectations are not often verbalized, but can change the teaching–learning relationship in ways that become unsatisfying.

Clear guidelines, regular communication, and responsive time together build a trusting relationship that rewards you both. Knowing who you are and the various people and institutions that will support you will help; see Table 1.1 for key terms to clarify your student teaching role. From the start, students begin to assume some of the responsibilities of teaching in a classroom. With more experience, the student teacher's role expands.

Think about the kind of "authority figure" you are looking for, and who your supervising teacher seems to be (Caruso & Fawcett, 1999). Building a relationship with this master teacher should be one of your first tasks, even as you begin to make friends with children or to build teaching skills. Concentrate on developing connections of trust and respect. Reflect on who was a good teacher in your life, and the qualities that person had that were important to you. Now see how you can have this experience with your master teacher. Try to be open about both what you are to learn and how you are to learn it. Successful student teachers sometimes start their practicum by simply observing, shadowing their supervisor, or sitting at an activity table with a child. There are many ways to get started.

Fieldwork Guidelines

Your student teaching experience can be an exciting time. Textbook theories come alive as children live out child development concepts. Student teachers expect to learn about individual child growth and development; many are surprised to discover that they also learn how children function in groups and with adults. For some students, the practicum may be the first hands-on opportunity to work directly with children.

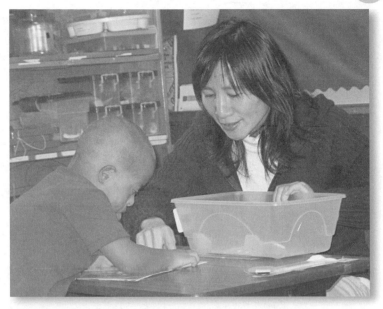

A student teacher has hands-on experiences with children.

Preparing for Student Teaching

Planning and executing activities that fit the needs and abilities of the children are usually part of the student teacher's role. This gives you an opportunity to test curriculum ideas, and to see what happens when children use the materials. The classroom tasks you are assigned will vary according to those assigned by your faculty instructor and the goals you set with your supervising teacher. College and/or state requirements for student teaching will determine the amount of time you spend in the classroom. When you finish, you should have many of the tools you need to become a successful teacher (Tyminsky, 2006).

You may have some choice in selecting a setting for your student teaching site, or you may be assigned one by the college faculty. Your practicum may take place in the college's child development center or in early childhood programs throughout the community. Ideally, your site will provide a high-quality program as determined by an external program review process or accreditation. Your faculty instructor may make on-site visits to observe and monitor your fieldwork progress.

Working with an experienced teacher who models highly polished skills is an important part of your teaching experience. Team teaching situations can be especially supportive, and identification with a number of professionals can help you find a teaching identity.

Although student teaching is enjoyable, it can also be a time for intensive self-searching and anxiety. The memory of a negative school experience of your own can undermine your confidence. You may still have doubts about being a teacher. It is uncomfortable to be evaluated by others, but this is part of the learning process. You will be assessed on, among other things,

- how effectively you participate,
- the variety and creativity in your planned activities,
- your classroom management skills,
- how well you meet timelines, and
- whether you behave professionally.

In Chapter 2 you will learn more about the student teacher assessment and evaluation process. If all this begins to feel like too much pressure, you might want to remember that even the most poised and confident master teacher was once a beginner like you. The Reflective Incident that follows tells about one student teacher's first-day experience.

Together, you, your faculty instructor, and the supervising teacher will set goals and expectations for your student teaching experience. From this you will get a concrete definition by the end of the semester of what you will gain from the time you spend in the classroom, whether it is creating a lesson plan or leading a group time. All three of you will be working toward the same goals to ensure a successful student practicum.

Reflective Incident "My First Day"

We started out with a brief orientation of my family child care home setting, and I familiarized myself with the different activity areas and went over the daily schedule. I observed while the teacher directed children with indoor activities. However, when outdoor playtime came, I offered to help out and that was when I felt a little overwhelmed. It was such a huge responsibility to watch all the kids, making sure the older ones were not hurting each other or fighting over toys, while ensuring the safety of two infants crawling around. Then when both of the infants started to cry, I didn't know what to do. I tried picking up a little girl, but it seemed to make her cry even more.—Anita

Your Thoughts

1. How would I feel?

2. What would I do?

3. What might the results be?

Planning Before School Starts

Beginnings are important as they set the tone for what will follow. You will want to plan your first steps carefully. Here are some strategies for easing the transition into the classroom that will help make your first days more satisfying and positive:

- *Contact and meet your supervising teacher.* Find out what time you are expected to arrive, where the classroom is located, what age group you will be working with, the size and makeup of the class, the daily schedule, and what hours you are expected to be on-site. Ask if there are children with special needs and if there are cultural considerations that you should know about. Find out what is expected of you the first few days as you get to know the children. If possible, meet the other faculty and staff of the school.

- *Look at this as an interview.* You will meet and interact with several people, you will have questions to ask, and it is the first impression you will all be making with one another.

- *Know the requirements.* You may already have a list from your faculty instructor, but you will need to check with the supervisory teacher for special requirements, such as tuberculosis (TB) clearance, physician's report, evidence of insurance, or fingerprinting. One requirement may be criminal history and child abuse clearances.

- *Visit the classroom where you will be teaching.* Become acquainted with its layout. Tour the yard. Find out where the janitor's room, kitchen, bathrooms, and storerooms are located.

- *Share with your master teacher any special skills or talents you may have.* Let the teacher help you use these skills in new ways with young children.

- *Complete a student information sheet that may be provided by your college instructor.* The basic information about yourself (address, phone number, previous experience, courses) will help your supervising teacher know more about your background. (See the sample format in Figure 1.4)

Getting Started

After the first few days of teaching, you will be familiar with the routines, you will know most of the children's names, and your presence in the classroom will be accepted. Your behavior is important (Browne & Dilko, 2005):

- *Dress appropriately.* Wear clothing that is comfortable, appropriate to the season, and easily covered by a smock or apron. Sturdy, waterproof shoes are good for outdoor activities. If you are uncertain about your clothing or items such as piercings or tattoos, call ahead or ask before you begin.

Figure 1.4
Student Information Sheet

A student information sheet provides your teaching site and supervisor with important information about you.

Name _____

Address _____

City, State, Zip Code _____

Phone _____ E-mail _____

    Worksite _____

    Address _____

    City, State, Zip Code _____ Phone _____

    Supervisor _____ Teaching hours _____

Have you worked with children before? YES _____ NO _____
Describe:

What other courses have you taken?
(If yes, where and when?)

Is there anything special about you that you'd like me to know?

In case of emergency, please contact _____

Phone _____ Relationship _____

Medical insurance plan _____

Number _____

Physician's name and address _____

Most recent TB test results _____

Date _____

(Give documentation to supervisor within a week of starting)

Do you have any important medical condition? YES _____ NO _____

Do you take medication? If YES, what? _____

Note: Permission is granted by the publisher to reproduce "Student Information Sheet" for evaluation and record-keeping. From K. W. Browne and A. M. Gordon. *To Teach Well: An Early Childhood Practicum Guide.* Copyright © 2009 by Pearson Education, Inc. All rights reserved.

- *Be prompt.* Arrive on schedule and always inform the supervising teacher if you will be late or absent. If transportation is an issue for you, alert your supervising teacher before you begin.

- *Know where things are.* Find out where important equipment and materials are stored. You may be given a map or list; if not, ask if you should look in cupboards or closets before you start to work in class.

- *Use professional ethics.* Avoid discussing children and families by name outside the classroom. Children's behavior is both delightful and upsetting, but their privacy should be respected. Keep confidentiality outside the classroom and also talk to your teacher regularly about what you observe.

Once you get started in your practicum site, you will be working directly with children, teachers, even other adults such as parents, janitors, and so on. Table 1.2 suggests guidelines as you interact with children and adults during your student teaching days.

Table 1.2 Guidelines for Working with Others in an ECE Setting

Interacting with Children	Relating to Other Adults
Move in slowly. Sit back and watch to see what children are doing and if you are needed before getting involved.	*Never interfere when another teacher is solving a problem between two children.* Unless specifically invited let the teacher deal with the situation alone.
Maintain your role as teacher. Avoid playing adult-centered games with the children or entertaining them so that you become the focus of their play. Keep their attention focused on each other or the activities.	*Ask questions.* Be sure to ask for help. You are there to learn, so feel free to question teachers as to why and how they handled various situations.
Give children time. Allow plenty of time for children to do as much as they can possibly do without help	*Maintain communication.* Keep the other staff members informed of significant events and problems that occur. Parents' questions and concerns should be redirected to the supervising teacher.
Help children wait. Be alert to times when children may have to wait until the next activity. Have songs and fingerplays memorized, or a short book ready to read.	*Be friendly with families, but do not try to be their friend.* Maintain a cordial relationship while keeping a professional distance.
Be alert to the whole group. Know where the children and other teachers are and what they are doing even when they are not in the immediate area.	*Consult your supervising teacher.* Work together on selecting and evaluating age-appropriate activities that will fit with the established curriculum goals.
Never leave children unsupervised. Notify the teacher in charge if you must leave the area and work out arrangements that will provide full coverage for all activities.	*Thank other staff members for their help.* Let them know you appreciate their support and that they make a difference.
Maintain the environment. Keep the room and yard in order as the day moves along, involving children in the cleanup process.	*Support and respect all families.* Find ways to acknowledge them and what they are trying to do, even if you have differing opinions.
Use your voice and tone effectively. Go over to a child, bend down, and speak clearly, rather than shout from across the room or yard.	*Keep the focus on the child.* All families appreciate hearing about their children, their day, and their accomplishments.
Never use force of any kind. Avoid picking up children and carrying them if they are supposed to move elsewhere. Learn to use verbalizations to get the child to cooperate.	

Source: From Gordon/Browne. *Beginnings and Beyond,* 7e. © 2008 Wadsworth, a part of Cengage Learning, Inc. Reproduced by permission. www.cengage.com/permissions.

"Welcoming a Student Teacher"

by Debbie Baker-Dailey

Teacher-Director, Circle of Friends Preschool

We have a student teacher! How nice!

Your First Day. In our classroom we welcome you, our new teacher, by introducing you to everyone. You get your own nametag, just like the children and teachers. We put a picture and a few sentences about you in our classroom newsletter. It can be a little overwhelming on your first day, so many names and faces. We will give you a photo page with all the children's names and faces so you can begin to "study" them.

You will notice this is a busy place. There is a lot going on. We will ask you to observe and get to know the children. Say hello, make eye contact, and talk with them. Ask them questions and get ready to listen. There is so much to see! How is the room set up? What are the children doing? How are they interacting with each other and teachers? What are the teachers doing and saying?

The Next Step. As you spend more time here, you will start to get more settled. You can begin to greet the families as they arrive for drop-off or pick-up. Some children will want you to meet their parents, grandparents, or nannies. Others may smile or hide as you introduce yourself. Know that they are all glad you are making a connection with their important "grown-ups."

Be sure to ask questions—find me, ask the teaching team, jot them down for yourself. Get on the level of the children and try to interact with them. Get comfortable with the environment and observe the children. Get familiar with the routines and habits. Remember that the best teachers are the children you are teaching.

Join In. We are glad you're here. ☺ You bring new knowledge, some expectations, fresh ideas, and perhaps some uncertainty. Teaching is a practice. Each day we reflect on our experiences, so plan to stay a little beyond your teaching time to talk with me. Every day we grow a little more as we prepare ourselves for our next day as teachers.

Welcome aboard! Getting started in your practice teaching is an exciting, complex process. For last-minute instructions, read the Lessons from the Field feature above. You are embarking on an amazing journey. Your bags are now packed, and you are ready to go.

Practicum Activity

Look at the top 10 list (Figure 1.1). Reorder it to match your priorities, or make one of your own. Find two other student teachers, and compare their thoughts with your own.

Journaling Assignment

Write a set of questions to ask when you get to your student teaching site. Follow up with your first impressions of the children, the setting, and your supervising teacher.

Resources

Baker, K. R. (1950). *The nursery school: A human relationships laboratory.* Philadelphia: Saunders.

Browne, K. W., & Dilko, P. (2005). *Guidelines for student teaching.* Unpublished manuscript, Cañada and Skyline Colleges.

Caruso, J. J., & Fawcett, M. T. (1999). *Supervision in early childhood education: A developmental perspective.* New York: Teachers College Press.

Derman-Sparks, L., and the ABC Task Force. (1989). *Anti-bias curriculum.* Washington, DC: National Association for the Education of Young Children.

Erikson, E. (1963). *Childhood and society* (2nd ed.). New York: Norton.

Gardner, H. (1993). *Multiple intelligences.* New York: Basic Books.

Gordon, A. M., & Browne, K. W. (1993). *Beginnings and beyond: Foundations in early childhood education* (3rd ed.). Clifton Park, NY: Thomson Delmar Learning.

Gordon A. M., & Browne, K. W. (2008). *Beginnings and beyond: Foundations in early childhood education* (7th ed.). Clifton Park, NY: Thomson Delmar Learning.

Jones, E. (Ed.). (1993). *Growing teachers: Partnerships in staff development.* Washington, DC: National Association for the Education of Young Children.

Katz, L. (1995). *Talks with teachers of young children: A collection.* Norwood, NJ: Ablex.

National Association for the Education of Young Children. (2005). *Code of ethical conduct.* Washington, DC: Author.

National Council for Accreditation of Teacher Education. (2006). *Standards, procedures, and policies for the accreditation of professional education units.* Washington, DC: Author. From "NCATE unit standards," retrieved from http://www.ncate.org.

Piaget, J. (1954). *The construction of reality in the child.* New York: Basic Books. (original work published 1937)

Read, K. (1950). *The nursery school: A human relationships laboratory.* Philadelphia: W. B. Saunders.

Sherk J., & Perry, J. (2005). *A mentor's guide.* San Francisco: California Early Childhood Mentor Teachers Program.

Tyminski, C. (2006). *Your early childhood practicum and student teaching experience.* Upper Saddle River, NJ: Merrill/Pearson.

Web Sites

California Early Childhood Mentor Program
www.ecementor.org

National Association for the Education of Young Children
www.naeyc.org

National Council for Accreditation of Teacher Education
www.ncate.org

chapter 2

Becoming a Professional Teacher

Congratulations! You are taking your next step in becoming a member of the teaching profession. Do you remember the four teachers you read about at the beginning of Chapter 1? They each had their own motivation for becoming a teacher. What about you? What is your incentive for joining the creative and dynamic profession of teaching? What does professionalism mean to you at this point in your student teaching?

The 10 fundamentals of teaching (see Chapter 1) are actually a roadmap you can follow on your journey toward professionalism. Two that you will explore further in this chapter are

- Adhere to professional and ethical standards of teaching
- Engage in reflective teaching

They are key elements in the professional life of a teacher. Teachers are the most important factor in determining the quality of an early childhood program (Spodek, 1972). An evaluation process, therefore, is critical in helping teachers become the best that they can be. Knowing about professional standards helps student teachers in their own teaching.

Setting Professional Standards

The field of early childhood education (ECE) has grown tremendously in the last 40 years. In part, this growth is due to the increasing number of young children in settings outside the home. This has given more visibility to those who engage in the work of caring for and educating children, particularly children under 5. The National Association for the Education of Young Children (NAEYC) has undertaken several initiatives to make the work more understandable and articulated those objectives to those both in the profession and adults outside classrooms. Writing a code of ethics, identifying developmentally appropriate practices, and developing a program accreditation process (see Chapter 5) are all efforts to make our field a legitimate profession. Another key element is setting professional standards.

This endeavor has support from other levels of education, such as elementary and secondary teaching preparation. The NAEYC, jointly with the Council for Exceptional Children's Division for Early Childhood (CEC/DEC) and the National Board for Professional Teaching Standards (NBPTS) (2003), has identified five standards for early childhood professional preparation. Programs that prepare student teachers are now incorporating those standards into the courses they teach. The practicum/student teaching course you are taking now may use them as well. Figure 2.1 outlines these standards.

In preparing to become a teacher, you will work on each of these standards. As you enter the field of early childhood education, you will find that these standards help you shape your ongoing professional goals and the objectives you need to reach them.

Figure 2.1 NAEYC Standards for Early Childhood Professional Preparation
Standards for early education teaching preparation can guide you toward teaching excellence.

Standard 1: Promoting Child Development and Learning

Key elements:

1a: Knowing and understanding young children's characteristics and needs
1b: Knowing and understanding the multiple influences on development and learning
1c: Using developmental knowledge to create healthy, respectful, supportive, and challenging learning environments

Standard 2: Building Family and Community Relationships

Key elements:

2a: Knowing about and understanding family and community characteristics
2b: Supporting and empowering families and communities through respectful, reciprocal relationships
2c: Involving families and communities in their children's development and learning

Standard 3: Observing, Documenting and Assessing to Support Young Children and Families

Key elements:

3a: Understanding the goals, benefits, and uses of assessment
3b: Knowing about and using observation, documentation, and other appropriate assessment tools and approaches

3c: Understanding and practicing responsible assessment
3d: Knowing about assessment partnerships with families and other professionals

Standard 4: Teaching and Learning

Key elements:

4a: Connecting with children and families
4b: Using developmentally effective approaches
4c: Understanding content knowledge in early education
4d: Building meaningful curriculum

Standard 5: Becoming a Professional

Key elements:

5a: Identifying and involving oneself with the early education field
5b: Knowing about and upholding ethical standards and other professional guidelines
5c: Engaging in continuous, collaborative learning to inform practice
5d: Integrating knowledgeable, reflective, and critical perspectives on early education
5e: Engaging in informed advocacy for children and the profession

Source: Reprinted with permission from the National Association for the Education of Young Children. For full NAEYC Initial Licensure Standards, please see www.naeyc.org/faculty/pdf/2001.pdf.

Goals and Objectives

How do student teachers develop teaching skills?

There are many proven strategies to improve your practice: observing other teachers; using a "try, reflect, try again" approach; asking advice from a supervising teacher and a faculty instructor; or talking to other student teachers. Through it all, beginning teachers set goals for themselves, and then craft objectives as a way to meet those goals.

Goals

Goals are the learning outcomes you need to attain in order to be a competent, productive, early childhood professional.

- What do you want to learn to do better?
- What would you like to work on?
- What areas would be best to stretch yourself?

Objectives

Objectives are measurable, finite steps that help you realize your goals. You can always tell if you've achieved them because you or someone else can observe and see what you are doing that shows your work. Objectives determine how you will meet your goals, and what you will do to get there.

Student teachers are often confused about the differences between goals and objectives. A goal is the "what" you want to do to improve your teaching, and the objectives are the "how" to do it.

- The goal is the big picture; the objectives the details.
- The goal is the forest; the objectives the trees.

Goals	Objectives
Are broad in scope	Specify an intent of some aspect of a goal
Are general statements of ends	Detail some type of result of an action
Reflect your philosophy or priorities	Set measurable stages toward a goal
Are long term or far-reaching	Are short term and narrow in scope
May not necessarily be measurable	

A goal may have several objectives aimed at reaching the outcome. Objectives can be for one day, week, month or year; goals are generally for longer than a year. Figure 2.2 provides sample goals and objectives established by a college instructor for students in a student teaching seminar. Compare this list with the goals for your student teaching course. What are your instructor's objectives for helping you teach well?

By the end of the course, I want my students to be able to reach these goals by meeting the stated objectives.

1. **Goal**: Articulate teaching goals and reflect on their teaching.

   Objectives:
   a. Setting goals in class
   b. Sharing those goals and getting feedback from
      i. Another student teacher
      ii. Their supervisor at their field site
      iii. Their faculty instructor
   c. Revising the goals during the term as needed
   d. Writing about their progress toward the goals in the journal
   e. Evaluating the progress toward the goals by the end of the term

2. **Goal:** Define the multiple roles of an early childhood teacher.

   Objectives:
   a. Hearing and listing multiple roles in class
   b. Observing and journaling about their site teachers
   c. Interviewing their supervisor
   d. Completing a project about one of those roles

3. **Goal:** Recognize problematic child behavior and indicate several guidance strategies to address those situations.

   Objectives:
   a. Observing children at their sites
   b. Journaling about problem behaviors and solutions tried or not
   c. Discussing situations and strategies in class

Figure 2.2
Sample Student Practicum Goals and Objectives
Goals and objectives help professionals set reasonable expectations for themselves. Note that the numbered goals each have several objectives that detail specific ways of accomplishing the goals.

Basic Teaching Skills

Goals and objectives will provide direction for the time that you spend in your fieldwork placement. Student teachers need to set reasonable goals for themselves.

First, consult your college course to see if you already have specific teaching competencies you must achieve. Many practicum courses set goals based on NAEYC teaching standards (see Figure 2.1), or follow certain community requirements. Some ask teachers to set goals based on a set of competencies. A set of *basic teaching skills* is essential for professional teaching, both now as a student and in the future (see Figure 2.3).

Second, talk with your supervising teacher about any expectations for your placement. Some sites ask that you participate in child assessments, develop curriculum, complete a child study, or lead a circle time. Others will want you to observe more than participate to begin with, then move into more responsibilities depending on your level of expertise. Many will require a specific number of lesson plans that you execute.

Finally, consider your own stage of teacher development. Are you a beginner, who needs to first learn to establish trusting relationships with children? Are you far enough along in your own teaching that you are ready to take on more guidance responsibilities? Are you ready to plan activities? What about working with families or team teaching and staff meetings?

Figure 2.3 Basic Teaching Skills
Students need to know what basic teaching skills they are to work toward mastering during their fieldwork placement.

The following is a list of the basic teaching behaviors on which you will be evaluated. You will receive feedback on this list from both your supervising teacher and your faculty instructor, and you will complete a self-evaluation on this same set of skills.

I. Personal Attributes
  A. Reliability
    Is prompt and avoids absences
    Prepares lessons carefully and age appropriately
    Learns the classroom/school routine readily
  B. Attitude
    Is eager to learn
    Has positive attitude
    Is willing to seek out new experiences
    Has positive work ethic
    Responds professionally to feedback and
      suggestions
    Shows initiative
    Reflects on and evaluates own behavior and
      actions
    Shows respect for people of all backgrounds and
      abilities
  C. Grooming and demeanor
    Dresses appropriately
    Is neat and clean in appearance
    Uses appropriate language in written and oral
      communications
    Behaves in an adultlike fashion
    Is aware of self as role model
  D. Professional conduct
    Prepares and completes work on time
    Maintains privacy and confidentiality about staff,
      children, and families
    Indicates growing understanding of professional
      code of ethics
    Participates in class and staff meetings
    Shows intellectual aptitude through written and
      oral assignments

II. Interactions with Children
  A. Knows and applies child development theory
    Understands developmentally appropriate
      practices
    Adapts to child's learning style
    Adapts to child's individual developmental needs
    Is informed by observations of child
    Uses variety of instructional strategies
  B. Builds relationships with children
    Learns and uses children's names
    Responds warmly and attentively when
      approached by child
    Treats children with kindness and respect
    Interacts positively with all children
    Encourages initiative and independence
    Is sensitive to individual differences and
      abilities

  C. Encourages communication
    Listens carefully to what children say
    Responds with interest, concern, and care
    Uses verbal and nonverbal communications
      effectively
    Uses child-appropriate clear language
    Uses body language well: gets down to child's
      level
    Tempers voice and volume to suit child's
      needs
    Applies communication skills to all children,
      regardless of ability
    Supports peer interactions
  D. Practices positive discipline
    Fosters independent problem solving
    Is alert to total classroom dynamics
    Uses positive statements with children
    Shows patience and understanding with children
      in conflict
    Provides emotional support when appropriate
    Uses variety of guidance strategies appropriate
      to the situation
    Recognizes the individuality of each child in
      choosing guidance measures

III. Relationships with Adults
  A. Builds relationships with families
    Understands the importance of knowing family
      culture, values, and beliefs
    Is sensitive to differences in gender, ability,
      culture, and language
    Is pleasant and welcoming to parents
  B. Works positively with other team members
    Coordinates with team members on
      planning
    Shows respect toward all team members
    Keeps team informed of critical incidents and
      concerns
    Feels comfortable asking others for help or
      information
  C. Works collaboratively
    Moves in to assist team members as needed
    Uses staff meetings to share information and
      contribute ideas
    Exhibits open and frequent communication with
      team members

IV. Program Planning
  A. Plans and carries out appropriate activities with
    children
    Demonstrates awareness of goals of program in
      planning

Figure 2.3 (*continued*)

Shows understanding of age group, abilities, and interests	Works effectively with supervising teacher in planning process
Creates experiences that provide opportunity for children to learn	Shows skill in preparing written lesson plan
Plans for children's involvement in their own learning	B. Evaluates planning process
	Reflects on children's response to the activity
Fosters a hands-on approach to learning	Shows flexibility in adapting activity as needed
Supports the theory that play is the medium for learning	Suggests ways to improve the activity
	Written evaluation indicates learning from the experience
Creates opportunities for children to make choices	

Your goal statements should be general statements on what you would like to accomplish during your field placement. For example, Philip decided one of his goals would be "to know and understand the multiple influences on development and learning." Think about how and why you selected these goals. What makes them valuable to your educational, professional, and/or personal growth? Philip identified with both Filipino and American culture; by reflecting on how these two cultures had influenced him, he wanted to understand the various cultures of the children in his center.

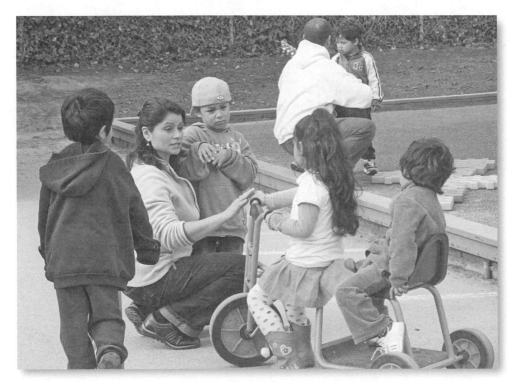

Student teachers can learn basic teaching skills by actively participating in interactions with children.

Creating Your Plan. To help you choose your goals, think about these questions:

- What subject areas interest you the most?

- In what area do you feel you need more work, information, or practice?

- What skills do you want to develop? What approaches or techniques are you hoping to practice?

- Is there a particular child, group of children, parent or family, or staff relationship you would like to include in your goals? Are there particular strategies that you want to explore further?

- What can be reasonably accomplished in the time frame of your practicum fieldwork?

- How will you measure whether you accomplished your objectives and met or made progress on your goals?

- How can your teaching team and/or supervisor assist and support you?

Next, your objectives are the concrete, measurable steps you will take to accomplish your goals. Be specific; use action verbs and words. Then, define a time frame, and be realistic about what you can accomplish in your student teaching experience. Philip chose four objectives:

1. Do some research about family theory.
2. Learn what the children's home languages are.
3. Find out the families' wishes for their children about maintaining home language and acquiring English proficiency.
4. Learn how to bring the home languages and family traditions into the center.

Figure 2.4 outlines another student teacher's goals and objectives.

Figure 2.4
Leticia's Student Teaching Goals and Objectives

Student teaching goals and objectives should be specific; use action verbs and words to describe what you want to know and be able to do at the end of your fieldwork.

Teaching Goal #1: *To improve my large-group-time skills with children.*
Objectives:

1. *Observe three teachers doing circle time for the month.*
2. *Write up five circle-time plans and get ideas from my supervisor.*
3. *Lead five circle times while my head teacher observes and gives feedback.*
4. *Lead five more group activities before the end of term.*

Teaching Goal #2: *To increase my knowledge of child growth and development.*
Objectives:

1. *Learn about my center's child assessment procedures.*
2. *Choose a child to observe weekly.*
3. *Make a portfolio on that child.*

Your goals and objectives should be reviewed and shared with your site supervisor. Seek out and use your supervisor's support and guidance in working toward your objectives. To reflect, use a journal or diary to evaluate your goals along the way. There is a journaling assignment at the end of each chapter. The following suggestions help student teachers use a journal, or an online discussion board, to articulate their progress on goals and objectives.

- Summarize your accomplishment of—or progress toward—each goal and objective.
- Describe any challenges or obstacles you faced and how you overcame them.
- Give examples of any successes or setbacks.
- Discuss the accomplishment you are most proud of and what area you feel you need more practice or experience in.
- Explain how you worked with your supervisor and teaching team in meeting your goals and objectives.
- Discuss how your fieldwork helped you and contributed to your overall professional and personal growth (Goines & Eto, 2000).

Teacher Assessment and Evaluation

There are many reasons that assessments and evaluations are part of the professional life of an early childhood educator (Hyson, 2003). In many schools, an annual performance evaluation is a professional requirement and the evaluation becomes a roadmap to follow as you work toward achieving specific goals. For the student teacher, the evaluation process helps identify strengths and areas for improvement. As your teaching improves, the skill set you have mastered increases.

An evaluation gives you an opportunity to address specific issues and think about what they mean to your teaching. Figure 2.5 illustrates the circular feedback

Figure 2.5
Evaluation Feedback Loop

Teaching goals and performance are part of a continuous process, as shown in this feedback loop.

Source: From Gordon/Browne. *Beginnings and Beyond*, 7e. © 2008 Wadsworth, a part of Cengage Learning, Inc. Reproduced by permission. www.cengage.com/permissions.

Figure 2.6
Top 10 Reasons for
Teacher Assessment
and Evaluation

Knowing the reasons for
evaluation can help ease
students' tension about
being assessed on their
teaching skills.

1. To uphold professional standards in the field of early childhood education
2. To hold you accountable and take professional responsibility
3. To identify your strengths and limitations
4. To benefit all the stakeholders: you, the children, teachers, families, and programs
5. To promote reflective teaching
6. To help you achieve your goals
7. To increase your skill level
8. To tell you whether or not you have met your goals
9. To promote healthy change
10. To increase self-confidence

loop that a good evaluation can take. Once you have set goals for yourself, you do something that shows your work—that is, you put the objectives to work. Your mentor, observing your behavior, can offer you feedback. Then you are ready to revise your goals to have something concrete to work toward. You strengthen your abilities and increase your skill level when you try to create a lesson plan, learn a new fingerplay, or set up an age-appropriate activity. The support of your faculty instructor and supervising teacher is an important factor in reaching those goals. Goals are usually set for a certain time period, and together you can monitor your progress so that you will achieve success.

The evaluation process promotes objective assessment based on articulated criteria that are given to you as you begin your student teaching. This overview of the teaching behaviors and expectations gives you the standards on which you will be evaluated. Student teachers should have a greater understanding that the purpose in the evaluation is to be fair and to help them make the necessary changes. Figure 2.6 lists the top 10 reasons for teacher assessment and evaluation.

Two Types of Evaluations

Because a key component of good teaching is the ability to reflect and analyze one's work, it stands to reason that self-evaluation is essential. Add to that important feedback from a seasoned teacher, a peer, or eventually even a parent, and the second element of evaluation is in place.

Self-Evaluation. A critical part of any assessment of teaching skills is the involvement of the person being evaluated. That's *you*, the student teacher. You have started working in a program, and have familiarized yourself with the children, teaching team, environment, schedule, and curriculum. You are starting—or continuing—to play a part in the actual teaching of the children. How are you doing? What do you bring to the enterprise? How are you faring in respect to the major responsibilities of a teacher?

An evaluation of your work is critical to your progress toward competence. Figure 2.7 is an example of a self-evaluation a student teacher could use to assess

Please complete the following self-evaluation form, using the process to reflect on your strengths as well as to identify where your professional skills need to be improved. Your supervisors—the instructor and head teacher—will meet with you to share their observations of your performance and discuss with you individual goals for your professional development.

Please use the following rating scale to respond to each question:

U = Usually,   S = Sometimes,   R = Rarely

Personal Qualities

_____ I arrive on time.

_____ I have a professional appearance.

_____ I work with a positive attitude, enthusiasm, and appropriate sense of humor

_____ I can stay calm in a tense situation.

_____ I am always alert to health and safety issues.

_____ I show flexibility with tasks and schedules.

Relationship to Children

_____ I listen and am responsive to children.

_____ My interactions are respectful and warm.

_____ I get down on the child's level to interact and converse.

_____ I use an appropriate voice tone and avoid using babytalk.

_____ I move toward children to talk rather than calling from a distance.

_____ I model appropriate behavior for children.

_____ I treat children of all races, religions, family backgrounds, and cultures with equal respect and consideration.

_____ I am aware of the entire group even when dealing with one child or a small group.

_____ I anticipate and modify situations to avoid negative behavior.

_____ I help children deal with negative feelings by giving comfort, identifying and validating their feelings, and helping them use words.

_____ I frame my statements to children in a positive way, avoiding the over-use of negative words (*don't, stop that, that's not nice*, etc.) or threats.

_____ I encourage problem solving by describing the situation so that children can evaluate the problem rather than imposing my solutions.

_____ I foster self-help skills and independence.

_____ I ask open-ended questions and speak individually to children.

Program Development

_____ I help create an inviting learning environment in the classroom.

_____ I permit children to use materials in a variety of ways.

_____ I plan activities that are appropriate to a child's stage of development.

_____ I am available to implement the program's curriculum, or I am prepared when trying my own activity plans.

_____ I record observations of children in order to plan activities that relate to their individual needs and interests.

_____ I can assist in helping children with transitions.

_____ I can make use of spontaneous happenings to help children's learning.

Figure 2.7
Self-Evaluation of Student Teaching
Self-evaluation is a critical part of the assessment process, allowing you to reflect on your strengths and challenges in teaching.

Figure 2.7
(*continued*)

Teamwork

_____ I am friendly and respectful with others.

_____ I understand the program philosophy and goals.

_____ I understand classroom responsibilities and assume a fair share of the work.

_____ I offer my ideas and materials.

_____ I interact with children and focus on their needs instead of engaging in unnecessary conversation with adults.

_____ I avoid discussing children in front of them at all times.

_____ I can communicate directly if a concern arises.

Please provide additional comments:

Note: Permission is granted by the publisher to reproduce "Self-Evaluation of Student Teaching" for evaluation and record-keeping. From K. W. Browne and A. M. Gordon, *To Teach Well: An Early Childhood Practicum Guide.* Copyright © 2009 by Pearson Education, Inc. All rights reserved.

basic teaching skills after starting to work with children in an early childhood program.

Another way to evaluate your work is to write about your progress toward self-selected teaching goals. The My Reaction feature gives an example of a student teacher's self-evaluation.

My Reaction

"Self-Evaluation: How I'm Doing on My Teaching Goals"

I work with toddlers in my regular job, and with 2-year-olds at my practicum site. Sharing is not something that comes easy at either age, so my goal is *to learn to help children deal with waiting for a toy they want.* I know that sounds simple, but it's a big task. There seems to be a lot of different ways children react to their wish to have a toy—some go try to take it from the other child, others start to cry, and some just look longingly for it. When a child grabs a toy, I would just give the one who lost it something else. Now I am trying to watch the child's reaction, and encourage him or her to start using words to let the other child know how he or she feels. But children don't always have the words yet!

So, I am going to work on talking to both children, helping them find the words that I give. I think I will have to be able to cope with more upsets, but if I acknowledge how hard it is to take turns, well—that's life, isn't it? Also, I am finding that we are lacking duplicate toys at my work, so I am going to talk about getting more, and trying to work on this goal at both places.

—Iben

Supervisor Evaluations. You need some feedback from your supervisor, and probably from your faculty instructor as well. Often supervising teachers give you informal feedback on a regular basis: in the moment while on the floor with children, in preparation or at the end of an activity, either before you begin or finish a session, and sometimes during weekly meetings with you or the teaching team as a whole.

Your faculty instructor may make site visits as well. All these experiences can get students feeling anxious and vulnerable, for this process opens one up to criticism. "I was worried when you set the day to visit me," writes Grace. "I thought you were there to inspect how poorly I was teaching, and I was afraid. But it didn't feel like that once you got there. You stayed in the background, and I actually forgot you were watching me! Afterward, your notes were so helpful—I have lots to think about, but I think you see me as a good beginner!" Figure 2.8 is a sample evaluation form that a supervising teacher might complete for the student teacher.

A final note: Anticipating an evaluation can be anxiety-producing, as noted in the My Reaction feature. At the same time, getting feedback helps you become a better teacher. Moreover, practicing or preservice teachers are sometimes mentored beyond their time as student teachers. In fact, you can still get help and advice to improve your work at any point in your development as a teacher. Once you become a member of a teaching team, look around for those teachers who have mastered what you still want to achieve. Katz (1977) notes that, at all of four developmental stages, teachers benefit from assistance and colleague advice. The California Early Childhood Mentor program (2005) has structured the mentor teacher and director mentor elements to include opportunities for postpracticum and extended mentor–protégé relationships. Read Stacey James's Lessons from the Field article at the end of this chapter.

My Reaction

"When the Faculty Come: Being Observed and Evaluated"

I feel disappointed in myself after your visit and tonight in class. I realize that as a shy person I need to work on my interactions with the children. It has never really proved a problem for me; actually, I find myself working much better with children than I do with adults. I'm struggling because I know that everything is constructive criticism that will only make me a more thoughtful and better teacher, but as the human that I am I want to defend myself in some sense. I know that you can only evaluate what you saw and I do realize that I kept myself in the background . . . but I don't want you to think that I haven't made any special connections with the kids. I realize that I need to create more interactions, but I don't just stand there and ignore them.

—KERRY

Figure 2.8
Evaluation of the Student Teacher

Meeting with your supervisor to discuss your progress may feel awkward at first, but the feedback you get may be the best advice you can get to improve your teaching.

Name _____

Evaluator _____

Date _____

This form is used by the supervising teacher to assess your competencies in basic teaching skills. It will be completed and given to you midterm and for a final evaluation. The faculty instructor will use it as a guide when assessing your total coursework.

Personal Qualities (reliable, positive attitude, personal characteristics)

Comments: *Shawna has come to work ready to go, with an enthusiastic focus on children every session. She keeps an enthusiastic attitude throughout her time with us, and has an open mind toward any new learning.*

Relationships with Children (child development understanding, child responsiveness, communication effectiveness, positive guidance, family sensitivity]

Comments: *Because Shawna has a 6-year-old son, she came to our preschool with some previous experience as a parent. However, she has had to widen that knowledge with our diverse group. She now says she wants to audit another child development class! As to being responsive to children, the class has really embraced Shawna and calls out for her help regularly. In particular, the children who are active and feisty like her—she is not intimidated by their energy, and doesn't get angry when they "act up." In terms of guidance, this is both an asset and area of challenge. Shawna needs to know when to intervene before a situation gets volatile, and calm it. She is working on our conflict resolution steps for the rest of the term. Building stronger family-teacher relationships is one of her special teaching goals. We had her work with our parent liason on a monthly newsletter, and this has helped her and the families have given me positive feedback on her work in this area.*

Program Implementation (appropriate activity planning and execution)

Comments: *This was Shawna's second teaching focus. She has worked hard on literacy and music projects, bringing in beautiful high-quality picture books to go along with our monthly themes. She is learning to use the autoharp, and the children love to sing along and play it as much as she will let them.*

Working with Staff (member of the team)

Comments: *We have come to look forward to Tuesdays and Thursdays, Shawna's teaching days with us. She has grown in her comfort in asking all of us questions before plunging into a situation, and is a thoughtful addition to our team. We have grown with her bringing in new curriculum ideas, especially the autoharp. We would like Shawna to apply for the teaching assistant opening next year.*

List the Student's Strengths and Challenges (1–3 of each)

Midterm

Strengths	Challenges
Enthusiasm	*Tends to "whip up" the kids*
Responsible in attendance	*Needs to ask more questions*

Final

Strengths	Challenges
Curriculum ideas	*Conflict resolution with the children*
Family connections	

Ethics in the Profession

Throughout your career in teaching you will be in the position of making difficult decisions regarding children, their families, and coworkers. As a professional educator, you will have an obligation to make a responsible decision based on your knowledge and abilities. What guides you in that decision-making process? What are the values and ethics that influence you?

First and foremost, you are guided by your own ethical and moral values. These are the ideals and principles that you learned from families and friends, from your culture, from teachers, and from your religious beliefs, that helped you learn right from wrong. They are a set of values that you reflect on every day when working with children, families, and other teachers.

As a member of the teaching profession, you also have a code of ethics developed by NAEYC (2005) to inform your response to moral and ethical situations. It is important because it contains the professional standards for the early childhood field. When you are faced with an ethical dilemma, the code removes the ambiguity of "Should I do this? Or that? Or what?" and gives you the backing of all early childhood educators everywhere. The four sections of the code are as follows:

- Section 1: Ethical Responsibilities to Children
- Section 2: Ethical Responsibilities to Families
- Section 3: Ethical Responsibilities to Colleagues
- Section 4: Ethical Responsibilities to Community and Society

Each section contains two parts: ideals and principles that inform our decisions. Here is an example:

Ideal	**Example**
The overriding philosophy and standard of behavior.	To recognize and respect the unique qualities, abilities, and potential of each individual.

Principle	**Example**
The guide for resolving ethical dilemmas.	To involve all those with relevant knowledge (including families and staff) in decisions concerning a child, as appropriate, ensuring confidentiality of sensitive information.

The full Code of Ethical Conduct can be found on the NAEYC Web site (www.naeyc.org). Figure 2.9 is a shorter, more personal statement from NAEYC that states the values and moral obligations set forth in the code. You might want to check back in Chapter 1 for the top 10 fundamentals of teaching and see how they relate to the Statement of Commitment and the code itself.

Figure 2.9
NAEYC Code of Ethics:
Statement of
Commitment
By committing to a
professional code of
ethics, teachers affirm that
they will engage in
professional behavior.

As an individual who works with young children, I commit myself to furthering the values of early childhood education as they are reflected in the ideals and principles of the NAEYC Code of Ethical Conduct. To the best of my ability, I will

- Never harm children.
- Ensure that programs for young children are based on current knowledge and research of child development and early childhood education.
- Respect and support families in their task of nurturing children.
- Respect colleagues in early childhood care and education and support them in maintaining the NAEYC Code of Ethical Conduct.
- Serve as an advocate for children, their families, and their teachers in community and society.
- Stay informed of and maintain high standards of professional conduct.
- Engage in an ongoing process of self-reflection, realizing that personal characteristics, biases, and beliefs have an impact on children and families.
- Be open to new ideas and be willing to learn from the suggestions of others.
- Continue to learn, grow, and contribute as a professional.
- Honor the ideals and principles of the NAEYC Code of Ethical Conduct.

Source: Reprinted with permission from the National Association for the Education of Young Children. Available at http://www.naeyc.org/about/positions/PSETH05.asp.

Using the Code of Ethics

Feeney and Freeman (1999) tell us that there are two vital aspects of ethical behavior in early childhood education. The first is to know and act on the core values as noted in the Statement of Commitment. The second is to know and use the

Ethical conduct includes maintaining confidentiality about children, families, and other staff members.

NAEYC Code of Ethical Conduct and practice it daily as you try to participate in early childhood programs. The following scenarios offer specific examples of how to use the code of ethics in your teaching.

Scenario #1: Ethical Responsibilities to Children

Maddy, who is 18 months old, began biting the children in her child care class after one of them bit her. Although this is typical behavior for the age group, the number of biting incidents increased to the point that another parent complained to the teacher and wanted Maddy removed from the group.

How does the Code of Ethical Conduct help? Section I. Ideal I–1.4, states that we are to " appreciate the vulnerability of children and their dependence on adults." Principle 1.4 states that "we shall involve all those with relevant knowledge (including families and staff) in decisions concerning a child, as appropriate, ensuring confidentiality of sensitive information."

These two statements guide our decisions. First of all, the teachers take the standard steps to prevent the biting. Maddy is given a rubber object to wear and told to bite it instead of the other children. Her parents are contacted and they acknowledge that Maddy's routine and schedule had changed quite a bit at home over the past month, which might be contributing to Maddy's biting behavior. They agree to come in and meet with the teacher to talk further. The teachers start to observe Maddy to find out what seemed to trigger her biting. The family of the other child is assured that appropriate measures were under way to ensure the safety of everyone, without going into detail about the conversation with Maddy's parents to ensure confidentiality.

Scenario #2: Ethical Responsibilities to Families

Josefina, a student teacher, has been given a small group of children to work with each day. Darrell is in her group. His cousin, Jess, is in another teacher's group. One day Jess's mother seeks out Josefina and asks that Jess be put in her group to be with Darrell. Josefina is aware that each child was assigned to the group that best suited his developmental abilities. She tells her supervising teacher.

How does the Code of Ethical Conduct help? Section II. Ideal I–2.7 states that we are to "share information about each child's education and development with families and to help them understand and appreciate the current knowledge base of the early childhood profession." Section II. Principle P–2.2 states that "we shall inform families of program philosophy, policies, curriculum, assessment system, and personnel qualifications, and explain why we teach as we do—which should be in accordance with our ethical responsibilities to children."

When the student teacher informed the supervising teacher of the parents' request, the staff realized it had not communicated the rationale for the small groups very well to this particular parent. The head teacher asked her for a conference and spoke with her about the wide range of developmental levels in the class.

She explained that the small groups were used to enhance language development in the groups, based on the individual child's needs. The mother seemed reassured that her child was being treated fairly and according to his developmental abilities. The student teacher was commended for bringing this issue to the attention of her supervising teacher.

Scenario #3: Ethical Responsibilities to Colleagues

Laverne, a student teacher, overhears Merleen, one assistant teacher, telling Anna, another assistant teacher, that she feels Laverne is not doing her share of the work, calling her "a lazy slob." This is the second time Laverne has heard Merleen make a negative comment about her. Laverne wants to talk to Merleen, but doesn't know if she should.

How does the Code of Ethical Conduct help? Section III. Ideal I–3A.1 states that we are to "establish and maintain relationships of respect, trust, confidentiality, collaboration, and cooperation with co-workers." Principle 3A.2 states that "when we have concerns about the professional behavior of a co-worker, we shall first let that person know of our concern in a way that shows respect for personal dignity and for the diversity to be found among staff members, and then attempt to resolve the matter collegially and in a confidential manner." In Section 3, Responsibilities to Employers, Principle 3B.4 states, "If we have concerns about a colleague's behavior, and children's well-being is not at risk, we may address the concern with that individual. If . . . the situation does not improve, we shall report the colleague's unethical . . . behavior to an appropriate authority."

Laverne decides to take this situation to her supervising teacher to ask if she should confront Merleen. The supervising teacher tells Laverne that she would speak to Merleen first. The supervising teacher talks with Merleen about her unprofessional behavior. Merleen takes it upon herself to go to Laverne and apologize for her comments. For the remainder of the semester, she becomes more supportive of Laverne. (See the Reflective Incident, "My Ethical Responsibilities.")

Reflective Incident "My Ethical Responsibilities"

Select one of the previous three scenarios of ethical responsibilities. Describe the dilemma and your responses to it.

Your Thoughts

1. How would I feel?

2. What would I do?

3. What might be the results?

Preparing for Your Career in Teaching

At this point in your early childhood education or career, you can begin to prepare for the next step in advancing your career. By the time you are student teaching, you have a good idea of why working with young children is so important, and are getting a better idea now of what early childhood educators do. Most careers in our field involve either working directly with children, or working with adults, such as families, students, or other teachers. Understanding your career options, creating a professional portfolio, and learning about teacher credentialing in your state are three ways to prepare yourself.

Career Options

Working with Children. There are many kinds of settings in which you can work with children; Chapter 10 of this book describes many of these educational programs. Related professional work includes children's librarians, child therapists or psychologists, specialists in speech and language or other special needs, and pediatricians. Each state has its own requirements for working with children, either as individuals or in groups, in public settings. Whereas most states require a bachelor's degree for kindergarten and elementary teaching, requirements vary for other teaching options. Figure 2.10 shows a kind of professional ladder that illustrates the varying levels of requirements.

Working with Adults. Many careers involve adults as well as children; indeed, most teaching positions in early childhood education require teamwork. Different kinds of professionals may work with adults on behalf of children, such as child care consultants or advocates, family services provider, or program directors. Supervisory positions may include working with children and also administering a program, although many ECE directors and home visitors work primarily with teachers and families. Professors and educational journalists educate future teachers. Job responsibilities and salaries vary, although unfortunately ECE professionals usually earn relatively low salaries considering the responsibilities (and often education and training) they have.

Professionalism as a commitment to the field includes advocating for young children, for quality programs in the early years, and for support in working conditions and compensation. The NAEYC is the world's largest ECE organization. More than 100,000 strong, NAEYC has a network of local, state, and regional affiliates whose goals are to

- Support excellent early childhood education
- Improve teaching and learning
- Build a profession
- Promote public support and policies

Figure 2.10
Choices on the ECE
Career Ladder

**Jobs Requiring Advanced Education
(College or University)**

Child and Family Therapist
Kindergarten and Primary Teacher
Preschool Director and/or Site Supervisor
Child Welfare Case Worker
Bilingual Advisor/Specialist
Child Development Specialist
Early Intervention Specialist
Child Development Professor
Family Support Coordinator
Speech Therapist
Community Advocate
Public Policy & Research Specialist

**Jobs Requiring Specialized Training
(Post Secondary)**

Parent/Family Educator
Child Health Paraprofessional
Recreation Leader
Preschool Food Service Director
Special Education Assistant
Early Intervention Aide
Art/Movement Therapy Assistant
Juvenile Court Probation Worker
Family Service Advocate
Preschool Teacher
Foster Parent
Computer/Graphic Designer Of Children's Products
Welfare Child Care Worker
Infant Care Provider
Playground Designer
Bilingual Assistant

**Jobs Requiring Limited Training and Experience
Entry Level (Secondary and Adult Education)**

House Parent Group Home
Special Education Attendant
Bilingual Aide
Kindergarten Teacher Aide
Children's Book Author
Preschool Food Service Worker
Summer Camp Counselor
Child Care Aide
Recreation/Playground Aide
Children's Tutor
Infant Care Attendant
Home Companion
Group Home Attendant
Nanny or Au Pair

Source: Reprinted with permission of Canada College ECE/CD Department, 2006.

Ask your supervising teacher and faculty instructor about this organization, and how you can join. You can also investigate its activities on its Web site, become a student member for a discount, and attend its annual conferences at both the national and state levels.

Additional state and local initiatives enhance the professionalism of the field by providing supports and program services to eligible participants. For instance, many state departments of education have a child development division or consortium that provides training, career incentive grants, or professional advising. As referred to earlier, in California the mentor program provides training and financial incentives in the form of courses for mentoring or adult supervision, a selection process for mentor teachers and director mentors who then receive ongoing stipends for professional growth, and for supervising student teachers and director protégés. These initiatives are often coordinated through local college departments or resource and referral agencies. Check out the opportunities in your area.

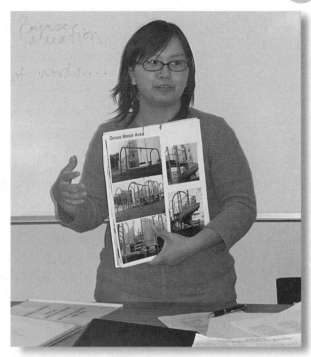

Attending and presenting at conferences helps teachers maintain their professional edge throughout their teaching careers.

Professional Portfolios

An innovative way to collect and present yourself as a professional has emerged in the last two decades. Student teachers at all levels of experience find making a professional portfolio useful and inspiring. A professional portfolio demonstrates your abilities as a developing professional, and saving student teaching artifacts can be put to use in a portfolio.

As a result of the standards movement in education, there has been a growing interest in developing portfolios both for children and for teachers. "A portfolio is a tool that helps a teacher make sense of his/her own experiences that contribute to his/her competence. It helps teachers track their own professional development and provides work samples for others to review" (Campbell, Cignetti, Melenyzer, Nettles, & Wyman, 2001, p. 2). A well-organized portfolio enables teachers to document their learning and their experiences, and "presents a clear picture of yourself as a growing, changing professional. Equally as significant, it can be a convincing, effective vehicle for you to demonstrate to others in a meaningful way the skills and knowledge you have gained in something as complex as teaching" (Campbell et al., 2001).

There are two kinds of portfolios: a working portfolio and a presentation portfolio. The former is a work-in-progress and is more inclusive than the latter. The presentation portfolio is a subset of the larger collection used in professional interactions with others. Teachers all start by creating a working portfolio, and then can pull from it what they need to present.

Include in your portfolio a collection of documents that will provide concrete evidence of your understanding of concepts, how you implemented theory, and your success in academic and teaching endeavors. There is no one standard way to create a portfolio, but you should have a system of organization. Some teachers use standards as categories (see Figure 2.1). Others prefer categories such as these:

- Academic
- Curriculum samples
- Conferences and workshops
- Leadership
- Personal statement
- References and recommendations

Take a moment to think about how to make your portfolio attractive and easy to understand and use. A cover page, table of contents, and introductory section that has a résumé and autobiography are inviting.

Creating a portfolio doesn't have to be difficult, but it does take time and personal reflection. Remember that you will be collecting work samples, or artifacts, that show your work, so you may want to use a large file box along with a large notebook that can be divided into sections. Once you have a filing system, become a packrat! And while you collect evidence of your work, notice the gaps so you can see what to work on.

Evidence of each goal met, and a reflection piece round out the portfolio. One student teacher we know used a lightbulb icon to signal the reflection; another attached large, colored sticky notes. As with children, documentation needs to be objective and accurate; a brief reflection adds your personal expertise and flavor. Figure 2.11 shows a sample list for a working professional portfolio.

Figure 2.11
What Do I Save in My Professional Portfolio?

A professional portfolio is a critical element in presenting yourself as a competent early childhood teacher.

Academic

Transcripts, grade reports, written evaluations from instructors, written assignments, course syllabi or summaries.

Conferences and Workshops

Signed verification forms, distributed materials, notes, description of how the activity assisted in meeting your goals

Leadership

Materials you developed, meeting agenda with your contribution highlighted, letter or editorial you wrote

Creative Endeavors

Photos or special project or activity, audiotape or videotape of project or activity, letters from participants, time log

Personal Statements

Autobiography, philosophy of early childhood education, statement of your commitment, your priorities and values in the field

References and Recommendations

Letters of reference, recommendations, awards and commendations

---

Source: Used with permission of San Mateo Compensation and Retention Enhances Stability (CARES) Program, 2000.

Finally, remember that you will be adding to this portfolio over time. Wherever you work, be sure to get a letter of reference when you move on; for instance, be sure to keep the evaluations you get from your student teaching and, if successful, ask your supervising teacher to write you a one-page letter about what you learned and did.

Teaching Credentials and Incentives

Each state has its own credentials and often sponsors incentive programs to recruit and/or retain teachers. Find out about this in your own state by going to your state's department of education Web site and checking the credential requirements and possibilities. For an example, Table 2.1 offers a

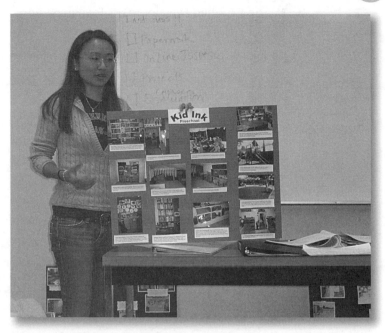

Creating a professional portfolio personalizes your student teaching experience and demonstrates your growth as a teacher.

condensed outline of the California Child Development Permit matrix for teaching in public early education programs for infant/toddler, preschool, and school-age children.

Many states offer certificate programs through postsecondary education. Either at the community college or 4-year level, these programs vary in their requirements. Many offer an Early Childhood Certificate program that verifies successful completion of particular ECE coursework; others offer associate or bachelor's degrees. Graduate programs are less common; some universities and colleges offer master's or doctoral programs in early childhood education; others may confer graduate degrees in human development, family studies, or other related fields.

Another avenue for professionalism comes from teaching incentive programs. Again, there is great variety and availability throughout the states, so contacting your state department of education or local resource and referral agency will give you current options. One program, financed by the voters of California, established local community agencies to establish and distribute funds to teachers who stayed at their program of employment and continued their education through college classes or professional workshops. This compensation and retention program has been continued to help increase the educational standards for early childhood teaching in that state.

You have learned about some of the criteria that make up a professional teacher's life. Some of it may have been enjoyable and some of it may seem uncomfortable. In either event, as you gain experience in these matters, you will be guided by experienced professional teachers who will help you meet the

Table 2.1 The CA Child Development Teaching Permit

	Education Requirements	Experience Requirements	Alternative Qualifications	Renewal
Assistant teacher	6 units of ECE or CD courses	None	Accredited HERO/ROP program	105 hours of professional growth
Associate teacher	12 units of ECE or CD courses, including core courses*	50 days of 3+ hours per day within 2 years	Child Development Associate (CDA) credential	15 additional units toward teacher permit (must be met within 10 years)
Teacher	24 units of ECE or CD, including core courses*	175 days of 3+ hours per day within 4 years	AA or higher in ECE or related field with 3 semester units of supervised field experience in ECE setting (SFE/ECE)	105 hours of professional growth
Master teacher	24 units of ECE or CD, including core courses*, plus 16 general education units**	350 days of 3+ hours per day within 4 years	BA or higher with 12 units of ECE, plus 3 semester units of SFE/ECE	105 hours of professional growth
Site supervisor	AA (60 units) with 24 units of ECE or CD courses, including core courses*, plus 6 administration units (Admin), plus 2 adult supervision units (Ad sup)	350 days of 3+ hours per day within 4 years, including at least 100 days of supervising adults	BA or higher with 12 units of ECE, plus 3 semester units of SFE/ECE; or administrative credential with 12 units of ECE, plus 3 units SFE/ECE; or teaching credential with 12 units ECE, plus 3 units SFE/ECE	105 hours of professional growth
Program director	AA (60 units), with 24 units in ECE or CD courses, including core courses*, plus 6 Admin., plus 2 Ad. Sup	Site supervisor status and one program year of site supervisor experience	Admin. credential with 12 units of ECE, plus 3 units SFE/ECE; or teaching credential with 12 units of ECE plus 3 units SFE/ECE; or master's degree in ECE or child/human development	105 hours of professional growth

* Core courses include child development; curriculum; and child, family, and community.

** General education courses include English or language arts; mathematics or science; social science; and humanities and/or fine arts.

Source: From *A Guidebook for Professional Growth Planning and Documentation,* by Child Care Training Consortium of California, 2000, retrieved from www.childdevelopment.org. Used with permission. A complete copy of the CD Permit matrix is available at the California Commission on Teacher Credentialing http://www.ctc.ca.gov, or through the Child Development Training Consortium, www.childdevelopment.org.

challenges. They can help you appreciate that this type of professional development can be a stimulating and positive reinforcement of your teaching commitment. Assessments and evaluations, ethics, and career preparation foster the reflective teaching you need to become a lifelong learner who grows and changes along with the children in the classroom (see "Lessons from the field: Becoming a Professional").

"Becoming a Professional"

by Stacey James

Mentor teacher, Geo-Kids Early Childhood Development Center

People engaged in many different types of work must participate in ongoing professional growth activities in order to remain informed, marketable, and skilled in their fields. Early childhood education is such a field. But to my mind, what makes teaching different from many other vocations is the need for ongoing *personal* growth. Personal development is professional development, and vice versa: they are inseparable and essential for us. Striving to become a more reflective, supportive, and responsive person makes me a better teacher; taking part in professional activities such as conferences, mentoring, and meaningful dialogue with colleagues makes me a better person.

I decided to become an early childhood educator at midlife, leaving a successful career in an entirely different field. The deliberateness of my choice, and the personal risk I felt I was taking, compelled me to take this career change very seriously, and I had little tolerance for people in the field who approached this work with a casual attitude. Despite my inexperience and the steep learning curve, I considered myself a "professional" from the start.

But I don't think I truly became a professional until I became a mentor teacher. Being a mentor teacher requires me to more closely examine the relationship between my theory and my practice, and to find ways to articulate both. I have become a more reflective teacher as a result, and this has made me a better teacher. I love to witness the "aha" moments as student teachers experience the richness of working with young children, and the excitement of discovering their role in the life of the classroom. These moments make my classroom experience richer, too. As my student teachers gradually take risks, I learn to become a more supportive presence. As we talk about their classroom experiences, I am drawn into more meaningful dialogue about this work. As they formulate and then succeed at achieving their goals, I feel more purposeful and hopeful about my own work with children.

"Professional development" has taken on a deeper meaning for me through mentoring. Although mentoring provides a path for my own development in this profession, it also allows me to feel that I am nurturing the development of other future professionals, as well as the development of the profession as a whole. The work that we do is too important to do less. We owe it to children, families, and ourselves to seek opportunities for personal and professional growth. Every time I stretch myself, I am rewarded with a measure of self-discovery and my practice is revitalized. I can't see how we could possibly enjoy this work if we become stagnant. After all, we clearly don't do it for the money! Speaking for myself, I do it because it is important work—endlessly fascinating, continually challenging, and frequently exhilarating. Just as the children are on an ever-expanding path of learning, so am I. I don't ever want to get to the day when I think I can stop learning—about children, myself, and teaching—because two things will happen on that day: The work will cease to be gratifying on a daily basis, and I will cease to be a good teacher.

Practicum Activity

Write two teaching goals for yourself. Now add at least two objectives for each goal. Refer to Figures 2.1 and 2.3 for help in setting and writing those goals. Compare your goals and objectives to those of a classmate and fellow student teacher.

Journaling Assignment

Do a self-evaluation based on Figure 2.5 during the first few weeks of your student teaching. Look at it as you finish your student teaching. See how much you've grown! Note where you would like to go next.

Resources

California Early Childhood Mentor Program. (2005). Introductory Brochure. Retrieved from http://www.ecementor.org

Campbell, D. M. Cignetti, P. B., Melenyzer, B. J. Nettles, D. H., Wyman, R. M. (2001). *How to develop a professional portfolio* (2nd ed.). Boston: Allyn & Bacon.

Canada College ECE Department (2004). *Your Career* (brochure). Retrieved from http://www.canadacollege/ece

Child Care Training Consortium of California. (2000). *A guidebook for professional growth planning and documentation.* Retrieved from http://www.childdevelopment.org

Feeney, S., and Freeman, N. K. (1999). *Ethics and the early childhood educator: Using the NAEYC code.* Washington, DC: National Association for the Education of Young Children.

Goines, V., and Eto, V. (2000). *Student teaching: Journal guidelines.* Unpublished manuscript, Canada College, Redwood City, CA.

Gorden, A. M., & Browne, K. W. (2008). *Beginnings and beyond: Foundations in early childhood education* (7th ed.). Clifton Park, NY: Thomson Delmar Learning.

Hyson, M. (Ed.). (2003). *Preparing early childhood professionals.* Washington, DC: NAEYC.

Katz, L. (1977). *Talks with teachers: Reflections on early childhood education.* Washington, DC: National Association for the Education of Young Children.

National Association for the Education of Young Children. (2005). *Code of ethical conduct.* Washington, DC: Author.

National Association for the Education of Young Children, Division for Early Childhood of the Council for Exceptional Children, and National Board for Professional Teaching Standards. (2003). *Guidelines for preparation of early childhood professionals.* Washington, DC: Authors.

Spodek, B. (1972). *Teaching in the early years.* Upper Saddle River, NJ: Prentice Hall.

Web Sites

California Early Childhood Mentor Program
www.ecementor.org

Child Development Training Consortium
www.chhilddevelopment.org

Council for Exceptional Children
www.cec.sped.org

National Association for the Education of Young Children
www.naeyc.org

chapter 3

Understanding and Guiding Behavior

Basic Beliefs About Guidance

Guiding young children is a challenge for all teachers. As you observe others teach and participate more in teaching yourself, you will learn some effective ways to guide children's behavior. You will also gain insight into your own feelings about children's behavior and find that teaching young children has less to do with "love and patience" and more to do with your ability to learn how to handle situations that arise as children grow and learn to control their behavior. Figure 3.1 lists seven of the basic beliefs about guidance that will help form your attitudes toward guiding young children. Look back to these basics as you move forward in this chapter to see how well you reflect them in your own teaching experience. You may find the examples helpful as each belief is discussed more fully.

Effective guidance practices can solve many behavior issues and prevent others from occurring. Positive guidance is based on attitudes and beliefs about children, families, and the guidance process. Most are learned over a period of time through classroom experience. These seven basic guideposts can be important as you shape your own approach to effective guidance.

Help children become responsible for their own actions.

Guidance is an interactive process between teacher and child with a strong emphasis on problem solving. Our goal is to help children learn by allowing them to work out solutions without undue interference; to make judgments based on their emerging inner controls; to model appropriate behavior for them; and to use guidance techniques that are appropriate.

Example: "They won't let you play with them, Rashad, because you knocked down their block buildings. What could you say so they know you want to play?"

Teach children to understand and respect differences.

The early years are the best time to help children develop attitudes and behaviors that help them live in harmony with one other. Children learn to see each

Figure 3.1
Seven Basic Beliefs
About Guidance

As you help children learn
the social skills they need,
these seven basic beliefs
can help you develop
more confidence in
guiding behavior.

> 1. Help children become responsible for their own actions.
> 2. Teach children to understand and respect differences.
> 3. Take into account a child's temperament, family, and community.
> 4. Learn how to apply developmental theory to guidance planning.
> 5. Appreciate that guidance is a system of strategies.
> 6. Become aware of your own potential bias.
> 7. Let children know you believe they are inherently good.

other with increasing understanding and respect for the many ways we are all different and unique. Good guidance practices teach these skills.

> *Example: "Takako is just learning to speak English and that is why she pronounces words differently than you do. Her accent isn't something bad, it is just different from yours. Let's ask her if she will teach us how to say 'hello' in Japanese."*

Take into account a child's temperament, family, and community.

Children's behavior is influenced by many factors. Each child has a unique style and temperament and is part of a larger community. Families, neighbors, and religious, ethnic, and cultural groups shape children's values and behavior. The essential partnership in guiding young children is between the family and the teachers and must be thoughtfully considered. Bronfenbrenner (1979) called this network the "ecology of development," recognizing the influence of the child's system of family and cultural relationships that significantly affect how the child develops. The complex interactions among the child's family and community connections are probably among the most important concepts you will learn as a student teacher, for they will impact your approach to teaching in the 21st century.

> *Example: "Has your grandmother come back from Mexico yet, Consuela? I know you miss her a lot. When she gets back, let's see if she can visit school again and teach us the special songs she sings to you."*

Learn how to apply developmental theory to guidance planning.

Child development theory teaches us about the individual nature of children; predictable patterns and stages through which they develop; variations in their growth; and what types of behaviors, fears, and interests are typical of various age groups. When we understand child development theory we gain the confidence to support the child's emerging self-control at each level of development. All teachers need to form developmental points of view so that they are able to use appropriate guidance strategies by matching theory to practice.

> *Example: "I know Ricky has been causing concern among the staff because he is taking so many risks on the climbers. Let's remember that although he has a highly developed vocabulary and is quite tall for his age he is just 3 years old, and needs more time for his physical development to mature. When he is near the climbers, let's make sure one of us is there to support his efforts."*

Appreciate that guidance is a system of strategies.

Guidance is not a single, quick-fix response to all behavior situations. Instead, guidance is an intentional course of action based on a teacher's knowledge of the individual child, the group of children, the family, and developmental theory. (See "My Reaction" for Jane's ideas.) Teachers use the appropriate guidance strategy at each step in the process in ways that encourage and support behavior changes at various age and developmental levels.

Example: "I know you have trouble sitting at group time and I know how you love stories, so I am going to help you. Tomorrow, come and sit close to my chair while I am reading. You can turn the pages for me. We'll do that for a few days and see if it helps."

Become aware of your own potential biases.

The ways you were raised influence the choices you make in guiding children's behavior. Teachers need to become aware of their reactions to certain behaviors and how their biases may impact their own attitudes and values. Stay open to different viewpoints of what is considered "right" or "wrong" while developing your guidance approach. This is especially important when working with families from cultures other than your own.

Example: "My mother taught us with the switch and would snatch us back. I know I can't hit the children, but they need stern discipline. Don't they need me to hold onto them so they know who's boss here at school?"

Let children know you believe they are inherently good.

Behavior is the only language children have to let us know something is bothering them until they are mature enough to use the words that will communicate their thoughts and concerns. All children will misbehave at some time; it is a natural part of growing up.

Example: "Wow, Pete. You are usually careful about other people's work. Is something bothering you? Can I help you use some words to tell me how you are feeling and why you threw Beth's papers on the floor?"

My Reaction

"Moments of Discipline"

I think discipline includes everything we do to teach our children to think for themselves, make good choices, solve problems, and express themselves. I consider the moments I have with the children in distress as a time to share: to talk with them, listen to them, support, guide, and instill in them some ideas of people other than themselves. One-on-one is the best; when there are two children it is good; three is more complicated; four. . . I don't know. I feel ineffective for not knowing what to do.

—JANE

Guidance, Discipline, and Punishment: What's the Difference?

You may find that early childhood settings use the words *guidance*, *discipline*, and *punishment* in different ways. Often the meaning of each word becomes confused when used interchangeably or without clear definition. To use appropriate guidance techniques, you need to first understand the basic differences among guidance, discipline, and punishment.

What Is Guidance?

Guidance is an ongoing system by which adults help children learn to manage their impulses, express feelings, channel frustrations, solve problems, and learn the difference between acceptable and unacceptable behavior. Effective guidance strategies are based on caring, respectful, and supportive relationships between children and adults. We call this positive guidance. As trust between the child and the teacher builds, teaching and learning the skills of social interactions and behavior becomes easier.

Through the use of positive, appropriate guidance methods, teachers create a balance between children's emerging need for independence and their need for outer controls, such as rules and boundaries of behavior. As children achieve greater self-control, teachers allow them to make more of their own decisions and govern their own actions. Taking responsibility creates self-confidence in children as they learn to handle challenging situations while building life skills in communication and problem solving.

Classroom management becomes easier when children are independent, self-directed learners. Good guidance strategies help them see the context of their actions along with understanding the consequences of their behavior. Learning about cause and effect of one's behavior will be of value to the children throughout their life.

Guidance is a way for you to be the guide, to lead children toward more positive ways to having healthy social relationships. The three elements critical to any guidance methods are the child, the adult, and the situation. All three elements must be addressed as you work toward a solution. Figure 3.2 elaborates on the guidance triangle. There is not just one "right" way to solve each problem. Each child, adult, situation, and relationship is different and the diagram can help clarify what is going on. Understanding is the first step toward solving a problem.

Keeping Guidance Positive

Positive guidance techniques usually begin with a positive statement rather than saying "Stop!" or "Don't." Here are some strategies for creating a more positive tone:

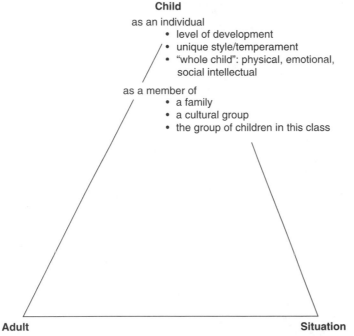

Child

as an individual
- level of development
- unique style/temperament
- "whole child": physical, emotional, social intellectual

as a member of
- a family
- a cultural group
- the group of children in this class

Adult
- the role: teacher, parent, coach, advocate, friend
- relationship to the child
- values, biases
- skills and guidance techniques

Situation
- the physical environment
- time of day
- who, what is involved
- what else is happening
- what is unique about it

Figure 3.2
The Guidance Triangle
The guidance triangle can help teachers establish effective guidance practices by highlighting three important elements: the child, the adult, and the situation.

Source: From Ann Gordon & Kathryn Williams Browne, *Guiding Young Children in a Diverse Society*. Published by Allyn & Bacon, Boston, MA. Copyright © 1996 by Pearson Education. Reprinted by permission of the publisher.

- *Emphasize* what a child should do by making positive statements. "Put the puzzle pieces on the table, Karly, so that other children won't step on them."

- *Foster* a child's ability to think of the consequences. "What will happen if you scribble on Orlando's paper, Josh? How do you think he will feel about it?

- *Accept* a child's need for autonomy when they are being assertive, testing limits, and challenging adults. "You are so sleepy and I know you want to keep playing with your toys. But it is naptime, so I'll put you in your crib and turn on some quiet music."

- *Encourage* a sense of empathy toward others. "Kiki dropped her pencil and it rolled under her wheelchair. Can you reach it for her, Patti?"

- *Set* an example to follow. "Sometimes when I feel angry, Shantell, I find a quiet corner away from the noise and that helps me calm down. Let's see if the book nook is available."

- *Help* children govern their own actions. "Good for you, Rocco. You remembered to use words instead of crying."

- *Recognize* the need to be consistent. Reinforce the same rules with all children at all times. "I know you *really* want a turn on the gym mat, Julio, but it's not okay for anyone to cut."

Understanding and Guiding Behavior

- *Give* directions and suggestions in clear, simple statements and give reasons for your request. "Look at your feet, Eunice, and you will see how to avoid stepping on Leo's hands. Put your foot down on the next rung after Leo moves his hands."

- *Provide* ways for children to refocus. "Luz, if you sit at the table you'll be able to finish dictating your story before going outside to play kickball."

- *Communicate* support and reinforce children when they change their behaviors. "Good. You were really careful when you put away the paints. You have gotten to be a very good cleaner-upper, Todd."

By choosing your words carefully and framing them in positive ways, you help children learn that they can become more responsible for their actions.

What Is Discipline?

Discipline is an important concept and a part of the guidance system. Discipline is frequently thought of in terms of punishment and negative responses to a child's behavior, but that does not have to be the case. Good discipline is good guidance. The word *discipline* comes from *disciple*, meaning a pupil, follower, and learner. That definition suggests an important concept of following examples and having adults model the kind of behavior that they would like children to learn (Gordon & Browne, 2007).

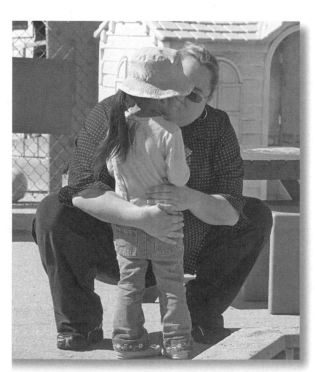

Positive guidance is fostered by warm and caring interactions so that children can develop positive self-esteem and social competence.

Discipline and guidance are similar in that good or effective discipline has the same foundation of positive, thoughtful, nonpunitive methods—that accept the premise that children will need time and support to learn appropriate social behavior—and that promote children's empathy and moral reasoning.

When discipline is used interchangeably with punishment, it loses its effectiveness and becomes a negative force in helping children change their behavior. When linked with guidance, discipline becomes a learning experience that relies on a child's interaction and involvement. Children should be disciplined, but in ways that foster thinking and problem solving. The challenging behavior should be seen from the perspective of "What should I do to help this child learn from this experience?" not "How can I punish this behavior?"

What Is Punishment?

Punishment is a harsh consequence for misbehavior. The punishment is a matter of degree of the consequence, which may or may not be connected to the offense. Negative strategies such as threats, withdrawal of affection or privileges, spanking, isolation, and other punitive methods that promote shame and humiliation are used to eliminate unwanted behavior. Punishment, because it is often a split-second reaction, is an adult release rather than part of a strategy to help a child learn self-control (Gordon & Browne, 2007). When punishment is used, there is an assumption that you can get rid of the behavior without understanding the cause. The behavior may stop but the reason a child misbehaves is still unknown. The adult who insists on obedience alone does not give the child an opportunity to learn both cause and consequences.

How Discipline and Punishment Differ

Three-year-old Maxine runs over to Lilly, grabs a book from her hand, and shoves her away. Maxine laughs and runs away. Lilly looks startled.

Solving Problems with Guidance and Positive Discipline. The teacher sits down with Maxine while another teacher comforts Lilly.

Teacher: Pushing other children is not okay, Maxine. We can't let you hurt other children just as we won't let them hurt you. Why did you push Lilly?

Maxine: I wanted her book. It's my favorite.

Teacher: I know how hard it is to wait for something you want, but I can't let you just grab it from her. She has stopped crying now. Let's go see if we can talk to her about giving you a turn with the book.

Together they walk toward Maxine and begin to negotiate a time when Lilly might be finished with the book.

The Point: Learning takes place for both Lilly and Maxine. The children learn from caring adults who acknowledge their feelings and guide them in problem-solving skills. Both children maintain some control over the situation: Lilly gets her book back and Maxine gets to have a turn. Lilly learns that she and her possessions will be protected. Maxine learns how to ask someone for a turn. The focus is directly on the children's behavior and there is a direct link between the action and the consequence. The adult models good communication skills to help the children verbalize their needs. The strategy is age-appropriate for 3-year-olds.

Using Punishment. The teacher grabs Maxine as she runs away.

Teacher: "That's a bad thing to do. You can't hit other children. Go sit in the time-out chair and wait there until I come back to get you.

The teacher keeps a hold on Maxine's arm, leads her to an isolated corner, and sits her down in a chair. Maxine begins to cry.

> **Teacher:** Crying won't help. You were bad. Now sit here for a while and think about what you did to Lilly.

The teacher leaves and returns to the center of the classroom.

The Point: The teacher took control over Maxine's behavior so very little, if any, learning took place. The teacher made no connection between Maxine's hitting and the punishment she imposed. Rather than help Maxine gain some inner control, the teacher imposed external controls over her, diminishing her self-esteem, and shaming her by calling her "bad." The teacher made no attempt to understand Maxine's behavior, no feelings were discussed, and the punishment had no direct relation to the behavior. Maxine does not know what to do if she feels like pushing another child again, not even the language to use. She has not been given any strategies for managing her urges. An isolated period of time sitting in a chair does not help her separate her feelings, actions, and thoughts so that she learns any effective strategies for coping.

Why Children Misbehave

There are many reasons young children behave the way they do. For the most part, children's motives arise from frustration and anger that they do not know how to express any other way. Misbehaving is a normal part of growing up as children test their limits. One of the teacher's most important roles is to help children learn the cause of their misbehavior and then provide appropriate and equitable guidance.

Misbehavior and acting out are signs that a child is somehow troubled and needs help and may be due to any number of circumstances. At least five factors affect a child's behavior (Gordon & Browne, 2008):

- *Environmental.* Sometimes the setting creates opportunities for inappropriate behavior. Class size, teacher–child ratios, and trained teachers have great influence on a child's behavior in any setting. There also may be too much or too little stimulation, inappropriate and insufficient materials and equipment, furniture that doesn't fit children's bodies, materials that are inaccessible, not enough time for activities, overcrowded work and play space, or too much time sitting and listening. The effect of environment on behavior and the importance of curriculum in guidance will be discussed at greater length in Chapter 5.
- *Developmental.* Young children are just beginning to acquire greater language and social skills that will help them learn acceptable behavior. Teachers need a solid background in child development to guide children according to their individual developmental abilities. A teacher's awareness

of the physical, social, emotional, and cognitive range of a child is necessary when planning guidance strategies. A schedule that requires 3-year-olds to sit for a 30-minute group time or an expectation to have toddlers share a single toy are both unreasonable and set the stage for misbehavior.

- *Individual.* When children are hungry, thirsty, tired, bored, restless, or ill, they may exhibit problem behavior. A child's basic temperament (i.e., easygoing, slow-to-warm-up, difficult) may also account for the way he or she behaves. When teachers are aware of the individual temperament of each child in the class, they can choose guidance measures that are tailored to meet the specific needs of that child.

- *Social and Emotional Needs.* Some behavior problems occur when children are trying to express social and emotional needs. A child who wants attention, or is fearful, embarrassed, or lonely, may act out those feelings for lack of words. Family situations, such as divorce, new baby, illness, or death, may cause young children to act out in inappropriate ways. Challenging behavior may also occur when adults have too high or too low expectations and when they do not set appropriate limits. Guidance strategies should be chosen that help children with language for solving conflicts and recognition of their emotions and feelings.

- *Cultural Influences.* When the family and the school cultures differ, children may be caught in the middle. Guidance and discipline issues are embedded in the values of each family. Behavior issues often arise when there are different expectations between home and school settings that highlight cultural child-rearing practices. Respect for these differences, valuing each child's family without bias, and working toward compatible solutions together creates a climate in which positive behavior will thrive. Figure 3.3 offers tips for teachers about how to choose effective guidance strategies.

Developmentally and Culturally Appropriate Guidance

The basic idea behind *developmentally appropriate practice* (DAP) is to start where children are and help them achieve their potential. In doing so, teachers make decisions about behavior and guidance based on what is *developmentally appropriate*.

Three Criteria

Three aspects of a program, activity, or teaching practice must be considered when planning guidance strategies and teaching methods.

Age appropriateness is what we know about how children learn and grow at certain ages of their development. These age-related characteristics allow us to

Figure 3.3
Twelve Tips for Teachers
By fostering cooperation and positive behavior in many ways, teachers encourage good behavior and problem solving.

Effective guidance and positive discipline happen when you:

- *Are aware of your body position.* Place yourself so you can see most or all of the room. Get down low to the children's level when you are talking to them
- *Ask, don't tell.* Ask the children, "What's going on?" "What happened here?" "What's not working?"
- *Acknowledge and express children's feelings.* You might say, "You sound angry/hurt/sad, etc." "I know you want that truck now." "I know it is hard for you to wait for a turn."
- *Enlist children's cooperation to solve the problem.* Ask, "What should we do next?" "How do you think we should handle this?" "What could everyone do to make this better?"
- *Use humor.* Say, "Oops! I guess someone forgot that the puzzles don't put themselves together at cleanup time."
- *Check the space arrangements.* Are too many children trying to play in one area? How can you enlarge it?
- *Know the teacher–child ratio for the classroom.* If there are 18 children and 3 teachers, where are "my" 6? Am I devoting too much time to one child?
- *Think before you speak.* Make sure the words you use are what you mean. For example, "Danny, run and get me a sponge." Do you want Danny to "run"?
- *Give children choices that are appropriate and acceptable.* "Do you want to go inside now?" is not a choice at certain times. A more effective approach is "Do you want to walk backward toward the door or on your tippy toes? "It's time to go home now. Do you want to put on your coat before or after the story?"
- *Recognize and acknowledge responsible behavior.* Tell the child, "What a great job you did in cleaning the fish tank." "That was kind of you to let him have the first turn."
- *State the positive.* Instead of "Don't ride so fast down the hill," say, "You're riding pretty fast. You might want to slow down." "Don't spill your juice" could be "Look at where you are pouring the juice. Find the edge of the glass and make sure it goes inside the rim."
- *Learn the group dynamics.* Which children are easily frustrated? Easy-going? Sensitive? Bossy? When do things start to fall apart for them?

predict within an age range what activities, materials, interactions, and experiences will be challenging and achievable to children of that age.

Individual appropriateness is what we know about each individual child: the strengths, challenges, and interests. This information helps us create flexible, open-ended learning experiences that are adaptable and respond to individual differences within a group of children.

Cultural and family responsiveness is what we learn about the family that helps us understand the influences on each child. We must be sensitive to a child's culture and background when planning guidance strategies. The ethics of the early childhood profession prohibits physical punishment, yet in some cultures, spanking and hitting children for their misbehavior are considered appropriate. To ensure that guidance techniques are compatible between the home and the school, teachers must work closely with families to understand their cultural needs and concerns. The NAEYC has criteria for making the connections between home and school. Chapter 9 will deal with these issues in greater depth.

When guiding children from different cultural backgrounds, we treat them with respect as we use various guidance techniques.

How to Apply DAP to Guidance Challenges: A Case Study

How does DAP work in choosing guidance techniques? All three criteria are woven together to plan appropriate methods for each child, as with Garth, for example:

> *Six-year-old Garth is having difficulty getting along with his classmates. He has a good sense of humor, but uses it to create unflattering drawings of many of the children in the class. Like any 6-year-old, he wants to have more friends but many classmates won't play with him.*

What would a developmentally appropriate guidance plan look like for Garth? His teacher would first look at the overall *age characteristics* and find that 6-year-olds, although charming, tend to show aggression through insults and name-calling. They are also seriously exploring art for the first time. These characteristics seem on target with Garth's acting-out behaviors. We also know that 6-year-olds are becoming proud of their accomplishments, have greater interest in the process of creativity than in the product, and like to work cooperatively on tasks and projects. At that age, they make their social connections through play and tend to have friends of the same sex.

Next, the teacher would focus on Garth as an *individual* and gain more insight into his behavior. Garth is one of the few boys in the class who participates readily and enthusiastically in art activities, and seems to enjoy honing his techniques and skills in drawing. When other children ask Garth about his drawings, he laughs and does not respond to their comments and questions, then moves on to another activity.

As to the third criteria of *family and cultural context*, Garth is the third boy of four children in a household that is boisterous and loud. Garth is often teased by his brothers for liking to paint and draw. His parents try to support his interest in art, but their time is taken up with Garth's aging grandmother, who lives with them.

Looking at all three criteria in relationship to one another gives us a more complete picture of Garth and some insights into a guidance plan that might help him change his behavior and gain more friends. Art seems to play an important but unappreciated role in Garth's life. The teacher talks with Garth about his drawings, showing sincere interest in his skills. She enlists his help in setting up a new art project that will be presented at Family Night. He agrees to be on the team of four students who will determine the scope of the project and is given the responsibility for much of the drawing. He also agrees to help other students learn to create some of the figures that are needed, and seems excited about being a "teacher" to his peers. The teacher was counting on the fact that 6-year-olds do like to be "know-it-alls," and Garth is no exception.

As the project proceeds over the next few months, Garth's ability to work with his peers improves. Some of the children are able to recognize and enjoy the cartoon quality of his drawings of people. Garth, in turn, begins to show them how to draw cartoons. At Family Night, Garth's family seems genuinely stunned by his artistic ability and his grandmother asks him to draw some pictures for her room. His parents make an appointment to see the teacher and discuss how to foster his talent in appropriate ways. Classmates now volunteer to work with Garth on other projects.

Developmentally appropriate guidance means that teachers have age-appropriate expectations, know about the individual children who are in their class, and have a working knowledge of the families of those children. With those criteria in mind, guidance strategies emerge as part of a well-thought-out approach to behaviors that are challenging.

Guidance Strategies That Work

Some guidance methods are subtle; others are more obvious. Each situation requires a strategy that best meets the needs of the child, the adult, and the group at that particular time. No one method applies to all situations—or children—at all times. The top 10 list of guidance techniques is shown in Figure 3.4. Guidance strategies run along a continuum, from the understated approach (ignoring the behavior) to the more obvious intervention (intervening physically), with a wide range of options in between. Just as the guidance triangle (Figure 3.2) helps you understand what is going on, the guidance continuum (Figure 3.5) helps you decide what to do to resolve the problem.

1. Set appropriate expectations for the age and individuals.
2. Model behavior and respect.
3. Observe and document behavior.
4. Have appropriate environments and curriculum.
5. Listen and reflect.
6. Reinforce positive behavior.
7. Redirect and give choices.
8. Set reasonable limits and follow through consistently.
9. Use problem-solving for conflict resolution.
10. Intervene and set consequences.

Figure 3.4
Top 10 Guidance
Techniques

Indirect Guidance

Children's behavior is strongly influenced by the people and environment in which they live, work, and play. When children enter a classroom indirect messages tell them what is expected of them. A room full of neatly lined-up desks says, "Sit and work here." A room with a long, open space leading from the entry to the outside says, "Run!" Daily time schedules that allow only a few minutes for transitions and/or cleanup create an anxious, tense climate. Too few teachers can lead to children who are undersupervised and out of control.

Indirect guidance is a teacher's way of establishing control and setting the stage for what they want to happen within the classroom. Teachers use their knowledge to ensure that their use of indirect guidance is based on their knowledge of the following:

- *Child development*, which helps them set appropriate expectations for children's behavior. For instance, group times for 4-year-olds are longer than for 2-year-olds who are not yet ready to sit and listen for 15 minutes.

- *The impact of the setting*, including space arrangements, schedule, materials, and resources. For each transition during the day, plenty of time is allotted for children to move from one activity to another without being hurried.

- *How to accomplish the goals of the program* by using the environment as a teaching tool. For instance, independence is fostered when materials such as puzzles, paper and crayons, glue, and scissors are situated on low, open shelves so that children can serve themselves and not have to wait for an adult to help them.

- *How to set the tone for positive interactions*. Teachers make sure that there is more than one truck, telephone, wagon, or easel so that children are not frustrated by a long wait, and to encourage social interactions.

- *How to create culturally responsive environments*. Throughout the classroom, books, photos, fabrics, arts and craft objects, multiracial boy and girl dolls, and multicultural dress-up clothing are used, especially those that reflect the heritage of the children in the class.

- *Curriculum that needs to engage children at all levels of their development.* Blocks and their accessories, books, puzzles, crayons, markers, and paper are the types of open-ended materials that children enjoy, no matter what their developmental age or ability is (see Chapter 6).

Indirect guidance, such as the examples just stated, involves some of the simplest guidance techniques that teachers build into the program. In Chapter 5 you will learn more about the environment and its influence on indirect guidance.

Direct Guidance

The indirect guidance elements create the conditions that promote optimal behavior. Direct guidance techniques are those that teachers use while interacting with children to help them solve problems, make friends, become self-confident, and learn new skills. Direct guidance methods cover a broad range of options. They may include:

- Giving a look of reassurance, approval, or concern, or questioning
- Offering a smile of encouragement (paying attention to positive behavior)
- Providing a touch of support, awareness, caution, or praise
- Observing and moving close to the situation
- Listening and reflecting at eye level
- Modeling behavior and respect
- Giving directions that are clear, consistent, and supportive
- Comforting a crying or hurt child
- Physically restraining a child
- Verbalizing negotiating skills

The following techniques, outlined in the guidance continuum (Figure 3.5) are all direct guidance methods. After analyzing what is going on the teacher selects an appropriate technique to address the child's behavior. Teachers take into consideration the needs of each child, the adult, and the situation (refer back to Figure 3.2, the guidance triangle). Each of the techniques should be used in the context of the overall goals and the guidance philosophy of the program. Your choices will change as children learn new behaviors and you alter your expectations.

Start with the least intrusive strategy to allow children time to work out the problem themselves. At each step on the continuum, there is a greater expectation for the child's involvement in problem solving. If teachers value helping children to master their world, they select strategies that are least intrusive yet still provide a level of intervention and support.

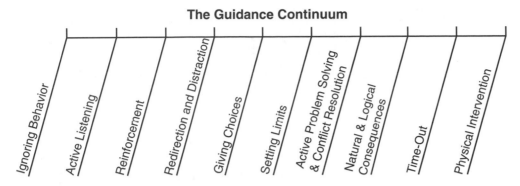

Figure 3.5 The Guidance Continuum

The guidance continuum identifies direct guidance techniques, from the least intrusive to more intervening strategies.

Source: From Ann Gordon & Kathryn Williams Browne, *Guiding Young Children in a Diverse Society.* Published by Allyn & Bacon, Boston, MA. Copyright © 1996 by Pearson Education. Reprinted by permission of the publisher.

Effective Guidance Techniques

The strategies listed along the guidance continuum begin with those that require the least amount of teacher intervention to those that have the greatest teacher involvement. This way a teacher can choose the most appropriate method for a workable solution for the situation.

Ignoring the Behavior. Some behaviors that are mildly annoying and are not harmful to a child can be ignored. When a child is whining, for instance, you do not respond while the whining persists and may even focus your attention elsewhere until the whining stops. This method also works for children who constantly call "Teacher, teacher, teacher." You pay attention to the child when the whining or calling stops. At some time, you may even tell the child, "I like to talk with you when you aren't whining (or calling me), and so I am not paying attention to you until you stop. That way, I'll know you are ready to talk and play again."

Active Listening and "I" Messages. In this method, you are looking for feelings as well as words by listening carefully to what the child says. You then reflect back in your own words what you think the child is saying. Knowing the child and the situation, you make an educated guess about why the child is upset.

- In *active listening*, your voice should convey interest, respect, and trust.

  Child: I hate school.

  Teacher: It sounds like you are really disappointed that Ruby and Danika wouldn't let you play with them.

  Child: I had some good ideas and they still wouldn't let me play. They wouldn't listen.

Teacher: You do have great ideas. It seems to me that you might not have heard some of their ideas.

Child: Well, I wanted mine.

Teacher: Because you have good ideas and Ruby and Danika have good ideas, let's go over and talk to them about how these ideas might work together. Do you think that would work?

Child: Sure.

● With *"I" messages*, adults can reflect back to a child how his or her actions affect other people. They are nonjudgmental statements that make an observation, without blame, about what has happened. Each statement a teacher makes begins with an *I*.

Teacher: I feel sad when you tell me you don't like me.

Teacher: I get angry when I see you hitting other children again. Remember our talk earlier? Let's sit down and review our agreement about hitting.

Teacher: I'm disappointed because no one cleaned up the art table today. What can we do to see that this doesn't happen again?

Reinforcement. Reinforcement is a method of rewarding positive behavior based on the belief that children will repeat the same action in the future because it has been noticed: "Tomas, you were very patient while you were waiting for your turn. I saw you find a book to look at until Mason finished his work on the computer." Social

Reflective Incident "I Didn't See It"

Mimi is a 4-year-old who lies constantly. She is not just making up stories, but telling lies that cause problems for other people. Yesterday, two other children saw Mimi take Ray's sandwich from his lunch bag, but she denied it when confronted by the teacher. Today, Mimi told the teacher that Marcy hit her with a book. Again, several children who had witnessed the incident said it was Mimi who did the hitting. Honestly, I don't know what to say or do!—Ani

Your Thoughts

1. How would I feel?

2. What would I do?

3. What might the results be?

reinforcers, such as smiling, talking, interest, and attention, are useful tools with young children at any time, but especially when you want to emphasize certain behaviors. To be most effective, the reinforcers should be focused on the action the child has taken, not on the child. The teacher specifically told Tomas that his patience was what she noticed so that he knows exactly what behavior she wants him to learn. Children will try harder to behave in appropriate ways when they are noticed for positive behavior. See if the Reflective Incident might call for some teacher reinforcement.

Redirection and Distraction. There are times when children's behavior is not *mis*behavior but is taking place at the wrong time or in the wrong location.

- *Redirection* helps preschool and school-age children. For example, on a rainy day, Neela and Ramona had been reading together in the Book Nook. They began throwing small pillows at each other. As the behavior escalated, the teacher approached:

    Teacher: Looks like you two are having fun throwing. This isn't a good place to do that because it bothers the other children who are trying to work. Let's go find the beanbags and put some small baskets in that corner. You can continue your game by tossing them in the containers.

The teacher first had to assess what the girls really wanted to do. In this case, they seemed to enjoy tossing pillows back and forth. The teacher considered some alternatives that allowed for tossing and redirecting the form of the activity to something more suitable. The substitute activity must be a valid one. In this case, the girls were not being deliberately destructive. They were expressing their curiosity, imagination, and social skills. Positive redirection helped them accept an alternative activity, taught them how to solve a problem, and enhanced their self-concepts.

- *Distraction* is related to redirection, but with some fundamental differences. Distraction is usually used to help focus a child's attention to another activity that may or may not relate to the previous behavior. Younger children, especially infants and toddlers, can be distracted fairly easily, as seen in the following example.

    Bruno, a 2-year-old, was lining up trucks in the block corner. Tyrese toddled over and grabbed two of Bruno's trucks. Bruno yelled, "No!" Tyrese raised his arm as if to hit Bruno. The teacher approached the boys.

    Teacher: Bruno is playing with those trucks, Tyrese. I see there's a place for you at the clay table. You can play there for a while and pound the clay. Let's go play with the clay.

Understanding and Guiding Behavior

The teacher knows that Tyrese likes to pound the clay, and that makes this an appropriate distraction for him. This method calls for well-timed intervention so that the child will accept the alternative.

Giving Choices. Choices are one of the easiest and most successful methods for helping children who are being resistant. When you give children choices you allow them to maintain some control over the situation as well as practice self-direction and self-control.

> **Teacher:** Su Jin, do you want to work with Rosie on her project or do you want to help Bonita with her story?
>
> **Teacher:** Armando, we're going to the library. Do you want to walk with Hector or Dale?

In each case, it is assumed that the child will make the decision and follow through. At the end of the day, when children are likely to be resistant, you might say, "It's time to go home now. Do you want to put on your coat now or wait until the story is over?"

Too many choices can be overwhelming. Suggesting two choices gives children the option and makes it easier to choose. Give simple choices that are legitimate and are given only when you mean for a child to make the decision work most effectively. Notice that either decision Su Jin or Armando might make would be acceptable to the teacher.

Choices have consequences and children need to know what they are before they make the choice. "You may play outside a little longer, if you like, Darragh, but you will miss snack time if you do."

Setting Limits. Limits are the boundaries we set so that children will not harm themselves or others. At various stages in their early lives, children need boundaries to help them learn to monitor their own actions. As they learn greater self-control and responsibility, the boundaries expand. In the classroom, limits are set to protect children and to present the destruction of materials and equipment.

In setting limits, we are teaching children to respect themselves and others. We know that it is in children's nature to test, explore, wiggle, giggle, talk, and act out at times. Our job is to keep school safe for

Children feel empowered when they are allowed to make choices.

all the children and help them learn to accept limits that are reasonable and equitable. Children need to know that you care enough about them to set boundaries on behaviors that may be harmful to them and others.

To be effective in setting limits, you should:

- *Match the situation, the child's age, history, and emotional development.* "Hans, I know it is the first day back at school since you broke your arm, but it is time to listen to the story. You and Aisha may talk later."

- *Be consistent in reinforcing the same rules.* "Monica, we walk inside. Both of the teachers have had to remind you several times today."

- *State limits simply, clearly, and directly.* "Nick, no pushing on the slide. Make a space between you and the person in front of you."

- *Follow through.* "Okay, Nick. You'll need to find another place to play because you keep pushing other children down the slide. Jackie has started a kickball game. Let's go tell her you'd like to play."

- *Accept the consequences and be prepared for the next step.* "I know you want to continue playing on the slide, Nick, but you need to find another place to play right now. You were hurting other children and I can't let you do that. If you don't want to play kickball, I can help you figure out something else to do."

- *Respect and acknowledge the child's feelings.* "I know you are angry, Franco. It hurts your feelings when they won't let you be on their team. Let's see if we can find another place to play with some other friends."

- *Act with confidence and authority.* "I won't let you throw things at other people, Mustafa, and I won't let them hurt you either. I want school to be a safe place for all the children. Put the book down."

- *Involve children in creating appropriate limits.* "We are going on our first field trip next week and we'll need to have some rules to follow so that we can all enjoy the trip. Let's make a list. Meera, do you have an idea?"

Active Problem Solving and Conflict Resolution. As children learn more and more self-control and social skills, they can learn to confront their differences with one another and work together to solve their problems. Children need to understand how to take someone else's point of view and to recognize their own feelings as well as others', a valuable process that can begin in early childhood.

Active problem solving calls for teachers who guide the process and see that children have positive experiences in conflict resolution. It is a collaborative effort in decision making and problem solving where teachers intervene, yet let the children create the acceptable solution. Teachers ask open-ended questions to help children focus on the problem and begin to suggest possible solutions.

"What could you do?"

"Do you have any ideas?"

"Have you noticed that . . . ?"

"How do you think he feels?"

"What might happen if . . . ?

The teacher's involvement is to help the children clarify what happened and help them explore the ideas that will lead to a resolution. Several other guidance techniques are integrated into this approach: active listening, reinforcement, making choices, and natural and logical consequences. As children suggest various alternatives to the problem, the teacher will need to help them think through the consequences of the actions they propose.

Figure 3.6 outlines a six-step process for active problem solving and conflict resolution. The children are full partners in creating a solution, giving them a

Figure 3.6 Six Steps to Problem Solving

Using a conflict resolution approach to problems helps adults listen rather than only talk, and allows children the time to sort through diverse solutions and views.

Step One: Approach (Initiate Mediation)
- Approach the conflict, signaling your awareness and availability.
- Get close enough to intervene if necessary; stop aggressive behavior or neutralize the object of conflict by holding it yourself.

Step Two: Make a Statement
- Describe the scene: "It looks like you both want the ball."
- Reflect what the children have said: "You both say you had it first."
- Offer no judgments, values, or solutions.

Step Three: Ask Questions (Gather Data, Define the Problem)
- Do not try to pinpoint blame: "Who started this?"
- Draw out details; define problems: "What is happening here?" "What seems to be the problem?"
- Help children communicate: "How did this happen?" "What do you want to tell him?" "How did that make you feel?"

Step Four: Generate Alternative Solutions
- Help children think of ways to work this out: "Who has an idea of how we could solve this?"
- Let children offer suggestions: "We could take turns." "We could use it together." "We could tell her she can't play here."

- Ask questions: "How do you think it would work to take turns?" "What would happen if you didn't let her play?"
- Avoid the common mistake of rushing this stage. Give it the time it deserves.

Step Five: Agree on a Solution
- When both children accept the solution, rephrase it: "So you both say that you can work on it together."
- If any solution seems unsafe or unacceptable, you must tell the children: "It is not safe for both of you to stand up and ride the wagon down the hill together. What is another way you could agree?" "We can't close the block corner because some other children want to play there."

Step Six: Follow Through
- Monitor the activity to make sure the agreement is going according to plan. If the decision involves taking turns, you may have to be the clock-watcher. "Okay, Maggie. Your 3 minutes are up. It's Cleo's turn now."
- Make a positive statement to the children who were in conflict and others who may have witnessed it: "Looks as if you solved your problem!"
- Use the power of language to reinforce the idea that solutions can be found and that children are capable of solving their problems.

Source: From Gordon/Browne. *Beginnings and Beyond*, 7e. © 2008 Wadsworth, a part of Cengage Learning, Inc. Reproduced by permission. www.cengage.com/permissions.

greater commitment to making it work, a sense of power and control, and a sense of self-worth.

Natural and Logical Consequences. As a child, you probably heard someone tell you "Don't touch the oven. It is hot and will burn you." You touched it anyway and burned your hand. The cause and effect were clearly defined and the outcome was a natural result of your behavior. There was no adult interference in your choice or judgments.

Natural consequences follow simple statements of what will happen if you choose a certain action. Other examples of natural consequences are:

- "If you don't eat dinner, you will be hungry by bedtime."
- "When you don't learn your spelling words, you don't pass the test."
- "If you don't practice the piano, you will play poorly in the recital."

The outcome rests with the child and the choices he or she will make. For behavior that consistently causes problems, natural consequences can be an effective change agent.

Logical consequences are similar. They are also the reasonable outcome for a specific behavior, but with adult intervention and guidance to ensure success.

- "Oops. You spilled the milk while you were pouring. Let's go get a sponge and you can clean it up."
- "Lenny, if you draw on another child's paper again, you will have to find another place to work."
- "Jessica, you interrupted me again. Please find a quiet place in the book corner and read until we finish this story."

The link is made with cause and effect and the consequences are immediate. Nelsen (2006) cites three criteria for using logical consequences successfully:

1. The consequence must be *related* to the action (cleaning the table after spilling milk).
2. The consequences must be *respectful* and without humiliation. ("Oh, oh. You spilled the milk," instead of "How could you be so sloppy and spill your milk?")
3. The consequence must be *reasonable* (finding another place to work rather than being punished, helping to clean up the milk).

It takes patience and creativity to ensure that logical consequences do not turn into punishment. These "three Rs" ensure that learning occurs in positive ways and that children's mistakes or misbehaviors are viewed as "teachable moments" rather than actions that require punitive measures.

Time Out. When children are removed from the group and placed in a chair or an isolated part of the room, it is referred to as a time out. This strategy is often overused and, in many settings, has taken on the proportion of punishment and humiliation of a child. Telling children to "sit here and watch other children play nicely" or "sit in this chair and think about what you have done" is ineffective at best. There is no link made between the behavior and the consequence and the strategy does not help a child learn the skills needed to behave appropriately.

There are times, in order to protect themselves and/or others, when young children need to be removed from the situation. Children whose intensity and emotions overwhelm them often need a place to bring themselves under control. With a teacher's care and guidance, the child can calm down, talk about the incident, and gain self-control. Used in a positive way, time out gives children the opportunity to monitor themselves, to assume some responsibility for themselves, and to choose when they wish to reenter play. In this way, time out is not a punitive action controlled only by the adult but is a supportive and caring way to help children learn about their behavior.

Time out is one of the more invasive strategies along the guidance continuum and should be used judiciously, if at all. A more effective approach would be to use active problem solving or logical consequences before the behavior becomes so disruptive.

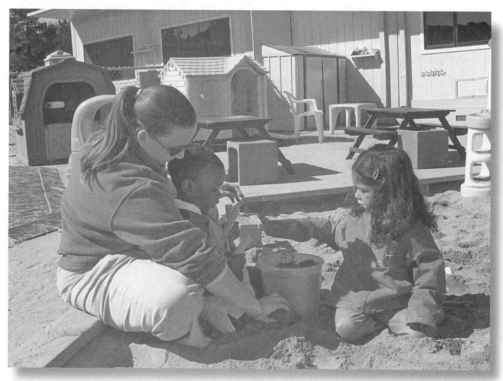

To keep one child from hurting another, you may need to use physical intervention and close proximity to stop the harmful behavior.

"Help Children to Trust You"

by Mary Jennings

Head Teacher, United Methodist Co-op

Reflecting on our first childhood experience, many of us remember our preschool teacher as a substitute for the warmth and caring of a parent. Having a caring and responsive relationship with their first teachers provides children a safe and nurturing environment, allowing them to grow socially and emotionally. A teacher who understands young children will help guide them to develop skills that will last a lifetime.

As children enter a facility, a teacher positions herself to greet each child. Olivia likes to hear "I've been waiting for you," while Will smiles when you tell him "How nice to see you this morning." A warm and accepting teacher will build a trusting relationship.

When Darlene came to student teach here, she did not know how to get the children to trust her. She began by observing, but seemed reluctant to talk much to them. By worrying about saying the wrong thing, she did not talk much to them—and they ignored her. Then we had a Valentine exchange, and she helped the children read each other's cards. They flocked to her to get her help. The next week, I noticed how she got acquainted with Tommy in the book corner, learning that he was ready to sound out a few words in a favorite story. Once she tried to enter the sand-digging, and was discouraged when they told her they didn't need her help, so that backfired. But then she tried to bring them some special shovels, and it worked!

A teacher will have numerous opportunities to strengthen the relationship with children by providing a program that understands children's needs. Student teachers become part of the routine that gives the children reassurance that each school day they are part of a group and together they will participate in activities, like having a snack and playing outside. Children feel comfortable with teachers who realize the importance of developmental needs such as time for large movement as well as activities to practice fine motor control like painting or working with playdough.

Student teacher Vikki discovered that in these classes, the children are given a lot of room for exploration, meaning that the teachers have limited "no's" and encourage the children to explore, question, and experience. I was pleased to see that she saw how children begin to trust teachers who want the children to experience and question activities, because that is how they learn, not because they are difficult or spoiled.

The child–teacher relationship will be further reinforced when the teacher shows respect for the child by using words that encourage and offer support. "I noticed you used a pattern with the colors" signals your interest in a child; "You were really concentrating while you cut the paper" ensures a child that you were paying attention and care about accomplishments.

A trusting relationship between teacher and child will provide a firm foundation for guiding behavior. Giving children choices will allow the child to have control over his environment. "Would you like to pick up the blocks or put away the dishes in the playhouse?" gives the child a choice and you authority.

Teaching expected behavior also helps guide children. Modeling appropriate manners—"please pass the crackers"—and setting limits provide boundaries to ensure accepting responsibility—"you need to put these books on the shelves." Using action statements will provide clarity and communicate a task. "Sarah is picking up the puppets," I overheard student teacher Ena tell the children, and James immediately joined in. Both Ena and James learned the value of encouragement as they built a trusting relationship together.

Physical Intervention. There may be times when you will need to step in and use physical restraint to prevent children from hurting themselves, others, or property. Jaxson jumps on Aaron and begins to punch him. The teacher moves quickly to protect Aaron, pulling Jaxson off of him saying, "Jaxson, stop!" He remains calm as he moves Jaxson away, holding his flailing arms close to his body. "I can't let you hurt Aaron. Let's move over here so we can talk about this." They sit together for a few minutes until Jaxson becomes calm.

Physically restraining Jaxson and moving him away from Aaron is only the first step in the process. The teacher also needs to determine if Aaron is seriously hurt and provide comfort to him. Sometimes another teacher will be able to comfort Aaron.

The teacher decides whether or not to talk with both children at the same time or if each needs to be spoken with separately. They all go to a quiet place after both boys have calmed down enough to respond to the teacher's questions. The teacher then proceeds with active problem-solving and conflict resolution techniques that engage the children in the problem-solving process. They learn to resolve their conflict in a positive manner. If either child has problems with aggression on a regular basis, a long-term strategy that includes observations and assessments should be considered.

The longer you teach, the more experience you will have in using the top 10 guidance strategies. Think of them as a "tool kit" for guiding young children. You have an assortment of choices for each situation. Choose the least intrusive first to allow children time to work out a situation themselves. As stated earlier, if we value helping children master their world, we will select strategies that are the least intrusive yet still provide a level of teacher interaction and support. Try the screwdriver before using the hammer!

Good guidance practices help teachers create the kind of atmosphere that promotes healthy social relationships, respect for self and others, and the ability to accept responsibility for your own actions. In "Lessons from the Field," mentor Mary Jennings shows how to help children to trust you.

Practicum Activity

Interview another student in your class and ask the following questions:

1. What is your approach to discipline?
2. What do you think influences children's behavior?
3. What are the "rules" at your school? How are they explained to children?
4. What happens when rules are not followed?
5. What guidance strategies do you find most successful?
6. Is there such a thing as developmentally appropriate discipline?

Journaling Assignment

Interview your supervising teacher on his or her approach to guidance and discipline.

Resources

Bronfenbrenner, U. (1979). *The ecology of human development*. Cambridge, MA: Harvard University Press.

Gordon, A. M., & Browne, K. W. (1996). *Guiding young children in a diverse society*. Boston: Allyn & Bacon.

Gordon, A. M., & Browne, K. W. (2007). *Beginning essentials in early childhood education*. Clifton Park, NY: Thomson Delmar Learning.

Gordon, A. M., & Browne, K. W. (2008). *Beginnings and beyond: Foundations in early childhood education* (7th ed.). Clifton Park, NY: Thomson Delmar Learning.

Nelsen, J. (2006). *Positive discipline*. New York: Ballantine Books.

Web Sites

Empowering People/Positive Discipline
www.positivideciphine.com

ERIC Clearinghouse on Early Childhood and Parenting
http://ceep.uiuc.edu

Floor Time
www.coping.org/intervention/ftpres

Observing and Assessing Children

Observation

Look outside the window. There is Nicholas, poised at the climbing pole. Feet aligned, he grasps the top of the side poles and climbs into the structure, a sliding tube, on his hands and knees. At the top, left arm grasping a rail, he pulls himself up with bent knees. He shouts at a peer in the distance and slides down the tube and looks back and forth as he stands up. Immediately he sprints, pumping with bent arms, across the yard of 150 feet! In the distance, he sits criss-cross style in a circle with two other boys and a teacher. Suddenly, he shoots up with both hands pushing on either side of his body, then runs away 20 feet and comes back, bending down on his knees. He has a stick and hits it against the ground. The other three people throw their arms over their heads, and he hands the stick to another boy.

Children are fascinating! Whatever Nicholas was doing, student teacher Theo tried to capture it. From this snippet of behavior, Theo could see that Nicholas had refined gross motor skills and was adept at climbing and running. He was able to observe some of his social skills such as initiating contact with peers and entering a game. Moreover, Theo gained insight into Nicholas's thinking, noticing his facial expressions and gestures and how he involved himself in this child-made game with rules.

How did this student teacher assess the child's development so quickly? In reality, Theo did not understand the significance of his observation until later. After making this observation, Theo tucked away his notes

What are children telling us about themselves as they play? We learn by observing what they do.

when he was called by a group of children to join them. Later, with his mentor teacher, he went over his observation. The two of them could make sense of what he saw, and verify it by rereading his documentation. They can use this observation in Nicholas's portfolio and in their curriculum planning for group games, as well as in determining how to develop a relationship with the child based on his interests and behavior.

Why Observe?

Observational skills are very important to being a good teacher. When you watch children, you see what they need, then provide the environment and tools they need to learn. You build relationships with them to understand better how they operate and why. Children notice that you value what they say and do when you are attentive and focused on them. Observational skills, comments student teacher Di,

> are as important to being a good teacher as they are to scientists. I have been working in cancer genetic research, where our focus was to find a new cancer gene. The results we got from the DNA and RNA samples looked very similar, and the previous researcher gave up. But when my group did very careful observations and repeated the experiment several times we found differences. We made a novel discovery and found a new gene, which is very important for cancer development. Our observations with children are no less important!

Scanning Versus Observing

Seeing children in a physical sense is different from seeing them in an observational sense. For instance, you can "see" children when you scan a room or yard: You can see who is there, how many children are in an area, and even supervise the activity in a broad way. Observing, however, requires closer inspection. You need to look carefully, focusing your attention instead of scanning. You have to narrow your view, and at the same time, stay a little apart from the activity. Theo would never have been able to capture the details of Nicholas's activity if he had been just watching the yard. He may have missed the small but significant detail of Nicholas's shouting to the group. Again, student teacher Di comments: "Without observation, we would treat children the same, and the result of teaching would be unsatisfactory. Only by doing very careful observations can we find the best way to teach children."

The Tools of Recording

In the 21st century, teachers have a number of methods for recording children's behavior. Teachers use digital and video cameras to capture children's behavior on tape, and can collect samples of the children's work. At the same time, much of children's growth in a naturalistic setting such as a center will be best documented by a teacher's written notes. Thus, student teachers should make time during their practicum to learn to observe and record children's behavior as it occurs.

Through careful listening, teachers can truly be "in the moment" with children. "Through listening, they are better able to spontaneously support and challenge a child to extend his thinking" (Gandini & Kaminsky, 2004, p. 9). Documentation is seen as "visible listening. . . . To ensure listening and being listened to is one of the primary tasks of documentation . . . as well as to ensure that the group and each individual child has the possibility to observe themselves from an external point of view while they are learning" (Rinaldi, 2001, p.). Your attention sends a message to a child that what thcy do has value and meaning.

This means that you must practice watching and listening to a child or children at play, and try to write what they are doing and saying in the moment. This isn't easy, and takes practice, as you will note in the following Reflective Incident. Start by equipping yourself with these tools:

- Small notepad and pencil (can be on a necklace; may include a camera)
- Clothes with a pocket (to stash the notes when duty calls)

Next, select a time and place to take notes. Place yourself in an area where children are interacting with materials and/or other children independently. This is usually

Reflective Incident "How Can I Do It All at the Same Time?"

Tanya is doing her first observation. The teacher assigns her to observe Jerome. She takes a chair behind the puzzle table where he is working and begins to record what she sees. A few moments later, Chandra comes up and plops herself on Tanya's lap. Alan walks up to them and asks Chandra what she is doing. Meanwhile, Jerome leaves the table and heads outside. As she breaks away from Chandra and Alan, Tanya wonders, "How can I do this? I do I keep up with Jerome and concentrate just on him?"

Your Thoughts

1. How would I feel?

2. What would I do?

3. What might the results be?

4. How can I teach and record at the same time?

5. Where do I go from here?

during free play (sometimes called choice time, interest area, or work time) rather than a transition or teacher-directed activity, which requires more adult intervention.

Student teachers often find themselves overwhelmed with how fast children move, talk, and change direction. Over time, they become more proficient at getting the important parts of behavior when they work at the skill.

Start by writing everything you see and hear; you are trying to capture in as much detail as you can the children's behavior, language, and interactions. Teachers often find it easier to write in their home language, scribbling what they see in shortened form and rewriting the key segment later.

> Carmine grabs a scarf and begins to dance, twirling and whirling, hopping and bending in time to the music. It is Greg and Steve, and he really likes the high rhythm of this stuff! Following the teacher's lead. Carmine balances on his toes and waves his scarf high over his head. Sarah and Juanita join him, ~~but he doesn't care about them.~~ He can keep time with the music! ~~I didn't know 3-year-olds could do that.~~ He keeps swinging it after the music stops. It doesn't matter to him that the tape is over—ha. ☺

Note the lines that are crossed out later, as the teacher selects those items that will describe the child's activity with *objectivity* and *accuracy*. Only with practice and reflection can we document in writing what we see in children's daily activities.

Observational Methods

Good records should reveal authentic child behavior and provide a detailed portrait of a child. Observing a child in multiple situations and over time should document individual progress. A teaching team with competent observation and documentation skills allows for evaluations from more than one person, validating both teacher observations and program accountability to families, communities, and colleagues. Check with your fieldwork site for its developmental record plan, and compare it to Figure 4.1. How many of these purposes does your plan fulfill?

Types of Observations

There are several types of observations. Some are more useful in clinical settings or for experimental purposes, and others work

Your eyes and ears are the best recording tools a teacher has.

Observing and Assessing Children

Figure 4.1
Building Authentic
Pictures of Children
Through Observation

Authentic assessments
must serve specific
purposes to be useful to
professional teachers.

Observational records should...	To discover...
• Document children's experiences	• How the child learns
• Document children's relationships and achievements	• How the child interacts and builds relationships
• Determine the child's abilities and strengths	• What each child is interested in learning
• Determine the child's present abilities in relation to program goals	• Where the child's development is and should be going next
• Serve as an effective tool in parent–child communication	• What will enhance the family–child relationships
• Serve as a basis for identification of special needs and from this, referral	• Where further evaluation is needed, as well as intervention or accommodation
• Be useful in determining program changes and staffing needs	• How development can be promoted

Source: Compiled from *Observing Development of the Young Child* (6th ed.), by. J. J. Beaty, 2006, Upper Saddle River, NJ: Merrill/Prentice Hall.

best for observing children in more natural settings. Three that teachers use most often are narratives, checklists, and behavior samplings.

Narratives are observations in the form of anecdotal records, and are the most common method of recording child growth and behavior. This is known as a "running record" or "anecdotal narrative" and is used in diary descriptions and journals. Narratives offer rich detail, but require a command of descriptive language. The running record makes a written sketch of a child, a kind of snapshot in time. It should be accompanied by a teacher's insights about what it means and what to do with the findings. Do not try to add your conclusions while you are engaged in documenting children's behavior; rather, you can make these interpretations either immediately afterward or at the end of the day while the situation is still fresh. Figure 4.2 shows a sample narrative recording form.

Checklists, at first glance, appear easier than the narrative because a teacher can simply make a mark (Yes/No, rating scale of 1–5, etc.) instead of writing longhand. However, the richness of an anecdote is lost. Further, a checkmark allows no verification for either objectivity or accuracy. Figure 4.3 illustrates a sample checklist.

Behavior sampling condenses the narrative record into small segments for easier recording. There are two major kinds of behavior sampling, one that focuses on time and the other on events. A *time sampling*, for instance, can help teachers see what kinds of play occur in their group. By breaking the record into timed segments and common play categories, they can capture what is happening efficiently.

Using Figure 4.4, a teacher can scan the room every 15 minutes and make note of how many children were engaged in each type of play. At the end of the

Figure 4.2 Sample Narrative Recording Sheet

- Child-initiated activity
- Teacher-initiated activity
- New task for this child
- Familiar task for this child
- Done independently
- Context (where, when, etc.)

- Done with adult guidance
- Done with peer(s)
- Time spent (1–5 min.)
- Time spent (5–15 min.)
- Time spent (15+ min.)

Child observed: _____

Date/Time: _____

Observer: _____

Desired results: _____

Developmental domain: _____

Observation:

_____

_____

_____

_____

_____

_____

_____

_____

_____

_____

_____

_____

_____

_____

_____

Interpretation:

What developmental theme did he or she engage in? What experiences, knowledge, and skills did he or she build on?

_____

_____

What did he or she find meaningful? Frustrating? Challenging? List questions, problems and solutions, and unique attributes demonstrated.

_____

_____

What question comes to mind about the child or your next step?

_____

_____

Source: From Mary Meta Lazarus Child Development Center, College of San Mateo, San Mateo, CA. Used with permission.

Figure 4.3
Sample Developmental Checklist

Note that checklists offer a quick assessment but lack the rich detail of a narrative.

Prekindergarten Checklist: Self-Help Skills	Yes	Needs Practice	No
Puts shoes on correct feet			
Can dress self independently			
Able to use buttons and snaps correctly			
Puts away personal belongings			
Pours liquid from small pitcher into cup			
Spreads soft food with blunt knife			
Uses spoon, fork, or chopsticks skillfully			
Washes hands correctly			
Toilets independently			
Blows and wipes nose independently			

play period, the team would then have a record of what happened in each time period. Further, they could look for patterns that may emerge to give them direction on what they might change or adapt. What patterns do you see in Figure 4.4 and what might this tell you about the effect of time during a free play period?

Event sampling is similar, making a recording sheet that is used for a predetermined event. Teachers can go about their ordinary work, picking up their sheets to record important data only when the event occurs. This technique is often used when teachers want to find out what is really happening in a problem situation. For instance, student teacher Michelle's team wondered why there seemed to be fighting in the classroom before circle time. They asked Michelle to observe this transition every day for a week. She made an event sampling sheet that noted the time the fight started, who was involved, what was said during the quarrel, how it was

Figure 4.4
Time Sampling of Children's Play

Time sampling is one kind of observational behavior sampling; teachers usually include an "interpretation" segment to add their conclusions and expertise to the record.

Time	Onlooker	Solitary	Parallel	Associative	Cooperative
9:00 a.m.	IIII	III	II	I	
9:15 a.m.	II	III	III	I	I
9:30 a.m.	I	II	III	II	II
9:45 a.m.		II	II	III	III
10:00 a.m.	I	II	II	II	III

Interpretation: *Children seem to "warm up" over the hour of play, engaging in more interactive play as time goes on. Should we invite children to join activities more, or is this pattern developmentally "on target" for this group at this time of the year? Let's observe where these activities take place, and consider rearrangements.*

Figure 4.5
Event Sampling of Children's Fighting
To look for a pattern or understand children's behavior better, teachers may choose an event sampling observation method.

Observer: Michelle

Children observed: Kid's Club After-School Care

Children's ages: 5–7 years; Kinders; Grades 1 & 2

Observation context: After snack & before circle time

Date of observation: February 8

Time begun and ended: 3:15–4:00 p.m.

Time	Children	Place/Material	Cause	Outcome
3:15 p.m.	Sam, Hiro	Computer	Both want a turn	Tchr. makes waiting list
3:25 p.m.	Jamie, Chris	Homework table	Pencil fight	Tchr. brings pencil box
3:50 p.m.	Jamie, Sam	Jigsaw puzzle	Fight over pieces	Tchr. holds pieces until they decide what to do
3:55 p.m.	Jamie, Sam	Same place	Flinging pieces	Tchr. sends them to block area
3:58 p.m.	Jamie, Sam	Block area	Grabbing blocks	Tchr. hands them each a block to put away

Interpretation: The same four children were involved in nearly every outbreak. Let's choose two to shadow next week and listen closer. They may need modeling or prompts with conflict resolution.

resolved, and the duration of the entire sequence. What do you think they discovered when they analyzed the results on Friday? (See Figure 4.5.)

Interpreting What You See

Children do more than we observe, and much more than we can ever record. However, to really see children, we must practice observing them carefully, and be planful about documenting what we see. As you focus your attention, you will discover the complexity of children's development, their personalities, and what influences them. To observe and record well, these three guides are helpful:

1. *Begin to recognize your own biases.* Ming discovered that loud and destructive behavior distressed her, and had begun to feel negative about the group of older boys that reveled in building and crashing block towers indoors and played active superhero games in the yard. By recording their behavior and talking over her interpretations with her mentor teacher, Ming began to address her attitude regarding what was typical 4-year-old behavior but which she had been taught was unacceptable in her culture (although more for girls than boys, she noted).

2. *Get familiar with the tools of observation and documentation.* Yuri had worked in a private center that engaged only in informal notes. His student teaching site was a publicly-funded program that required annual child portfolios to be developed in the fall and updated in the spring. By learning to observe and record children's behavior, Yuri added to his teaching skills and his own professional development.

3. *Decide what to do with the information gathered.* Notice the questions at the bottom of the observation form in Figure 4.2. Once a teacher has made an objective and accurate observation, the next step is to consider its significance and implications. Think carefully about what children "teach" us with their behavior. Their strengths and interests can be used to build curriculum. What is challenging to them can also be woven into classroom experiences. And the unique flavors of each child are ready to permeate the environment, if only we notice and use them well.

What is the next step? Observing and recording children's behavior takes a lot of effort. Interpretation needs to be part of the learning process for teachers, too. Make the process meaningful by tying it into your ongoing work with children, rather than recording behavior and then saving it for a conference or formal assessment later. By reflecting on what you see, you gain insights that will help you work with them.

Interpretation puts the observation into perspective, making sense of what has been recorded. It helps teachers decide if they need to observe further to see the cause of a child's behavior, or if they need to make environmental and curricular changes for the child. It can serve as a springboard into action about the schedule or strategies for working with a group of children. Perhaps most important, interpretive notes add the teacher's expertise and make meaning of the observation itself. Look back on Figures 4.4 and 4.5; following the observation section there is space for interpretation that includes analysis, evaluation, inference, and conclusions. Figure 4.6 provides guidelines for interpretation.

Figure 4.7 shows an example with both narrative observation and interpretation. Student teacher May is observing Frankie as he arrives at the preschool co-op with his mother, who is participating that day.

Figure 4.6
Guidelines for
Interpretation

By following professional guidelines for interpretation, teachers use what they observe to promote quality education and accurate information about children.

- Look for behavior that is repeated.
- Look for circumstances under which repeated behavior occurs.
- Ask yourself how the observed behavior is affecting the child's learning and relationships with others.
- Look for specific efforts the child is making to satisfy needs and accomplish developmental tasks. Are the efforts appropriate? Are they getting results?
- Listen carefully to the conversations of the child. Try to pick out the questions children ask. This will help determine what they want to know about the world around them.

Narrative Observation	My Interpretation
F. sits at art table, points to pen & looks at mom. He takes it and begins to color on the table. Mom gives him another pen, and paper; he colors on that. The pen then drops to the floor, he says "Uh,oh" and looks under the table, then sits back up. He picks up another pen and tries to color on the table again. Mom asks if he is all done, he shakes his head no. He looks at the other children at the table, continues to color on the table. He leans over and colors on 2 children's papers. He puts the cap on, then takes it off again. Repeats twice, struggling with getting it on securely. He looks to his mom and grunts as if to ask her.	Is he trying to get her attention? Does he know how to use the pens on paper already? His grasp of the pen makes me wonder about his level of experience with this media. What is his relationship with his mother and their usual level or kind of communication? What is his level of language development? I don't hear any words to know his articulation or speech level. He appears to find this activity appealing but frustrating. He seems intrigued and not sure why the cap is not going on. I need to ask my mentor teacher about Frankie's level of development in ALL domains!

Figure 4.7
Frankie and his mother

Assessment

In the last two decades, American education has undergone a shift toward standards-based teaching at nearly all levels. With learning standards for children come processes for checking the progress toward those goals.

> Policymakers, the early childhood profession, and other stakeholders in young children's lives have a shared responsibility to . . . make ethical, appropriate, valid and reliable assessment a central part of all early childhood programs. To assess young children's strengths, progress, and needs, use assessment methods that are developmentally appropriate, culturally and linguistically responsive, tied to children's daily activities, supported by professional development, inclusive of families and connected to specific, beneficial purposes: (1) making sound decisions about teaching and learning; (2) identifying significant concerns that may require focused intervention for individual children; and (3) helping programs improve their educational and developmental interventions. (Hyson, 2003, p. 9)

Check with your program for its goals and assessment plan to define and then monitor what children are to know and be able to do.

Assessment of children's skills must include regular observation and recording of their behavior in their natural settings.

Assessing Early Development

Assessment is "the process of gathering information about children from several forms of evidence, then organizing and interpreting that information" (McAfee, Leong, & Bodrova, 2004). Figure 4.8 offers the top 10 characteristics of good child assessment.

Older children may be able to demonstrate their knowledge in structured, testlike conditions, whereas younger children, who have a limited repertoire of behaviors that can be assessed, are best studied through observation.

In fact, to assess young children, who are unable to express themselves fully with words, with any other than direct observations may not be possible. Further, young children reveal themselves through their behaviors. Unlike older children and adults, young children are incapable of hiding their feelings, ideas, or emotions with socially approved behaviors, so observing them often yields accurate information. (Seefeldt, 1998, p. 251)

Child Assessment Systems

Because using systematic observation has become an important part of a classroom staff's daily responsibilities, student teachers will need to become acquainted with the many child assessment systems used in contemporary programs. One

Figure 4.8
Top 10 Characteristics of Quality Child Assessment

Incorporating these characteristics into your child observation and assessment plans will ensure accuracy without unnecessary interference.

1. It is an ongoing process.
2. It cannot be based on what is wrong with a child.
3. It must be authentic and cannot be based on tests in artificial situations.
4. It must be based on what you see, not what you think you should observe or the child should be doing, and have meaningful artifacts and work samples.
5. It must be diversified with multiple measures; that is, it cannot be based on a single observation or situation.
6. It must state the facts, not interpretations, judgments, or conclusions.
7. It must be confidential, with note-taking materials kept handy but easily set aside.
8. It must have an interpretive piece based on your expertise to put it in perspective.
9. It must be based on your center or program learning standards.
10. It needs to raise relevant issues that require action.

practicum class was polled about how the centers assessed children. Responses included:

- An initial assessment within 45 days of enrollment
- A home visit, family conference, and individual learning plan within the first semester
- Biannual anecdotal assessment done in fall and spring
- Narrative assessment by parent request only
- Spring prekindergarten motor and language checklist

Gabriela found that her center's assessment process was at first overwhelming; see her reaction over time in the My Reaction feature that follows.

Good assessment tools will define the behaviors to be observed and provide space for teachers to write what they see that describes the specific learning goal. For example, the state of California has identified four goals, or desired results, for children in publicly-funded programs:

- Children are personally and socially competent.
- Children are effective learners.

My Reaction

"From Observing and Documenting to Portfolios and Curriculum to Me!"

I talked with my supervising teacher about child observation and assessment today. I was quite overwhelmed with all the information that I received about the process. I assumed it to be a complex process, but—oh man—I didn't think it would be this much work!

In summary, each teacher observes a designated group of children in four basic areas of development (physical-motor, cognitive and language, socioemotional, and creative). The three of them can use their preferred method of observation, but they have to create a portfolio for each child. Along with their notes, they include children's work and photographs to capture a thorough picture.

But this is not the end! The head teacher writes a final summary of findings and completes group summaries that show how the class is doing as a group. They use this to plan curriculum. Whew! Just explaining the process was exhausting!

So how do I take my skills to the next level? When my teacher observes me, she documents the children's responses to my directions and interaction. Since I'm working on small-group activities, she records what happens there, and then debriefs me by going over together what she saw. It inspires me to try to get some of this down on paper myself. You sure can use these skills everywhere.

—GABRIELA

- Children have physical and motor competence.
- Children are healthy and safe.

The assessment tool, called the Desired Results Developmental Profile (DRDP-R), further articulates the behaviors for each desired result, described in terms of the various age groups (infant/toddler, preschool, kindergarten, primary). Both public and private centers have adopted this tool or have adapted their own assessments to parallel these results. One program used the tool to develop a method of documenting levels of competence within each category, leaving room for the observer to note the date it was observed and requiring anecdotal notes to be attached that validate the rating. A few of the areas can be seen in Figure 4.9.

As we conclude this section, we wish to emphasize again that observations are the backbone of assessment. Whether you are preservice or a paid intern, you are involved in discovering the development, strengths, and challenges of a group of children in your care. So much can be done with accurate observations: You will be more effective in guidance, more able to create environments and schedules to suit the group, better prepared to plan curriculum, and far better suited to assess their skills if you hone your observation skills now during your student teaching.

Cautions About Evaluations

Authentic assessment can capture who the child is. To do this, it must occur in a variety of settings, over time, drawing on many sources of information. As the teacher, you observe and then record what you decide is significant. You are making a choice about what to record, and this is based on what you value. Anyone involved in evaluating children should appreciate the challenge and try to avoid the following pitfalls (adapted from Gordon & Browne, 2008):

- *Unfair comparisons.* Do not use assessments to compare children with one another in a competitive manner.
- *Bias.* Evaluations can label unfairly or prematurely the very people for which they are intended.
- *Overemphasis on norms.* Remember to individualize the process rather than try to fit a child into the mold created by the assessment tool.
- *Interpretation.* There is sometimes a tendency to overinterpret or misinterpret results.
- *Too narrow a perspective.* Sampling only children's skills as the single measure would lead to conclusions that are neither reliable nor valid.

F i g u r e 4.9 Sample Child Assessment Competencies Form

One example of a child assessment is an adaptation of California's Preschool Desired Results Developmental Profile (Revised) for Personal & Social Competencies.

Personal and Social Competencies			
Exploring	**Developing**	**Building**	**Integrating**
Self-Concept: Identity of Self			
Shows recognition of self as individual, recognizing own name and names of familiar people	Describes self or others in terms of basic physical characteristics	Describes self and others in terms of preferences	Accurately compares self to others
Date:			
Self-Concept: Recognition of Own Skills and Accomplishments			
Shows interest and/or pleasure when someone reacts to something he or she has done	Characterizes self positively in terms of specific activity that he or she is doing or has just finished	Characterizes positively own skills involved in doing a task	Characterizes self positively in terms of generalized ability or skills
Date:			
Social Interpersonal Skills: Expressions of Empathy			
Shows awareness when others are unhappy or upset	Offers simple assistance when he or she thinks it is needed—even if not really needed	Accurately labels own and others' feelings	Uses words or actions to demonstrate concern for what others are feeling
Date:			
Social Interpersonal Skills: Building Cooperative Relationships with Adults			
Seeks interaction with familiar adult for company, help, or comfort	Attempts to establish a relationship with an adult by cooperating and interacting	Seeks to share experience or get information from adults	Works cooperatively with an adult to plan and organize activities and to solve problems
Date:			
Social Interpersonal Skills: Developing Friendships			
Interacts with another child side by side as they play with similar materials	Names another child as a friend or seeks out a particular child with whom to play	Engages in social games and pretend play with a particular child	Prefers to play with a particular child who also expresses preference for him or her
Date:			

Source: From Mary Meta Lazarus Child Development Center, San Mateo, CA. Used with permission.

To be authentic, information is gathered over a period of time through multiple observations.

- *Too wide a range.* It is appropriate to measure a child's ability to print at age 6 but not at age 2.
- *Too little or too much time.* The evaluation that is too lengthy loses its effectiveness in the time it takes.

Think about these issues as you read about the standards movement in the following section.

A Pressure Cooker

In the United States, federal funding for education comes primarily from the Elementary and Secondary Education Act (originally passed in 1965, with regular authorization from Congress). Since the end of the 20th century, there has been a systematic focus on closing the achievement gap between disadvantaged and minority students and their more privileged peers through legislation titled No Child Left Behind (NCLB). Major provisions of the act pertaining to early childhood include:

1. Adequate annual progress must monitored, as evidenced by testing at third grade of reading and math (with a third area left to states' choice).
2. All teachers must have a BA degree and be state certified in their assigned teaching level.
3. Reading and literacy are highly funded with the goal of all children achieving grade-level reading proficiency by third grade.

Many educators worry that these provisions are creating an unbalanced curriculum and too much time and focus on testing. Such pressure can "trickle down" to earlier grades in elementary school and even into programs for 4-year-olds. Early learning standards could

- lead to teaching to the standards only in a cookie-cutter-style curriculum. Then, the uniqueness of early childhood education is lost.
- bring a pressure of accountability with the risk of a push down in curriculum and inappropriate expectations for younger children. (Gronlund, 2006)

Developmentally appropriate practices indicate a broader curriculum emphasis on the whole child and play; moreover, DAP and child development knowledge imply that our assessment practices avoid inappropriate testing.

Assessing Children with Disabilities

Although there are many ways that children are more alike than different, watching and working with them exposes the many ways in which children are diverse. Developmental theory tells us that, although development is predictable and follows a sequence, individual children will grow at different rates and will display a range of temperaments and learning styles. In addition, genetic and environmental differences can be seen. Student teachers often wonder if the differences are evidence of special needs.

Approximately 15 to 20% of all children in the United States will exhibit some form of atypical development and need special services. Public educational policy since 1975 entitles everyone from 3 to 21 years of age to a free and appropriate public education (FAPE), and states that every child with a disability be educated in the least restrictive environment (LRE; Allen & Schwartz, 2001). In addition, parents may bring concerns about a child's development to the center's attention. Equally likely is the possibility that teachers will observe unusual behavior within the context of school. Therefore, student teachers will probably see a range of both typical and atypical behaviors in their practicum sites (NAEYC, 2006). Whereas most teaching staff are not trained in special education testing, many programs may use some kind of tool to determine if and how a child has mastered developmental milestones. Figure 4.10 is a sample child questionnaire that might be used to describe atypical development.

Because early diagnosis and intervention are important, student teachers should ask about their center's policies. Common practices include careful observation, concurrent discussions with families, and calling in specialists to verify or dispel concerns.

The teachers' role is to observe the child and provide current information, to support the parents through their concern, to find appropriate resources for them, and to be available for consultation with others who are working in the best interests of the child. The early childhood professional is not an expert in diagnosing learning disabilities but can be effective in helping parents secure proper referral and treatment. (Gordon & Browne, 2008, p. 256)

Figure 4.10
Sensory Regulation and
Social Interaction:
A Rating Scale

Use the following questionnaire to determine which milestones your child has mastered and which still need work. Use the rating scale to rate your child in each one, as he or she is now. If the skill is always present, record at what age it was mastered.

Rating scale: N = ability never present; S = ability sometimes present; A = ability always present; L = child loses ability under stress (hunger, anger, fatigue, etc.)

Milestone: Purposeful Emotional Interactions (4–9 months)		
Ability	**Current Rating**	**Age Mastered**
1. Responds to your gestures with intentional gestures (e.g., reaches out in response to your outstretched arms, returns your vocalizing or look)		
2. Initiates interactions with you (e.g., reaches for your nose or hair or for a toy; raises arms to be picked up)		
3. Demonstrates the following emotions: • Closeness (e.g., hugs back when hugged, reaches out to be picked up) • Pleasure and excitement (e.g., smiles joyfully while putting a finger in your mouth or while taking a toy from your mouth and putting it in own) • Assertive curiosity (e.g., touches and explores your hair) • Protest or anger (e.g., pushes food off the table or screams when desired toy not brought) • Fear (e.g., turns away, looks scared, or cries when a stranger approaches too quickly)		
4. Recovers from distress within 10 minutes by being involved in social interactions		

Source: From Floortime: DVD Training Series: Sensory Regulation and Social Interaction, by S. Greenspan and S. Wieder, 2006, Bethesda, MD: Interdisciplinary Council on Developmental and Learning Disorders. Used with permission.

A Child's Portfolio

Many early childhood educators have embraced the idea that a portfolio of children's work samples and teacher assessments is an excellent way to document individual learning and faithfully capture the child's development. If your practicum site creates child portfolios, ask to see one. Look for a collection plan, and check how the work samples are stored and organized. Make a note of how teacher commentary is incorporated into the portfolio, and how it is shared with families or other professionals.

> During the past few years in my teaching career, I find myself adjusting my assessment system to work optimally with my work load. I use a portfolio assessment system whose categories are based on the state standards. I rely on my teaching team to help collect and analyze the data for the portfolios. Novice teachers or teachers who are instituting an assessment system for the first time, tend to provide short, simple observations and sometimes have difficulty interpreting the data while more seasoned teachers tend to have more detailed documentation with reflective evaluations. (Wiggins-Dowler, unpublished correspondence, 2007)

Student teachers often find documenting children's learning overwhelming. Student teacher Gordon found that "my biggest challenge in engaging in the assessment process was learning the assessment terminology and also learning the sequential process of how to get from point A to B to C and that the process builds on itself. It reminds me of, 'Now that I have my driver's license, how do I drive?'"

Portfolios present an image of each child as a competent learner who actively constructs knowledge within a social and cultural context. What is visible is the child's classroom history and learning, complete with a window into temperaments, styles, strengths, interests, and disposition. Molly and Luisa's mother offers this note:

> The portfolios that Karen created for my two children remain among my very most treasured possessions. This record of all the different parts of their emotional and cognitive growth gave me such a clear picture of how they were developing, and let me into their inner world. The contents of the portfolios were so helpful during our parent–teacher conferences in expanding the connection between what was happening at school and what I could be doing at home to provide reinforcement. At the time, I never thought I'd forget any of "those moments," but now that my children are in grade school, I regularly pull out their portfolios to show other parents "what they were like when they were little." I love them! (Wiggins-Dowler, unpublished correspondence, 2007)

Check with your supervising teacher about the learning standards and assessment tools in your site. Ask yourself these questions:

1. *What is their purpose?* Legitimate needs are to support learning, identify special needs, and monitor program quality.

2. *What methods are used?* Appropriate methods include observation, samples of children's work, teachers' anecdotes, and documentation.

3. *What resources are available?* These include materials for parents and for you to learn about how to deal with concerns and also to work with children who have identified special needs in your program.

Remember, just as it takes practice to improve observation skills, it takes time and reflection to identify, define, and understand a variety of assessment techniques and to analyze how they can be used to measure specific child and program goals. Still, it is good to assess children. To help children grow and learn, we need to know exactly who they are and where they are in their development. Frequent observations, accurate recording, and clear documentation help us get up close and personal with the children. "Observing and assessing is not just about being a good teacher, it's about serving the children—our observations and assessments should be used to benefit them, not just so we can call ourselves good teachers, [but also] it helps us help the children" (Yuen, 2007, personal correspondence).

We end the chapter as we began: Children are fascinating. Learning to observe and assess their growth and development is a fundamental part of becoming a competent teacher and this takes time to master, as described in the "Lessons from the field" that follows. Practice makes better, so incorporate regular observation and documentation into your daily student teaching.

lessons from the field

"My Personal Journey into the Land of Child Assessment"

by Kären Wiggins-Dowler

Mentor Teacher, Mary Meta Lazarus Child Development Center

My historical journey as an early childhood educator has kept me constantly revisiting the concept of assessment and documentation and how to best facilitate an appropriate assessment system. As a new teacher, I viewed assessment as a necessary requirement to fulfill my duties and responsibilities as a teacher. During my first year of teaching, I was given a checklist to fill out on each child. I relished the fact that checklists are easy to comprehend and quick to fill out without much mental debate. Get the children to perform certain tasks, record their responses, and then, at a future date, inform the parents as to the progress of their child.

Without much formal training, I successfully replicated my own "report card" experiences and used the checklist as a framework for my parent–teacher conferences. The assessment tool exuded power in the simple declarations of can she/he do or not do, know or not know. As a new teacher, this brought me a sense of security and relief, especially as it related to talking with parents. One of my mentors, Jennifer, a seasoned teacher of several years, remembered her parent–teacher conferences at the beginning of her career: "I wasn't so honest about negative behavior due to fear of parental actions. I didn't have the ability to internalize; everything was so external. After years of experience I now know how to approach parents when talking about child concerns in a non-blaming manner. I also now do a disclaimer for the paperwork. The assessment list that I use is just a theoretical benchmark of growth that doesn't take into account the individualism of your child."

After several years of gaining confidence in my abilities as a teacher, I began to feel that the assessment tools that I had been using were inadequate in revealing who each child was. I also hated the feelings associated with an assessment system based on a *deficit model* . . . is the child able or not able to perform, know, or do. Growing up, I myself never performed well on tests and I spent much of my energy trying to make the grade instead of engaging more deeply in the learning experience. Life would be so much better without the stress of tests! I found myself starting to read articles and books about assessment, testing, and different ways to document children's growth. I laugh at myself now when I think back to the beginning of my teaching career—I would have never guessed that I would be interested in testing and assessments.

So, how was I going to adequately represent the child? The more I stood back and observed the children under my care, the more I realized that my role as a teacher included being an anthropologist and a historian. What the children were learning and how they were learning it needed to be documented more fully with the due respect that the children's efforts deserved. Finishing his practicum experience, Gordon remarked that "it was a joy getting inside a *child's* world. Through the observations I noticed the little subtleties and nuances that I just would not see without taking the time to observe. I now understand the significance of this information for them as individuals and for the program. Now my eyes are open all the time. My problem now is to develop the knowledge of what to record and what not to record."

Another student teacher, Lisa, said, "I had the absolute luxury of only observing one child without any other responsibilities." Honing in on your observational skills is one thing; try the observational challenge of a classroom of twenty-four children.

Scores do not reflect the uniqueness, knowledge, skills, and dispositions of each child. What I needed to do was to collect more data and work samples in order to develop a more complete picture of each child.

Making close observations of children had to become a part of my regular classroom behavior because trying to recall details at the end of the day was next to impossible due to mental exhaustion. Tiana, a new teacher, reflects that she finds "it difficult to pull back and write observations because it interrupts my relationship with the child." This comment reminds me of my own concern with the development of optimal teacher–child interrelationships during my initial teaching years.

Many years later, I now perform a balancing act of interacting with the children and then stepping back to make written observations. With the intense daily coordination of two dozen children, families, and a team of teachers, I find that these written observations, pictures, and work samples provide me with the necessary details to reveal and to understand the development of each child. A well planned and ongoing system of observations and work samplings informs us how a child learns, what stage of development that he/she is at, how the child develops relationships with peers and adults, what are their interests, strengths, and dispositions, what will be our next steps with the child, and are we, as teachers, actually accomplishing our program goals and objectives.

When this system is incorporated into the classroom culture, even the children feel its importance. I once had a four-year old child approach me and insist, "Support me!" I asked, "Support you, what does that mean?" He replied, "Write down what I'm doing. It's important!"

So where does my journey go from here? I am working on refining my techniques to include data from the beginning, middle, and end of the learning experiences that the children are involved in so that I can focus more on the learning process of each child. I also want to develop more analytical systems in order to help others use the portfolio system more efficiently. As Lillian Katz said, "No one was ever born an expert." This is a lifelong journey of learning and it still intrigues me. Also, if you have any suggestions about how to get more hours out of every day, please let me know! I am up to the test!

Practicum Activity

Bring to the practicum the assessment tools that your center uses for assessment. Compare them with those from other centers. Which ones do you like (and why)? Which ones have problems, and what are they? Make a chart together, compiling the forms, their purpose, and a joint list of their assets and liabilities.

Journaling Assignment

Write about how your center assesses children. Be sure to ask your supervising teacher about the goals, strengths, and challenges the team sees in this effort.

Resources

Allen, K. E., & Schwartz, I. L. (2001). *The exceptional child: Inclusion in early childhood education* (4th ed.). Clifton Park, NY: Thomson Delmar Learning.

Beaty, J. J. (2006). *Observing development of the young child* (6th ed.). Upper Saddle River, NJ: Merrill/Pearson.

Gandini, L., & Kaminsky, J. A. (2004). Reflections on the relationship between documentation and assessment in the American context: An interview with Brenda Fyfe. *Innovations in Early Education, 11*(1).

Gordon, A. M., & Browne, K. W. (2008). *Beginnings and beyond: Foundations in early childhood education* (7th ed.). Clifton Park, NY: Thomson Delmar Learning.

Greenspan, S., & Wieder, S. (2006). *Floortime: DVD Training Series: Sensory Regulation and Social Interaction.* Bethesda, MD: Interdisciplinary Council on Developmental and Learning Disorders.

Gronlund, G. (2006). *Make early learning standards come alive.* St. Paul, MN: Redleaf Press.

Hyson, M. (Ed.). (2003). *Preparing early childhood professionals: NAEYC's standards for programs.* Washington, DC: National Association for the Education of Young Children.

McAfee, O., Leong, D. J., & Bodrova, E. (2004). *Basics of assessment: A primer for early childhood educators.* Washington, DC: National Association for the Education of Young Children.

National Association for the Education of Young Children, Division for Early Childhood of the Council for Exceptional Children, and National Board for Professional Teaching Standards (2006). *Joint position statement on preparation of early childhood professionals.* Washington, DC: Authors.

Rinaldi, C. (2001). Documentation and assessment: What is the relationship? In C. Giudici, C. Rinaldi, & M. Krechevsky (Eds.), *Making learning visible: Children as individual and group learners.* Reggio Children. New York: Routledge.

Seefeldt, C. (1998). Assessing young children. In C. Seefeldt & A. Galper (Eds.), *Continuing issues in early childhood education.* Upper Saddle River, NJ: Merrill/Pearson.

Web Sites

Council for Exceptional Children
www.cec.sped.org

National Association for the Education of Young Children
www.naeyc.org

National Center for Research on Evaluation, Standards, and Student Testing (CRESST)
www.cresst.org

National Institute for Early Education Research
www.nieer.org

Environments and Schedules

Two fundamental aspects of developmentally appropriate programs for children are the environment and daily schedule. When creating environments and schedules for young children, teachers must take a realistic look at what they have to work with—and with whom they need to collaborate—to make the best of what is at hand. The first part of this chapter introduces you to the basic elements of environments, and the second offers key points for schedules.

Environments for Early Childhood Programs

Early education teachers think about the physical environment as a key ingredient when planning program and curriculum for young children. The environment is a powerful teaching tool, for children in the early years are sensitive to the world around them, and take cues and lessons from what is offered to them both indoors and outdoors, all during the session.

Considerations

Ask your supervising teacher what to consider when creating the indoor and outdoor space. Chances are, teachers are very aware of the limitations: Your program may be in a church basement, a portable trailer, or space intended for other uses. Resources are usually limited, and the environment is often not optimal for young children. Still, early childhood teachers can be creative, flexible, and innovative in how they use the space they have.

Physical Plant. How can you make the setting beautiful and inviting? The environment may be a powerful teaching tool but it is also a place where children experience their childhoods and where teachers live their professional lives. We give meaning to the spaces in our lives, and in turn, we are deeply influenced by them.

One influential program model in environmental and schedule design is that of Reggio Emilia. Developed in Italy in the mid-20th century, the Reggio approach builds on Italian community values of esthetics and creativity, and its philosophy grows out of attention to beauty and the creative process. The environment reflects these priorities in several ways: Visual appeal to both children and adults is a primary consideration in how space is arranged. Often an area or room is set aside specifically for artwork (see the Lessons from the Field article about an atelier). Time periods and experiences are arranged so that children can study deeply objects and space and make creations that reflect their thinking.

Environments for various types of programs have unique spaces, resources, and program goals. At the same time, every physical plant must be created with children in mind. First, you must rescale the space to fit their size. A good way to do this is to get on your knees at the door and look around at what the children will see. For infants and toddlers, the floor is where their primary activity takes place; preschoolers are able to reach low shelves and tables; school-age children can make use of higher cupboards and counters.

In the United States, each state sets its own standards for the licensing of educational centers; often this responsibility is given to smaller regions or counties. The National Academy of Early Childhood Programs (a division of the National Association for the Education of Young Children) recommends a minimum of 35 square feet of usable playroom floor space indoors per child and 75 square feet of play space outdoors per child (Bredekamp, 1998). Check with your local area for its requirements for physical space. At the same time, look at how the space functions when in use, not only square footage. Spaces that are insufficient or in poor repair can lead to conflicts among children, materials becoming disorganized,

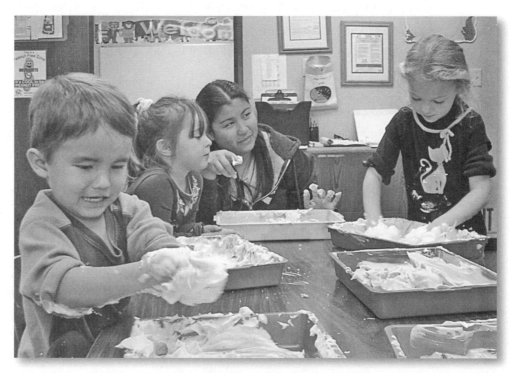

Blending the center's philosophy and goals with the environment, quality schools strive to become models of lively places for children and adults.

and tensions among staff (Cryer, Harms, & Riley, 2003). Environments that are safe, clean, attractive, and spacious is the goal.

Program Goals. Before placing furniture or stocking shelves, teachers must think about their goals for children. Social interaction is a likely goal; therefore, the environment will need to be arranged so that children can play together. Small tables near shelves of toys and spaces that are protected from constant intrusion will suit this purpose better than rows of desks or wide-open areas that invite running more than focused connections. See if you can infer the goals of your program from the room and yard arrangement.

An educational focus is an important part of a program's goals. One such goal is a *self-help* focus. A community supermarket is a good example of a self-help, or self-reliant, environment because the shelves are set so customers can reach and select for themselves. Some stores now have self-help checkout areas as well. An early childhood self-help environment will have toys on reachable shelves marked with pictures or names of the items, and tables or floor space nearby. Easels are set up for children to put on an apron, paint jars are already in a tray, and a drying rack is nearby with pins that children can use to hang their paintings.

Another example of an educational goal is the *antibias* approach in which the focus is for children to learn tolerance and acceptance of diversity. These environments reflect a variety of styles in family life; for instance, the house corner is likely to have woks, tortilla presses, and pasta rollers as well as soup pots and frying pans. Dress-up clothes will go beyond a business suit or party dress to include dashikis, sarongs, and other items worn by diverse families (Gordon & Browne, 2008).

Health, Safety, and Connectedness. "Our designs shape children's beliefs about themselves and life. In a well-designed area, children are engaged and feel secure. A well-designed area can facilitate predictable, consistent and intimate care for each child" (Olds, 2000). These basic considerations hold for every early childhood environment. Regardless of program philosophy or physical plant, the teaching staff keeps in mind these four areas as fundamental priorities. Providing for children's health and safety is essential:

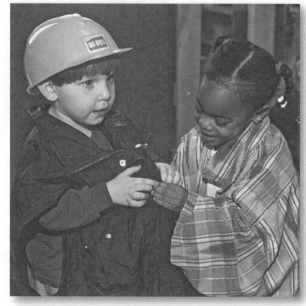

Good environments for children promote cultural diversity and antibias sensitivity by providing a variety of clothing, dishes, and other materials for children to experience.

- Keeping children healthy involves sanitation, temperature, ventilation, lighting, and proper nutrition.

- Keeping communicable disease at a minimum includes strong practices and good health assessment of children and adults.

Environments and Schedules

- Guarding children's safety involves creating a hazard-free environment that still offers challenges and risks, and monitoring for potential problems as well as being prepared to administer first aid and deal with natural disasters.

- Handling vehicle safety includes attention to arrival and departure places and routines as well as transportation on field trips.

Finally, maintaining children's well-being involves setting the emotional tone, preserving children's play (see Chapter 6), and addressing threats to children both in the program and beyond, such as at home or in their community. Children who are emotionally connected to the "important others" in their lives—including you as their student teacher—will be better able to take advantage of what an early childhood environment has to offer.

Planning Space

The prepared environment, a phrase Maria Montessori coined over a century ago, describes a wealth of ideas about the environment as the key to children's educational experiences. Child-sized furniture, a sense of order, a place for everything, and materials accessible to children are all hallmarks of the Montessori influence (Montessori, 1967).

Although you will encounter a variety of places and spaces in early childhood programs, there are some key elements that all good early educational environments will share. Activity areas should be located for predictability and flow, with boundaries that include ways to move within and between them, with freedom to explore and privacy (Community Playthings, 2006). Figure 5.1 describes space and furnishing items from one of the most well-known and researched environmental rating tools.

In addition, the following key dimensions should be considered when planning indoor and outdoor space (Prescott, Jones, & Kritschevsky, 1972):

- Softness (pillows, grass) and hardness (tile floors, cement)
- Open (dress-up clothes, sand) and closed (puzzles, slide)

Figure 5.1
Space and Furnishings in ECE Settings

Indoor space

Furniture for routine care, play, and learning

Furnishings for relaxation and comfort

Room arrangement for play

Space for privacy

Child-related display

Space for gross motor play

Gross motor equipment

Source: From Thelma Harms, Richard M. Clifford, & Debby Cryer, *Early Childhood Environment Rating Scale. Revised Edition* (New York: Teachers College Press. © 2005 by Thelma Harms, Richard M. Clifford, & Debby Cryer). All rights reserved.

- Simple (climber) and complex (with slides and ropes)
- Intrusion (blocks area) and seclusion (loft)
- High mobility (trike lanes) and low mobility (board games table)

Look at your environment with an eye for these environmental components and key dimensions. Chances are, the better they match up, the more functional and productive the children's play and learning becomes.

Children's positive behavior can be enhanced by attending to the physical environment. It is said that the environment is the children's third teacher (Dodge, Colker, & Heroman, 2002). The physical space communicates to children about where they can go, what they can and cannot do, even how they are to behave. For instance, leaving a large open space in the center of the room may invite preschool wrestling; reconfiguring it into several areas for small groups encourages children to choose and stay in an area. The 2-year-olds who pull all the lids off marking pens are also the young children who enjoy pushing the pens back into the lids that are affixed to the bottom of a pen tray (Lally & Stewart, 1990). School-age children who see sign-up sheets near the computers and the ball room are more likely to engage in an orderly process than if there are no environmental cues about how to get a turn.

Adapt and accommodate best describes what early childhood professionals do to provide productive environments for children. Few programs have a perfect environment. Moreover, as soon as children enter a space, their teachers find themselves making changes so that the group and each individual can succeed (see the My Reaction feature). Other circumstances such as weather, scheduling problems, staffing changes, even unexpected guests, mean that teachers need to add adapting and accommodating to their outlook. Young children are new to the world and easily overwhelmed; when changes occur, it is easier for the adult to adapt. When Mike comes to school announcing his displeasure about his new sister, you may need to adapt the dramatic play area by adding some dolls and baby bottles, and accommodate this "big feeling" by locating books about becoming a big brother for the library area.

For example, the fingerpainting activity you had planned may need to be postponed when you are told to host a group of prospective parents and explain your program while in class; or the surprise thunderstorm cancels the planned walking field trip, and means you need to get the parachute and soft balls out onto the patio instead of simply doing a clay project. The physical environment will need to be adapted as the circumstances of a day unfold.

Space is often used in many ways, so teachers find themselves adapting the environment frequently. Look at your practicum site: What is the primary use for each area of the environment? What else happens there in the course of a day or week? A countertop may start the day as a staging area for preparing materials, then for drying art projects, and setting up snack trays—all before 10 a.m. The block area transforms into the area for circle time and then gets several nap cots on it for naptime. The same asphalt driveway that is the trike lane gets used for relay races and for parachute play.

My Reaction

"Is This a Good Environment for Young Children?"

When I first walked into the classroom, I immediately focused on the small desks and chairs in a "U-shaped" formation. I was caught off-guard: Why would a structured set-up be of value with 3- to 5-year-olds? Then I reconsidered the thought that maybe the more structured setting is developmentally appropriate for these children with special needs, to keep them connected from one activity to the next. Don't get me wrong, they have tremendous activity centers for children to play together and personal cubbies to mark individual spaces for privacy. While the desks surprised me, now that I am working here I can see each child is receiving and meeting his or her personal needs and education plan.

—RACHYL

Sample environments are helpful for student teachers to examine as they become more proficient in teaching young children. It is said that there are as many ways to make a school space as there are teachers to plan them. Indeed, NAEYC deliberately avoided dictating specific arrangements or yard items in its work on developmentally appropriate practices in recognition of the diversity of environments, and space challenges, in early childhood programs. Figures 5.2 to 5.5 offer a few ways to organize space for the three age groups. Compare them with your space to see what elements you have in common, and how the environments differ.

Equipment and Materials

Consider your resources. As with physical space, programs vary widely in the financial resources they have for equipment and materials. Teachers often find themselves having to make-do with plastic equipment instead of hardwood and with donated materials rather than new items. Yet, because the investment will have to last for years, it is worth considering purchases carefully.

Equipment, such as the furniture in a room, should fit the children who inhabit your program, and often will need to be employed for multiple uses. For example, chairs will need to be stable, match the tables, fit the children, and be able to withstand use for activities, snacks, art projects (as easels), audience space (for puppet shows, for instance), and even as train cars. Early childhood environments are demanding, and equipment must be able to withstand the children's use.

Center use of equipment is at least ten times as hard as home use. Sharp edges or corners? Parts to swallow? Toxic finishes? Will the item be pulled or tipped

F i g u r e 5.2 Infant and Toddler Environment

A toddler environment has safety and accessibility in mind, while helping children work in small groups so they can be maximally involved with a minimum of distraction from others.

Source: From Gordon/Browne. *Beginnings and Beyond,* 7e. © 2008 Wadsworth, a part of Cengage Learning, Inc. Reproduced by permission. www.cengage.com/permissions.

over? Will it wear or break in a manner that then makes it dangerous? Does it allow for cleaning and disinfectant? Right size and scale for all children also with special needs? (Greenman & Stonehouse, 1996, p. 195)

Ample storage shelves and tote box units help a program display what is available and put aside items for rotation.

Stocking the room or yard happens once the furnishings are in place. It is time to put materials into the interest areas. Adequate, reachable, and labeled (with a

Figure 5.3 Preschool Environment

A preschool child care center needs clearly defined boundaries and obvious pathways to make it easy for children to use this space independently.

Source: From Gordon/Browne. *Beginnings and Beyond,* 7e. © 2008 Wadsworth, a part of Cengage Learning, Inc. Reproduced by permission. www.cengage.com/permissions.

Figure 5.4 School-Age Environment

A school-age environment has learning centers to allow children to make clear choices and engage in active learning through play.

Source: From Gordon/Browne. *Beginnings and Beyond,* 7e. © 2008 Wadsworth, a part of Cengage Learning, Inc. Reproduced by permission. www.cengage.com/permissions.

Figure 5.5 ECE Playground

A playground/yard, suitable for ages 4 and older, will give children a sense of security and adventure.

Source: From Gordon/Browne. *Beginnings and Beyond*, 7e. © 2008 Wadsworth, a part of Cengage Learning, Inc. Reproduced by permission. www.cengage.com/permissions.

picture) materials are vital for orderliness in every age group. All children learn through their senses and with concrete, hands-on materials. In addition, the inclusion of children with disabilities in a regular classroom has benefits for all when teachers have materials that are universal in design that work for many levels of age and ability. Look at the activity areas in your room and yard, and think about the group of children you teach as you compare your materials with the list in Figure 5.6.

Figure 5.6 Basic Materials in an Early Childhood Classroom and Outdoor Playground/Yard
Although not comprehensive, this list starts to organize the environment for a variety of play, both indoors and outdoors. Note the adjustments that must be made to accommodate different ages.

Classroom Art Supplies

Easels, paints, watercolors

Play dough, clay

Pens, pencils, brushes

Scissors, holepunches

Glue, paste

Collage materials

Assorted paper

Infants/toddlers: Limit materials.
Use open shelves with few choices.

School age: Have self-help table and
teacher-guided projects.

Discovery and Science

Nature materials

Textured materials

Water/sensory table and materials

Magnifying glasses, mirrors

Scales

Small pets

Infants/toddlers: Simplify, watch for
safety. Aquarium.

School age: Display to read. Computer.

Dramatic Play

Safety mirrors

Furniture: child-sized, versatile

Clothing: variety, nonstereotyped

Dolls: variety, and accessories

Cooking utensils

Food items

Purses, suitcases, briefcases, backpacks

Infants/toddlers: Limit the choice, add
hats or dolls that can get wet.

School age: Varied units such as
prehistoric cave, moonscape.

Blocks

Unit blocks, hollow blocks (may also be outdoors)

Props: people and animal figures, doll house,
transportation toys

Accessories: transportation signage, doll furniture, gas
pumps, cloth scraps

Infants/toddlers: Substitute soft blocks and cardboard
blocks for unit blocks; limit props and accessories for
safety; push–pull toys.

School age: Include "village" or "castle" blocks; pattern
blocks; increase number and types of unit blocks,
add paper and pencils for child-made signage; make
homemade blocks from milk cartons.

Manipulattves/Table Toys

Puzzles

Construction toys: Legos, Tinkertoys, etc.

Math toys: Unfix cubes, Cuisenaire blocks, attribute
blocks, colored cubes, lacing, stringing toys,
pegboards

Dressing frames

Montessori materials: pink tower, graduated cylinders,
golden cube, etc.; collectibles: buttons, keys, shells,
etc. cooperative games: lotto, dominoes, matching
games

Infants/toddlers: Provide a few simple puzzles, with
knobs, or soft ones; eliminate math toys and replace
with large plastic beads, nesting boxes, stacking
toys, easy dressing frames for toddlers.

School age: Emphasize construction, math toys and
cooperative games. Add cards, board games.

Language and Books

Books

Flannel board, accessories

Photos

Lotto games

Records, tapes

Writing center: typewriter, pads, and pencils

Infants/toddlers: Cardboard books; use others with
adults only.

School age: Readers, listening post.

Figure 5.6 (*continued*)

Outdoor Playground/Yard

Grounds: Various surfaces (grass, asphalt, gravel/sand, tanbark), as much natural habitat as possible

Equipment: Climbing apparatus with ramps, slide, pole, ladder; swings (various types); house/quiet area; ramps and supports to build; tires, "loose parts"

Sand/water area and toys

Riding area and various wheel toys

Large building blocks

Dramatic-play props

Balls and game materials

Workbench and woodworking/clay materials

Easel and drying rack

Dancing/parachute/tumbling mat materials

Pet and garden areas

Infants/toddlers: Have plenty of simple riding toys, eliminate woodworking, have apparatus correct size and simplicity and/or foam wedges.

School age: Increase game area; may eliminate number or kinds of wheel toys; substitute a stage, mural, boat, creek; increase "loose parts" for child-created forts.

Source: From Gordon/Browne. *Beginnings and Beyond,* 7e. © 2008 Wadsworth, a part of Cengage Learning, Inc. Reproduced by permission. www.cengage.com/permissions.

Finally, just as the overall environment should be responsive, materials and equipment should be flexible. Having a variety of materials offers children many ways to learn in their environment. For example, materials such as puzzles and self-correcting graduated cylinders can be used in only one way, so it is important to have some materials that can be used in various ways, such as Tinkertoys, blocks, and dramatic-play items. Teachers can make equipment supercomplex by adding water to dry sand, rollers and garlic presses to play dough, or different kinds of brushes to the paint jars.

> Children can use [these materials] in a variety of ways, depending on their maturity, ability, past experience with the materials, interest and involvement. . . . Programs should include lots of materials that have an abundance and variety of uses to give children a sense of creativity and control. (Wardle, 1999, p. 34)

Reuse and *recycle* are catch words for most early childhood programs. Along with the overarching goal of being mindful of the environment as a whole, and of the heavy footprint most Western habits make on the planet, early childhood educators find it necessary to stretch their budgets by being resourceful in reusing and recycling materials. One student teacher made recycling her curriculum focus, sending a letter to families with items to save and send with their children, and having them ask their children how they could reuse items at home. Note the items requested and the uses the student teacher offered to families:

Cereal boxes	Make a puzzle, create a matching game, cover with paper to create building blocks
Water bottle tops	Put in beans for shakers, use them for Bingo counters, make a ring-toss game
Plastic coffee and frosting lids	Use as a base for a bird's nest, punch holes for a lacing card, make a stepping-stone game.
Bubble wrap	Tape to floor with duct tape and let kids stomp on it, tape to table and use toy hammers to pop, let children cut it out for collage work

- Simplicity of detail
- Versatile in use
- Easily comprehended design
- Easily manipulated
- Involve the child in play, including large muscle
- Encourage cooperative play
- Material that is warm and pleasant to touch
- Durable
- Work as intended
- Safe
- Generous in proportions and quantity
- Price is based on durability and design
- Sized to fit children
- Work for children with disabilities

Figure 5.7
What Makes Good Playthings?
Appropriate materials for young children must have certain characteristics to be useful and educational.

Source: Excerpt from *Children Come First,* used with permission from Community Playthings, www.communityplaythings.com.

Selecting materials for young children is as varied as the environments for children. Consider using the list in Figure 5.7 to evaluate what you find in your practicum site.

Appropriate Schedules for Young Children

The daily schedule defines the structure and flow of each program. If the environment defines where things happen, the schedule determines *when* they occur. The format tells children and adults in what order things will happen and for what length of time.

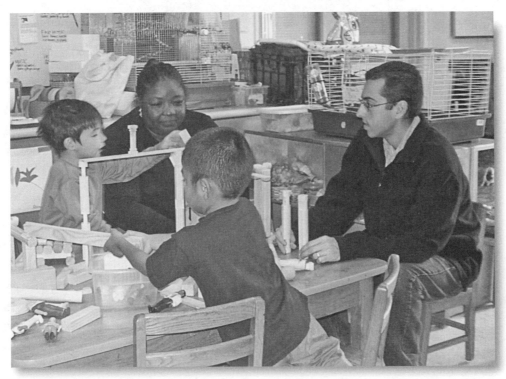

Children play and work best in classrooms that are equipped with age-appropriate materials and equipment.

Schedules and Program Goals

Daily schedules reflect children's ages and their needs while meeting the program goals. The time of day and timing of activities show what is valued in the program. Programs that focus on children's self-care skills will allow the time needed for children's dressing, eating, and toileting. An academic program would likely have substantial time set for teaching subject matter such as math and literacy.

Priorities in Scheduling. Look at the schedule at your center and calculate the minutes for children's-choice and teacher-directed activities, for transitions and routines, for small-group and whole-group times—the more minutes given, the higher the priority. Then ask your supervising teacher to rank those activities and see if the stated priorities match the time given to each.

For instance, student teacher Candice discovered "the daily schedule does provide enough time for unhurried play, because the first hour is for free play. The periods that create tension are the transitions because they are hurried and very rushed. At the beginning of the day the pace is more leisurely; even for cleanup, the Barney song is put on and all the children participate in the process. But as the end of the day nears it often seems more rushed and the children back off and teachers are nagging everyone. We should build in cleanup time at both ends of the day."

Components of Schedules. As a schedule is created, teachers should keep in mind variety, choice, pace, and balance.

> Our homes are where we feel secure and competent and *it* reflects us when *it* is familiar and predictable. Children's places need ordered time and space that furthers the program goals while making the program a pleasant place to live and work for all those (large and small) who inhabit the program. . . . The order provides a comforting framework that does not harshly interrupt the activities of children; instead, the order allows for more experiences and for children to anticipate their day. (Greenman, 2006, p. 53)

For example, Michelle found at her center an "open-door policy" where the children have the choice to go inside or outside from 10:30 a.m. until lunch. Her supervising teacher Nataliya pointed out that children choose to play inside when there are new or interesting things on tables, or when they are pursuing a theme or activity with certain friends. Some children head outside as soon as the door opens, and return after vigorous play; others will play outside even in wet or chilly weather. The choice seems to be encouraging to children; Michelle observed over the course of the semester that participation levels increased for *all* children during the semester for that time slot.

Figure 5.8
Top 10 Tips for Building
Developmentally
Appropriate Schedules

1. Include time for routines, transitions, and groups.
2. Alternate quiet, sedentary activity with loud, active play.
3. Offer time indoors and outdoors.
4. Allow both structured and unstructured time.
5. Include teacher-directed and child-choice experiences.
6. Make time for children to be alone, in small groups, and with the whole group together.
7. Set the schedule with the group age range and their developmental level in mind.
8. Allow for flexibility to change because of weather, emergencies, children's moods and interests, and spontaneous surprises.
9. Have a beginning and an end, so each child or family is greeted and dismissed warmly.
10. Turn the unexpected into "teachable moments."

General Guidelines

What is important for children is the security of knowing a sequence, rather than a certain number of minutes.

Common Elements. There are common elements in all schedules, regardless of the age or time period. Figure 5.8 outlines these elements.

Flexibility. Even while following these guidelines, teachers should adjust their schedules to fit the needs of the group as well as be flexible for individuals. See

A common element of all schedules is time to eat.

the "Reflective Incident" for flexibility in response to the unexpected. In addition, keep these four ideas in mind:

1. *Offer more choices as children grow.*   Two-year-olds need fewer toys on the shelf than do 4-year-olds. Toddlers can be either indoors or out, but preschoolers may be able to handle making a choice, and certainly school-age children can.

2. *Transitions are handled differently with age.*   Older children may be able to move as a group from the classroom to the library, but preschoolers will do better in small groups and certainly with more adult help. Kindergartners can walk along with partners, but 2-year-olds will need an adult's hand or a rope to hold.

3. *The daily structure changes over time.*   "The balance of free-play and teacher-directed activities shifts from relatively few directed activities for younger children to some more for the nursery school and child care ages. The kindergarten schedule provides more structure in individual work projects and teacher-focused time" (Gordon & Browne, 2008, p. 369).

4. *The content and duration of circle time expands with age.*   Toddler group time is short and simple, perhaps a song and a story. In preschool this increases to include acting out a familiar story or fingerplay, brainstorming how to solve a problem. By kindergarten the circle time has expanded to include concept introductions and more elaborate discussions.

Think about what changes you might make to accommodate children's developmental stages and skills at your fieldwork site.

Sample Schedules

Because early childhood practicum courses involve teaching in settings for children from infancy to school age, the schedules you will encounter will be varied. These sample schedules outline programs for children ages 2 to 8. Charlotte, doing fieldwork at her worksite, notes that "creating a schedule is a difficult task, and it is hard to plan it when you haven't yet met the children. We make it up so that the children are, hopefully, intrigued by what they will be doing throughout the day. The schedule may not always be followed, but it is important to have some sort of map for all of us to know."

Look at the schedules in Figures 5.9 to 5.12. They offer ways to plan a day for children in each of the major age groups. Compare them with the schedule at your placement site. Remember, daily schedules provide structure so that children have time to learn and thrive.

● **Reflective Incident** *"The Fire Drill During Circle Time"*

I finally did large group time. I've been dreading it for weeks now, as I watched Bushra and Theo do it so effortlessly. It seems that Bushra just lights up when she is in front of the whole group, and the kids love whatever Theo tries. I've become a trusted teacher to these children over time, and have a small group of my own now—well, it's really my mentor teacher's group, but she has given it over to me by now.

So, I got the children settled with a good song ("If You're Happy & You Know It"), then we read a story (*The Very Hungry Caterpillar*), and they were practicing on their carpet squares how to wiggle like caterpillars . . . when there was a fire drill!

It was almost funny; the kids kind of froze but they were still wiggling. Then we all lined up at the door to go outside. But one child was very upset because she wanted to stay standing on her piece of rug. Preschoolers really make you look at how something you are doing affects them emotionally, as well as physically!—Monica

Your Thoughts

1. How would I feel?

2. What would I do?

3. What might the results be?

8:00 a.m. Welcome children and families
Free play indoors: Easels, play dough, books, blocks, ramp
8:45 a.m. Optional music/dancing group
8:50 a.m. Cleanup song
9:00 a.m. Door opens to outdoors
Free play outdoors: Slides, bridge, climber, sand
9:45 a.m. Optional organized game
9:50 a.m. Cleanup song
10:00 a.m. Handwashing and Toileting/Diapering
10:15 a.m. Snack at small groups
10:25 a.m. Optional stories at small groups
Indoor or outdoor free play
11:20 a.m. Cleanup song
11:25 a.m. Circle time: (optional: families join group for story)
11:30 a.m. Goodbye to children and families

Figure 5.9
Toddler Half-Day Schedule

A sample daily schedule for toddlers includes options for flexibility, a consistent routine, and responsiveness to individual children as they learn self-regulating skills such as toileting.

Figure 5.10
Preschool Full-Day Schedule

A program for preschoolers involves a comfortable pace with time for play, routines, and transitions.

7:30 a.m. Arrival: welcome and breakfast

8:00 a.m. Indoor free play

9:00 a.m. Cleanup song

9:15 a.m. Circle time: songs, games, today's events

9:30 a.m. Focus choices: art, cooking, science

10:30 a.m. Cleanup and handwashing for snack

10:45 a.m. Snack at small groups

11:00 a.m. Outdoor free play

11:00 a.m. Fieldtrip or walk, swim lessons, music or art teacher

Noon Cleanup and Handwashing for lunch

12:15 p.m. Lunch

12:30 p.m. Put away lunch, toilet, prepare for nap

1:00 p.m. Naptime, individual stories or storytape

2:00 p.m. Nonnappers do quiet activities and snack prep

3:00 p.m. Snack time

3:15 p.m. Circle time: music, special options

3:30 p.m. Indoor or outdoor free play

4:00 p.m. Walk to park, play group game or movie

5:30 p.m. Departure: check in with families

Figure 5.11
Preschool Half-Day Schedule

The traditional preschool program is half-day with an emphasis on play and social interactions.

9:00 a.m. Arrival and greeting

9:00–9:45 a.m. Free play indoors: art, blocks, dramatic play, table toys, water table

9:45 a.m. Cleanup and handwashing

10:00 a.m. Circle time

10:15 a.m. Snack at small groups

10:45 a.m. Outdoor free play: climbers, swings, sandbox, woodworking, wheel toys, group games

11:45 a.m. Cleanup

Noon Story time and dismissal

Figure 5.12
School-Age and Kindergarten Through Grade 3 Schedule

With older children, schedules include plenty of group opportunities as well as support for homework.

Noon Kindergarten arrival: welcome, handwashings, lunch

12:30 p.m. Kindergarten circle time: news, choices

12:45 p.m. Choice time: indoor free play and cooking

1:45 p.m. Outdoor playground available and games

2:45 p.m. Cleanup and all indoors

3:00 p.m. Grades 1 and 2 arrival: welcome, put away belongings

3:10 p.m. Circle time for all: news, choices

3:20 p.m. Snack time

3:30 p.m. Grades 1 and 2 homework; kindergarten art project

4:00 p.m. Grades 1 and 2 outdoor teams, indoor clubs; kindergartens free play indoors

5:00 p.m. Indoor or outdoor free play, bus, departure

Planning environments and setting schedules are critical aspects of teaching, and each includes a complex array of tasks to master. At the same time, it is these elements that set the stage for the curriculum to come alive. Although student teachers can feel overwhelmed at first, early childhood professionals—indeed, all teachers—find tremendous satisfaction when their plans can be realized, as in the "Lessons from the Field" feature that follows.

lessons from the field

"Creating the Atelier, One Box of Recyclables at a Time"
by Patricia Dilko
Co-Coordinator, San Mateo, CA Regional ECE Mentor Teacher Program

In August 1998, a small child care program opened its doors for the very first time to a community of children and families who had eagerly anticipated its arrival. I must admit this was not the first "start-up" that I had facilitated, but it was special: it was a child development laboratory for a small community college in the San Francisco Bay Area. Not only did we have 50 children and their families to think about, but we were also responsible for students stopping in to do child observations or administrative interviews, and semester-length student practicum placements. While I had run larger programs before, I had never had such responsibility to the community; our college housed the ECE Department and we were the child development laboratory. You can imagine how nervous I became knowing that students and faculty from many classes would be observing us and talking about the program in ECE classes!

Opening a state-of-the-art early learning environment in a 2,000 sq foot, one room, re-locatable building can be tricky. The plan was to become NAEYC accredited after we had been open for a few years, so for everything we did we kept an eye on those requirements. The building sat on the crest of a hill overlooking a beautiful valley with the coast mountain range beyond, so we wanted to mirror the natural beauty that surrounded us. We decided that the classroom environment should tend toward natural materials and neutral colors; the furniture was light maple, with baskets

on the shelves holding manipulatives, the textiles and furnishings blended into the background. We wanted the brightness and joy of the children to be the focal point of the environment.

At the beginning we chose a traditional classroom design with the usual interest areas including a pretty basic art area that was easy to close off during other activities. At the end of the first year the staff met to talk about our plans for the next year and I brought up the concepts that I had been hearing from the preschools in Reggio Emilia, Italy: Projects, Documentation, Transparency, Planning Time, Parent Involvement, and the Atelier. After lengthy discussion, we decided to open up the art area into a mini-atelier!

The concept that captured our imaginations was "transparency." We began to look at our space as if to make it borderless . . . without walls. We installed deep, metal kitchen shelving so that children could see all of the wonderful materials that we had gathered. We transitioned to all clear boxes or low baskets for materials to accomplish the same visual effect. And we went to two local recycled materials centers to gather interesting, open-ended supplies.

When we re-opened the center for fall semester the children were fascinated, the parents were curious, and the teachers were overwhelmed! At first it seemed like we could not establish any boundaries, and the children did not understand the freedom that they had with materials. Frankly the place was a mess, and we weren't seeing anything positive from our experiment. But as the semester rolled by, and we developed a language of expectation for the children, the mess subsided, and the creativity exploded! We found it to be true that even very young children can manipulate colored pencils and pastels if they are given repeated opportunities. And we found that the more precious the materials we used, the more gentle and respectful the children became. They learned, as we modeled for them, the importance of caring for the environment.

Slowly we began to see ourselves as a Reggio-inspired program, and yet we were uniquely ourselves.

Much of our culture came from being part of the college community. The ebb and flow of the semester cycle became a part of our project planning and the materials in the atelier reflected the seasons and needs of the projects. Parents became involved with gathering and displaying materials as well as photographing children and assembling documentation panels. We learned not to be afraid of taking big risks because the children will guide the way. We learned to trust the team of teachers that we worked with because our collective wisdom was far greater than anything one person could develop on their own. And we learned to honor and respect the competencies of young children.

Practicum Activity

Make a sketch of the indoor and outdoor environments where you teach. Note the problem areas—too many children, not enough space, an area ignored. Now design your own environment for the age level in which you teach. Show how your environment improves on your placement.

Journaling Assignment

What "trouble spots" do you see in the daily schedule where you teach? Are there times where children are hurried? Parts of the day where children chronically have behavior problems? Identify these in the schedule, and make recommendations for changes that would remedy the problems.

Resources

Bredekamp, S. (Ed.). (1998). *Accreditation criteria & procedures of the National Academy of Early Childhood programs*. Washington, DC: National Association for the Education of Young Children.

Community Playthings. (2006). *Spaces: Room layout for early childhood education*. Retrieved from http://www.CommunityProducts.com

Community Playthings. (2006). *Children come first: Selecting equipment for early childhood education*. Retrieved from http://www.CommunityProducts.com

Cryer, D., Harms, T., & Riley, C. (2003). *All about the Early Childhood Environmental Rating Scale*. Raleigh-Durham, NC: Pact House.

Dodge, D.T., Colker, L.J., Heroman, C. (2002). *The creative curriculum for preschool* (4th ed.). Washington, DC: Teaching Strategies, Inc.

Gordon, A. M., & Browne, K.W. (2008). *Beginnings and beyond: Foundations in early childhood education* (7th ed.). Clifton Park, NY: Thomson Delmar Learning.

Greenman, J. (2006, July/August). The importance of order. *Exchange Magazine*, 53–55.

Greenman, J., & Stonehouse, A. (1996) *Prime times: A handbook for excellence in infant and toddler care*. Redmond, WA: Exchange Press.

Harms, T., Clifford, R., & Cryer, D. (2005). *Early Childhood Environmental Rating Scales* [FACERS, ECERS-R, ITERS-R, SACERS]. New York: Teachers College Press.

Lally, J. R., and Stewart, J. (1990). *Infant-toddler caregiving: A guide to setting up environments.* Center for Child and Family Studies, Far West Laboratory for Educational Research and Development.

Montessori, M. (1967). *The Montessori method.* Cambridge, MA: New York: Frederick A. Stokes Company.

Olds, A. (2000). *Child care design guide.* New York: McGraw-Hill.

Prescott, E., Jones, E., & Kritschevsky, S. (1972). *Group care as a child-rearing environment.* Washington, DC: National Association for the Education of Young Children.

Wardle, F. (1999, January/February). Educational toys. *Earlychildhood NEWS,* 38.

Web Sites

CABE (Commission for Architecture and the Built Environment)
www.cabe.org.uk

Community Playthings
www.communityplaythings.com

FPG Child Development Institute
www.fpg.unc.edu

High/Scope Educational Research Foundation
www.highscope.org

Teaching Strategies
www.TeachingStrategies.com

Program for Infant Toddler Care
www.pitc.org

Curriculum

Start at the Very Beginning

Long before a room is designed and arranged, the daily schedule set, and before the curriculum is created, the early childhood professional reflects on the "how," "what," "when," and "why" of young children and the learning process. Experienced teachers will almost unconsciously run through the underlying factors that affect their thinking before they plan the curriculum. Beginning teachers can benefit from reviewing the process of creating sound learning environments and curriculum for young children.

How Young Children Learn

A group of kindergarten and first-grade children are kneeling on the floor of the after-school center, making a large map of the neighborhood where they live. They have markers, scissors, magazines, glue, and colored paper. The conversation is lively:

Corey:	My house is around the corner from Luke's. Where is yours, Nedi?
Nedi:	On Second Street; that's two blocks away. I'll get some string and we can measure from each house to the school. I wonder which one is closer.
Luke:	We should go past the fire station today and see what's in the lot next to it since Nedi says the drug store is there and Rosalie says it isn't.
Merleen:	This doesn't look right. How do you draw a fence?
Rosalie:	We have to do street signs. I'll print their names. My street is easy, but yours is hard. Mrs. Garcia, how do you spell "Montgomery Street"?
Ms. Garcia:	Let's sound it out together, Rosalie, and I'll print it on the board for you.
Corey:	Oops. There's no road to get cars through. Let's make the road go all around the town. Luke, you start at that end and I'll start over here.
Joey:	I'll cut out some real neat cars and glue them on the streets.

Watching children interact, you notice they are active, curious, eager to learn, and creative. They question, explore, and experiment with ideas, language, and imagination. The children collaborate, negotiate, and learn from one another as they construct their own knowledge in making the map.

Hands-On Learning. *Hands-on learning* is the most effective way young children make sense of their environment and form their own understanding of how the world works. As active learners, children have to explore and manipulate materials in a variety of ways. Pushing, pulling, stacking, building up, taking down, sorting, measuring, digging, taking apart, putting together, pouring, and climbing are some of the ways children learn. The value of discovery cannot be underestimated as children find out for themselves how things work. The concept of "balance" is meaningless until children have built block structures, watched them fall, and learned how to make them stable. This is a tangible, physical experience necessary for learning the concept of balancing. Much of the map-making is physical and takes place on the floor, as children move around the space, working on different parts of the map with different materials and responding to each other's comments and suggestions.

Firsthand Learning. *Firsthand experiences* are the beginning of learning. Young children construct knowledge by expanding on their own experiences. In the block area for the last few weeks, the children in the map-making story have been building

Children are eager to learn and need meaningful experiences to help them create their own knowledge of the world.

complex structures and have created a town. To extend their interest and learning, Ms. Garcia suggested they create the town on butcher paper. Daily activities in the community provided the firsthand understanding the children needed to begin their map, starting with their own home and street. The children's own experience in the park, at the drug store or at the fire station fueled their interest and excitement. As the children created a visual representation of their neighborhood their concepts of spatial relationships, area, volume, and measurement were more clearly defined. The knowledge and skills the children acquired through this project began with block building and will expand in the future as the children make more sophisticated maps with three-dimensional objects, create dioramas of buildings, and use graphs to build their structures to scale.

Meaningful Learning. *Meaningful learning* makes for optimum results. Involvement is guaranteed when the learning experience touches on children's own interests, needs, and concerns. For the young child, this means activities that include children and their families, friends, pets, community, and the environment in which they live, work, and play. Making the map was exciting because the project related to the children's own neighborhood and called on them to think about things that are important in their daily life, such as how far they walk to school and who else lives and works in the neighborhood. As they play, these children will build on what they have learned and apply that to how they understand and define the meaning of neighborhood. Later, that knowledge expands to other maps of the city, state, country, and world.

Cooperative Learning. *Cooperative learning* takes place when children work and play together. Children can be resources for one another and expand one another's awareness and knowledge as they play together. Cooperation and shared learning are important lifelong skills that young children learn by being actively engaged with others in the learning process. Throughout the mapping activity, children and adults discussed and solved problems together, stimulated creativity, expanded social skills, and fostered new concepts. Children gain social skills as they find the need to share both materials and space with others and strengthen their communications skills as well. Working and playing together enhances their enjoyment as well as their learning, as seen in the My Reaction feature from a student teacher.

Learning Through Play

Play is the way children learn how to learn. Children have a natural curiosity that motivates them to stop and watch a bug make its way across the sidewalk or to pour water over and over into different-sized cups. The intensity, persistence, and creativity of their play are the tools children use to learn about learning.

My Reaction

"Cleaning Pennies"

Today's activity was to clean pennies. The first group of children was enthralled with the solutions used to clean the pennies (vinegar, salt, and/or baking soda). The objective was for the children to dip their brush into the vinegar and then choose either the salt or the baking soda to scrub the penny with. They started doing it this way but it became more of a science experiment to see what happens when you combine the solutions together. So they started adding the salt to the vinegar and it would fizz and bubble a little. Their expressions were priceless. They were in awe. I asked the questions, "Which do you think would have the most reaction when you add it to the vinegar, the salt or the baking soda?" Half said the salt, the other half said the baking soda so they tried them both and came to the conclusion that the reactions were about the same. The next group of children that came to the table were not interested in the solution, but in the cleaning of the pennies. I explained what they were supposed to do. They showed me their pennies and were so proud that you could see the copper shining through. The question I asked this group was, "Which do you think cleans the pennies better, the salt or the baking soda?" Again, some said salt, a few said baking soda, and a couple said both. So they tried them both and even mixed the salt with the baking soda. Their consensus: They both worked! I really, really liked this activity.

—VIKKI

Play is a natural way for children around the world to express themselves and is a basic need of children throughout their school years. Piaget (1962) defined three basic forms of play: practice play, symbolic play, and games with rules.

Practice or Functional Play

This type of activity is a child's earliest form of play and forms a basis for the types of play that follow. Practice play, sometimes referred to as functional play, occurs primarily in the first 2 years as the infant and toddler learn their physical capabilities and the cause and effect of acting on their environment.

Symbolic Play

This kind of activity includes both constructive play and dramatic play and begins around age 2. In symbolic play, children use an object or toy to stand for or represent something else, such as gathering twigs and pinecones to make pretend food.

Constructive Play. This type of play is more intentional than practice play as children plan and construct, using a variety of materials. A long, rolled-out piece of clay becomes a snake or an arrangement of blocks becomes a skyscraper. Concrete materials are used to make a representation of objects and experiences in children's lives.

Dramatic Play. Dramatic play is a highly developed form of symbolic play and is based more on reality. Children imitate real-life people and situations and incorporate make-believe elements as needed. In the dress-up area of the classroom, Cora, pretending to be the doctor, tells Bahraim, "You need a shot. Don't cry, it won't hurt." She reaches for a crayon, saying, "This is the needle." Bahraim pretends to cry. Cora reaches for a pretend tissue and hands it to him. "Here. Wipe your nose and I'll give you a balloon." Dramatic play allows children to "think" out loud as their learning comes together, strengthening their knowledge and understanding of the world.

Games with Rules

Games with rules increase around age 6 or 7 when children are mature enough to accept and adjust to preset rules. Children acquire the ability to play games with rules gradually as they grow in cooperative social behavior and cognitive abilities.

In planning for play, teachers must consider how each of these three forms of play relates to the child's maturity and level of social development.

Kinds of Play

Children need opportunities for all levels of play and to incorporate materials and activities that allow for a variety of social interactions. Two chairs at a table of Legos will encourage social interactions with one another; an isolated area with soft pillows will give a child the chance to be alone for quiet time, and a stack of firefighter hats and hoses will encourage group and cooperative play. Parten (1932), in her now-classic study, defined six kinds of play and types of social interactions that occurred (see Figure 6.1).

The value of play as a means of social growth and development is one important aspect of play in early childhood environments.

The Value of Play

Play is often referred to as the child's "work," or as a window into the child's world. Play is all of that and more. Through play, children learn to:

- Use their imagination and be spontaneous
- Invent new uses for materials and equipment

Unoccupied Behavior: Stuart stands by the cubbies watching the general activity in the room. A few minutes later he sits down and spends the next 5 minutes glancing around the room, getting on and off the chair, and standing again.

Onlooker Behavior: Seth sits near the easels watching children paint. He continues to watch the children, speaking infrequently to them as they work. He makes no effort to join in painting.

Solitary Play: Lois is sitting alone at the puzzle table, working and re-working the same two puzzles, oblivious to what is going on elsewhere. She interacts with no one.

Parallel Play: Francesca and Mary Jane sit near each other at the clay table. Mary Jane is molding the clay into various shapes while Francesca is slapping and rolling the clay around the table. The girls play independently, in close proximity of one another, but with no interaction.

Associative Play: Corita, Terry, and Danna are playing in the block area. Corita has placed a series of cars along a strip of building blocks. Terry is building a tower and Danna is making an enclosure for farm animals. They pass blocks to one another, but do not play together. The three children are aware of and associate with one another at this beginning stage of group play.

Cooperative Play: Joel and Sammy are digging in the sand pit and are joined by Kurt, Kerry, and Liza. Joel and Sammy tell the other children where to dig and how to enlarge the hole they are making. All five children work toward the common goal. The digging effort becomes more complex as bridges are added and a water hose fills the "river." Each child takes on a specific role as the play continues. Kerry is in charge of the hose, Liza is finding wood for boats, Kurt and Sammy are building the bridges, and Joel continues digging. Creating a goal, negotiating roles, and building activity around cooperative interactions are all components of this stage of group play.

Figure 6.1
Kinds of Play
Take a look in any early childhood classroom and you are likely to see these play behaviors.

Source: Adapted from "Social Participation Among Preschool Children," by M. Parten, 1932, *Journal of Abnormal and Social Psychology*, 27, pp. 243–369.

- Be adventurous
- Practice their physical skills and learn new ones
- Negotiate and cooperate with others
- Use an important avenue for self-expression and express their emotions
- Make choices for themselves
- Problem solve with words, ideas, people, and materials
- Develop greater social and cultural understanding of others
- Have fun

Some parents and teachers do not easily recognize the value of play. It is the job of the childhood professional to help families understand what is happening when children engage in play. Look around the classroom where you teach and notice where children are playing, how they are playing, and what they are saying as they play. Learning is taking place in every interaction. Share these examples with families as illustrations of their child's imagination, abilities, competence, and creativity.

Play is an important way for children to learn.

Developmentally Appropriate Play

When planning for developmentally appropriate play, early childhood teachers bring to bear all of their knowledge about how children grow and learn, as well as an understanding of the cultural context in which the children live. From that base, play experiences are woven into the curriculum to meet the developmental needs of the children in the class. Two key concepts in developmentally appropriate planning are to set reasonable but challenging goals for each child and to meet children where they are (Copple & Bredekamp, 2006).

Joyce, a 3 1/2-year-old, lives on a hilly street and has never ridden a tricycle. Her teachers plan the curriculum with Joyce in mind. Indoors, music activities call for children to create bicycle motions with their legs. Outdoors, pumping on swings and running games help Joyce develop some of the large motor skills she needs as she learns to ride a trike. Although this activity is focused on Joyce, the teachers are also aware of how this part of the curriculum will help Richie find ways to handle his excessive energy and Gina participate in more group activities. The teachers intentionally build on the children's known abilities but at the same time provide challenges for them to meet.

The significance of play in the development process cannot be underestimated. All the developmental domains are enhanced through play. The children in the mapping activity, described at the beginning of the chapter, for instance, are building social (cooperation, sharing), cognitive (problem solving), emotional

An effective teacher:

- Guides the play, but does not direct or dominate.
- May participate in the play, but does not overwhelm the children.
- Starts with the children's thoughts and ideas and does not enforce a point of view on them.
- Models play when necessary. Shows children how a specific character might act, or how to ask for a turn, or how to hold a hammer.
- Asks questions and clarifies for the children what is happening.
- Helps children start, end, and begin again.
- Gives them verbal clues to enable the children to follow through on an idea.
- Focuses the children's attention on one another and encourages them to interact with one another.
- Interprets children's behavior aloud, when necessary, to help children learn to verbalize their thoughts and ideas.
- Assists in verbalizing feelings as children work through conflict.
- Expands the play potential by making statements and asking questions that lead to discovery and exploration.

Figure 6.2
Teacher's Role in Facilitating Play
The teacher is to be a facilitator and uses teachable moments in which further learning is enhanced.

Source: From Gardon/Browne. *Beginnings and Beyond*, 7e. © 2008 Wadsworth, a part of Cengage Learning, Inc. Reproduced by permission. www.cengage.com/permissions.

(self-identity, competency), physical (gross and fine motor), intellectual (measuring distance), and creative (drawing) skills as they play. Play challenges children to use all of their abilities and in doing so, the *whole* child is affected when play is developmentally appropriate.

Through unstructured play, children take a part of their world and rehearse, restructure, and refine it in order to understand how it works. Practicing for life is an important job for young children and they need teachers who appreciate and value the role of play in the early childhood setting. Figure 6.2 highlights the teacher's role in facilitating play.

Curriculum in the Early Years

Curriculum does not just happen. A great deal of planning is needed to create a high-quality early childhood setting with an appropriate curriculum. Long before children enter the classroom, teachers make decisions on what is developmentally appropriate for the age group, the strengths and interests of each child, and the cultural context of the children in the classroom. The goals of the program, the school's underlying philosophy, and needs of the families are also woven into the planning.

Setting the Stage

To set the stage for learning, the environment, schedule, and curriculum merge to create a program that children will enter into with enthusiasm and interest. Teachers use the space, room arrangement, outdoor play area, materials, and daily schedule as a scaffold on which to build learning experiences to meet the varied interests, abilities, and needs of each child. How well the curriculum and environment are blended is reflected in the children's independent use of materials, how free they are to explore and satisfy their curiosity, and how they practice and master skills as they develop competencies. The role of the environment and schedule were previously explored in Chapter 5.

Teachers also set the tone, the emotional framework in which children work and play. The classroom atmosphere is influenced by a teacher's body language, facial expressions, tone of voice, as well as nonverbal and verbal gestures (Gordon & Browne, 2007, 2008). The interpersonal climate within the classroom is as important as the arrangement of furniture and the quality of the curriculum. Young children are very sensitive to an adult's manner and attitude, as well as how children treat each other. A positive atmosphere supports a child's need for a safe and nurturing place to learn. (Chapter 3 discussed strategies for guiding children's behavior.)

What Exactly Is Curriculum?

Curriculum for young children addresses all aspects of a child's growth, including social, emotional, physical, cognitive, and language development. The whole child is challenged when planning includes each of the developmental areas.

Curriculum is not just a lesson plan, a fieldtrip, or a project. Curriculum is fluid: It moves with the children's interests and needs. Flexibility can be challenging for teachers, yet provides them with the raw materials for a fascinating conversation about worms, or a detour from a planned activity to a surprise earthquake drill response. Figure 6.3 illustrates the broad scope of curriculum.

Bredekamp and Rosegrant (1995) define curriculum as an "organized framework" with four areas of focus:

- The *content* consists of *what* children should learn and how it reflects their interests, needs, and experiences.

Figure 6.3
Scope of Curriculum

Curriculum is fluid and flexible and happens throughout the day.

Curriculum happens everywhere and includes:
- What needs to be taught and how to teach it.
- Everything that happens in a school day, planned and unplanned.
- Formal, written lesson plans and spontaneous on-the-spot change of plans.
- Small- and large-group-time experience, story times, transitions, free play.
- Interactions children have with others: what they say, how they reflect their understanding of the world, what questions they ask.
- Exploration and creativity that happens when children manipulate materials and equipment.
- Learning through play to make friends, be creative, follow rules, make mistakes, solve problems, make choices.
- Challenging children to master appropriate developmental tasks by building on their current strengths and knowledge.

- The *process* includes *how* and *when* learning takes place, the choice of activities, how they are integrated with one another, and the time frame within the daily schedule.

- The *teachers* are the people who *use* their knowledge of child development theory to individualize the activities to meet the needs of all the children in the class.

- The *context* is *why* certain projects and activities are chosen and is based on the program's philosophy and goals in conjunction with families and the community

These factors work together during the planning process to help teachers develop curriculum. The goal of the process is to translate theories of education and development into practice, based on the children's interests and the adult's awareness of children's needs.

There are curriculum models that promote good practices in developmentally appropriate learning for young children and that have their own philosophical thrust. These include High/Scope, Bank Street, the schools of Reggio Emilia, Montessori, and the Creative Curriculum, among others. Many schools adopt one particular model or integrate elements from several into their planning. By now you may have taken a course in curriculum that describes these approaches in greater depth. During your student teaching experience you may be placed in schools that partially or fully implement these philosophies.

Developing curriculum is a decision-making process. You make decisions about what materials children will use; what activities will bring balance to the day; what small group a child may be assigned to; what teacher will be responsible for science this week; and how the room arrangement is set up for learning. These decisions are based on your knowledge and insight about young children.

Essentials for Creating Curriculum

The most effective curriculum happens when teachers consider the essential elements, as noted in Figure 6.4, when creating meaningful and appropriate curriculum.

Essential Elements for Planning Curriculum

The Curriculum Is Age Appropriate. What do you know about how 2-year-olds learn? Five-year-olds? Seven-year-olds? What do you know about their social skills, physical dexterity, language capacity, and intellectual abilities? You need an understanding of each age group in order to plan for children's growth and development. Teacher Maya is aware that 2-year-olds are beginning to share, like to watch each

Figure 6.4
Top 10 Questions When Creating Curriculum

Ask yourself these 10 essential questions whenever you plan a lesson or activity.

Is the curriculum

1. age appropriate?
2. individualized?
3. culturally responsive?
4. inclusive?
5. integrated?
6. emergent?
7. balanced?
8. related to learning standards?
9. written?
10. evaluated?

other, and often play parallel to one another. With this knowledge, Maya can plan appropriate activities that encourage more social interaction throughout the day. She also knows that as they turn 3, the children will enjoy simple poems and humor. Maya includes this information in her planning. Knowing the characteristics of the age levels above and below the ages she teaches, Maya will make sure that the curriculum for her class of 2-year-olds will include appropriate challenges for developing new skills.

The Curriculum Is Individualized. Children have different learning styles and intellectual strengths that help them process information. Both are important considerations when planning and implementing curriculum.

There are three basic sensory styles young children use to learn: visual, auditory, and tactile-kinesthetic. Each child has a preferred mode, although it is not the only way a child integrates knowledge.

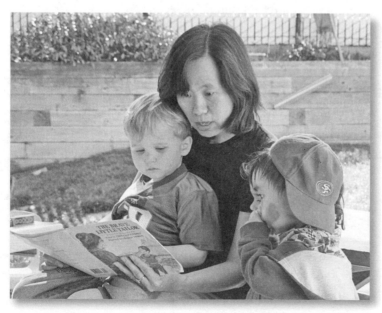

Knowing the age level and interests of the children in the class helps the student teacher plan appropriate and appealing curriculum.

- The *visual* learner likes to represent learning by reading, writing, and drawing. After a fieldtrip to the aquarium, Inez writes and illustrates a story about sharks.

- The *auditory* learner listens to others to learn and talks to others about what they learn. On the way home from the fieldtrip, Darius makes up a song about a starfish. The teacher asks him to teach it to the rest of the group.

- The *tactile-kinesthetic* learner is a physically active learner who learns by doing rather than by listening. Back in the classroom, Miranda and Noemi head straight to the water table filled with plastic fish and begin to sort them into the groups they saw at the aquarium.

The teaching staff assesses children's skills, behavior, play patterns, and the effectiveness of the curriculum by observing and documenting what each child does during the school day. A teacher's notation may look like this:

Luz and Dario spent over 30 minutes going through the rocks and minerals display, sorting by color, size, and texture. We could expand their interest by taking a "rock walk" around the schoolyard later today. Let's ask them for suggestions about what else they might like to do with the rocks and minerals. This might become a project.

To individualize the curriculum further, the teachers must also know how each child is "intelligent." Gardner holds that children have multiple intelligences, which give them eight "different ways of knowing" (Gardner, 1983). Gardner's eight intelligences are listed in Figure 6.5.

We all have these eight intelligences to some extent but we differ in the degree and combinations. Each person, including you, has sets of abilities and talents that reflect your experience, culture, and motivation. What do you think is your primary way of being smart?

The Curriculum Is Culturally Responsive. Teachers are challenged to present a curriculum that reflects contemporary American society and adapt the curriculum to the diversity represented in each class (Gordon & Browne, 2008). All children learn best when the school environment is welcoming and says we care about and support you and your family. This is especially true for children and families whose culture and background differ from that of the teaching staff. Families need to see that their culture is woven into the curriculum in the books and literature, songs and dances, activities and fieldtrips. Positive relationships with children's home and community begin with honoring the family's cultural values and creating avenues for working together in the child's best interests.

---

1. *Body-kinesthetic:* Uses one's body to solve problems and communicate; wants to be a participant, not a spectator.
2. *Intrapersonal:* Is sensitive to one's inner feelings and knows one's strength and weaknesses.
3. *Interpersonal:* Is sensitive to and understanding of others; is often a leader.
4. *Linguistic:* Uses words and language in many forms; reading and writing come easily.
5. *Logical-mathematical:* Can discern patterns, and is precise and methodical.
6. *Musical:* Is sensitive to nonverbal sounds and connects with rhythms and melodies.
7. *Spatial:* Can visualize and think in images and pictures; excels at representational drawing.
8. *Naturalist:* Can discriminate among living things (plants, animals); is sensitive to features of the natural world.

Figure 6.5
Gardner's Multiple Intelligences
Planning curriculum with Gardner's eight intelligences in mind is one way to plan children's experiences.

Source: Compiled from *Multiple Intelligences,* by H. Gardner, 1993, New York: Basic Books.

The Curriculum Is Inclusive. An inclusive curriculum is a step beyond creating curriculum that meets the needs of the individual child. An inclusive curriculum is broader in scope and challenges the teacher to provide opportunities for *all* children, regardless of gender, abilities or disabilities, language, culture, ethnicity, and religion. The activities and materials in an inclusive classroom are chosen to enhance the growth potential of each child and are sensitive to the diversity of abilities within the classroom.

All children need the same things from their learning environment. The question becomes how you accommodate this wide range of differences in children while planning curriculum. The true test of an appropriate activity is whether or not it will adjust to children with a wide range of skills and abilities. Quality curriculum is flexible enough to accommodate the needs of each child, where children can participate at their developmental and ability level, yet be challenged in their learning. Figure 6.6 shows how an art activity can be changed to support children who have disabilities.

The Curriculum Is Integrated. In a child development class you learned about the concept of "the whole child," and how it affects planning for their growth and

Figure 6.6
Adapting Art for Children with Special Needs

Many activities can be adapted for children with special needs.

Visual:
Verbally describe materials and how they might be used.
Provide a tray that outlines the visual boundaries.
Offer bright paint to contrast with paper.
Go slowly and encourage child to manipulate the items as you talk.

Auditory:
Model the process, facing the child and using gestures for emphasis.
Use sign language as needed.

Physical:
Make sure there is a clear path to the art table.
Provide adaptive art tools such as chunky crayons and large markers.
Provide double ambidextrous scissors so you can help, or a cutting wheel.
Attach Velcro to marking instruments or paintbrushes.
Use contact paper for collage, or glue sticks instead of bottles.

Attention-deficit and/or hyperactive behavior:
Provide children with their own materials and workspace, minimizing waiting and crowding.
Offer materials like clay or play dough to express feelings.
Limit children to a few choices rather than overwhelming them with everything in the art center.

Source: From Gorden/Browne. *Beginning and Beyond,* 7e. © 2008 Wadsworth, a part of Cengage Learning Inc. Reproduced by permission. www.cengage.com/permissions.

development. The whole-child approach stresses the interaction and relationship among the physical, social, intellectual, language, and cognitive areas of the developing child. So it is with integrated curriculum. Rather than teach subject matter (such as science, math, geography, or art) as separate topics, early childhood teachers teach them "across the curriculum." The subject matter becomes planned components of the total curriculum. To some, cooking in the preschool may simply be a fun activity. To the teacher, it is a coordinated learning experience in science, reading, math, social skill, small motor development, and multiculturalism. Any number of developmental areas can be woven into any aspect of the curriculum to reinforce concepts in the broadest possible way. This approach reflects Dewey's philosophy of education as meaningful, active learning, and is used extensively in the schools of Reggio Emilia. Integrated curriculum is often used with a theme or project approach to developing curriculum. Figure 6.7 shows how sensory skills are enhanced through an integrated curriculum.

Week Of: _April 10_   **Teacher:** _Mariko_   **Group:** _3-Year-Olds_

Focus: _Sensory stimulation_

Objective: _To explore the world through the five senses_

Day of Week	Activity and Learning Focus	Small-Group Activity and Learning Focus
Monday	_Soap painting: Encourages use of fine and gross motor skills; and creativity_	_Guessing game of textures: Cognitive exercise to identify soft and hard_
Tuesday	_Water table: Promotes social interaction, motor skills, and cognitive learning_	_Guessing game of smells: Memory exercise (cognitive) to identify familiar scents_
Wednesday	_Fingerpainting: Encourages use of fine motor skills and creativity_	_Guessing game of weights: Cognitive exercise to distinguish heavy and light_
Thursday	_Make a collage of materials collected on walk: Enhances social and physical skills_	_Identify and sort familiar objects: Exercise to develop memory and cognitive skills_
Friday	_Play dough: Promotes social and physical motor skills_	_Sample finger foods: Exercise to identify size, shape, texture, and taste; extends language and cognitive development_

Figure 6.7
Exploring Sensory Skills: An Integrated Approach
Integrating the curriculum enhances the ability to learn on many levels.

The Curriculum Is Emergent. Emergent curriculum begins with assessing children's needs and interests. Through observations and awareness of children's play, teachers find out what children are attracted to and what captures their attention and their eagerness to learn. This information is blended with the teacher's knowledge of what the group and the individual children need to learn and what activities, materials, and equipment will enhance those specific skills. Together, teachers and children will cocreate the curriculum.

Each class or group of children is unique, so through continuous examination and dialogue, topics of interest emerge. The teacher who took notice of Luz and Dario's avid interest in the rocks and minerals display also noted that this activity might become a project. Mrs. Garcia helped the children extend their learning about maps for an activity that could emerge into a longer-term project. Emergent curriculum begins with an idea or activity that can be expanded for greater learning potential and that will reinforce children's interest and excitement about learning. Often, a project continues for days or even weeks. The project approach is an in-depth study of a theme, and is especially appropriate in the older end of the early childhood years. Through projects, children learn to work cooperatively, do research, collaborate with adults, and evaluate their work (Chard, 1998). Emergent curriculum embodies the characteristics of integrated and inclusive curriculum as well.

Topics are chosen in many ways for different reasons: children's interests, teacher's interests, developmental tasks, resources available, the value of the topic, and curriculum requirements or standards. Emergent curriculum is a planning process where teachers question children about what they know, what they might like to know, and how they might find out what they need to know. Emergent curriculum is an interactive and collaborative experience where "children are our models and coplayers" (Jones & Nimmo, 1994).

Figure 6.8 is an example of a project created and conducted by a student teacher. Called "Project Blueprint," it emerged from the children's interest in seeing a construction site near their school.

The Curriculum Is Balanced. Balance is key to an effective curriculum. Quiet times alternate with more active play. A story time follows outdoor play periods. Active play is scheduled after naptime or rest time. Look again at the scheduling section of Chapter 5 to see how this balance is achieved throughout the day.

Balance, too, is needed in the type or themes of activities. Those that focus on only one aspect of development, such as intellectual growth, ignore the social-emotional and physical growth aspects so necessary to learning. Some activities may stress social-emotional concerns, creativity, or literacy. The focus of themes should be diverse and balanced as you plan throughout the year.

A third way to provide good balance in the curriculum is to allow children the experience of playing alone, with one or two other children, or in a larger group. A balance of child-directed activities and teacher-guided activities provides opportunities for children to be self-directed at times and learn to make choices

Figure 6.8
Project Blueprint

The months-long curriculum that emerged from interest in a nearby construction project demonstrates how children's interests can be used to build skills.

Source: From Margaret Lam and Kären Wiggins-Dowler, "Project Blueprint: A construction project." College of San Mateo Child Development Center, 2005.

and decisions for themselves. Take a look at the classroom in which you teach and assess how balanced its curriculum might be in terms of small and large groupings.

The Curriculum Meets Learning Standards. Across the country early learning standards are being developed to create a set of expectations for preschool children. The terms *child outcomes*, *benchmarks*, and *performance standards* are used to measure the kinds of development and learning that is taking place.

Most of the individual states have adopted some form of standards or expectations of children aged 3 to 5 years and in school-age settings. You are more than likely teaching in a state that requires you to meet its standards (see Chapter 4). As an early childhood educator you will want to know whether your state has mandated early learning standards and, if so, what they encompass.

Early childhood standards can benefit children, in numerous ways: by being linked to primary-grade standards they ensure school readiness; they can define the foundational skills for learning; they help teachers identify the next steps and have appropriately higher expectations for children; and they professionalize the field of early childhood (Gronlund, 2006).

Early learning standards pose potential risks as well as benefits. Too often, the standards do not address all the developmental domains necessary, and are not adaptable for children with disabilities or those who are culturally and linguistically diverse. Many early childhood professionals are concerned that the current standards push direct instruction, inappropriate expectations and assessment of preschoolers, and lead to "teaching to the test" mentality. (see Chapter 4, which dealt with the

Table 6.1 Linking Standards to Curriculum

By developing appropriate curriculum to meet learning standards, teachers ensure that children are engaged in meaningful activities while also progressing in their skill development.

Standard	Activity	Demonstrates Mastery
Personal and social competence: Identifies self by categories of gender, age, or social group.	1. Graph children's ages. 2. Make an "All About Me" book. 3. Create self-portraits with dictation.	1. Says correct age and shows correct number of fingers. 2–3. Says "I'm a girl," "I'm 4 years old," or "I'm Vietnamese."
Effective learner: Completes increasingly complex puzzles.	Play with knob-puzzles, puzzles with and without frames, and floor puzzles.	Uses puzzles with interlocking pieces without the help of frames.
Physical and motor competence: Manipulates two or more objects at the same time.	String beads; play with Legos or Duplos; practice buttoning, zipping, lacing cards, and cutting paper.	Two hands manipulate object at the same time to complete task successfully.

Source: Adapted from Kim Yuen, San Mateo Country Office of Education, San Mateo, CA. Used with permission.

topic of standards.) Table 6.1 shows an example of how one state's preschool learning standards are linked to developmentally appropriate curriculum.

Written Lesson Plans Are Created. A *lesson plan* is a written outline that helps teachers articulate and implement the goals they have set, yet are flexible enough to adapt to changes. Goals may be short or long range and may focus on skill development, themes, or projects. Written lesson plans stimulate teamwork and in-depth planning, and also provide a concrete format from which evaluation and assessment can be made (Gordon & Browne, 2008).

Student teachers often struggle with making lesson plans. With practice and a few simple guidelines, your planning skills will improve.

- Observe children in your program to find out what they are interested in. In Sam's class the children were interested in bugs.

- Decide on a topic and check it out with your supervising teacher. Sam asked his lead teacher if bugs were an appropriate topic for 3–1/2-year-olds.

- Look at children's assessments to see where they are developmentally and what skills you wish to enhance. Looking at the children's portfolios, Sam found that most had unrefined fine motor skills, so he chose that as the focus.

- Plan the activity to promote the development of those skills. "The collection and investigation of bugs" became Sam's activity.

- Create a list of materials needed. Sam's list included small bags for collection. Then at the table he had small trays, flashlights, magnifying glasses, and plastic tweezers, and a clipboard for himself.

- Outline the steps children will take and what they will do in the activity, including cleanup. Sam took his small group outdoors to collect bugs, then came back to the classroom and investigated them by putting them on a tray, looking at them with the tools provided, and making a list together of what they discovered.

- Write a list of open-ended questions you will ask while they play: "What do you see? What does your bug look like? What are the differences between yours and someone else's? What will happen if you turn the bug over?"

A written lesson plan provides a map that may outline a single activity, an entire daily plan, or the focus for a longer period of time or project. A good lesson plan will also have a space for review and/or evaluation. Figure 6.9 is a sample of an individual activity lesson plan.

Activity name: _____
Purpose/goal: _____
Context:
    Location (indoor/outdoor, in what section of yard or room): _____
    Time of day: _____
    Type of and size of group: _____

Materials needed and how you will have children use them:
_____
_____

How you will introduce it and what antecedents are necessary for this group:
_____
_____

Cleanup provisions (will children be involved? How?):
_____
_____

Results:
    What were the children's responses? _____
    Did you achieve what you wanted? _____
    Problems? _____
    Solutions for next time? _____
    Implications for other activities _____
Next steps/other activities: _____

Figure 6.9
Planning an Activity
Good planning takes time and thought, and these questions can help a teacher focus on the important aspects of curriculum planning.

Another way that teachers create written plans is the process known as *webbing*. Webbing is done in a variety of ways: alone, with other teachers, and often with children. Webbing involves identifying a key theme or topic that becomes the center of the web. Radiating from the center are other aspects of the theme, such as concepts and activities. This type of planning is fluid and continues to change with the participants' ideas. Figure 6.10 illustrates a curriculum web on the topic "Summertime." Starting with what children already know about the theme, or with what the teachers want the children to learn, the web grows with new ideas. Often, the activities, experiences, and materials that may be needed are included in the web.

Curriculum Is Evaluated. Developmentally appropriate curriculum doesn't just happen. To keep meeting the needs, interests, experiences, and abilities, of each child, curriculum needs to be evaluated and refined frequently. Each day informal evaluations occur among the teachers.

- "No one spent much time at the woodworking table today. Should we put it away for a while?"
- "I noticed that three or four of the children are having difficulty cutting with the scissors. We'd better plan some activities that will help them learn that skill."

Evaluating the curriculum is an ongoing process as children change, grow, and develop new interests and abilities, and their teachers implement appropriate changes.

In more formal evaluations, children's responses to the curriculum are documented through a variety of assessment and observation methods, such as those discussed in Chapter 4. Evaluation points out the relevancy the curriculum has in the children's lives. A theme unit on subways was not particularly popular with a group of 4-year-olds in rural Indiana, but it may have great appeal for children living in the Bronx. Because both programs require that the children learn about principles of motion in their science curriculum, the midwestern teachers focus instead on the trailer trucks that ply their highways. Taking their cues from the children, early childhood professionals adapt the curriculum to activities that are more culturally meaningful to the class.

An effective curriculum is based on the goals and objectives of the program's philosophy, indicating what children are to learn and experience at each age level. The goals are intentionally broad because the developmental levels of the children in a classroom are so diverse. Ongoing evaluations inform the staff as to how well the goals are being met.

Mastering the art of curriculum planning is a challenge for teachers, yet one of the most satisfying aspects of working with young children. The plans come

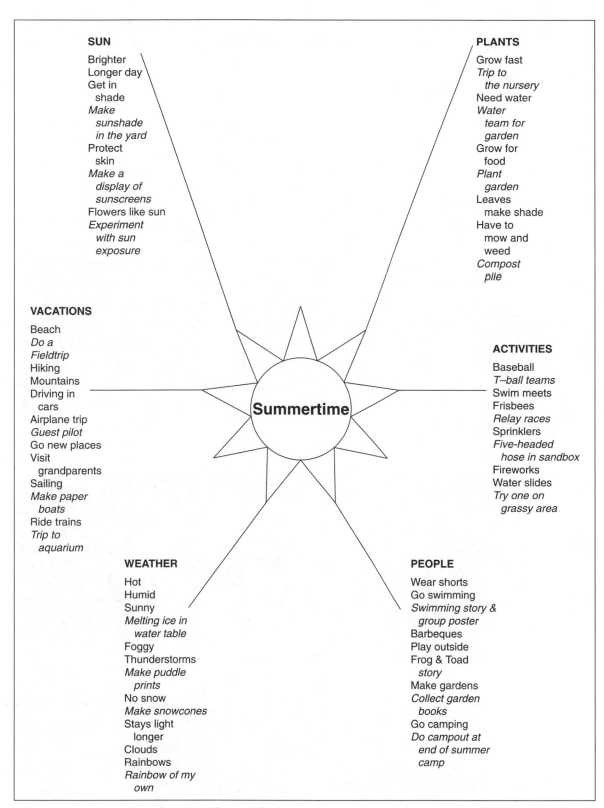

SUN
Brighter
Longer day
Get in
    shade
*Make
    sunshade
    in the yard*
Protect
    skin
*Make a
    display of
    sunscreens*
Flowers like sun
*Experiment
    with sun
    exposure*

PLANTS
Grow fast
*Trip to
    the nursery*
Need water
*Water
    team for
    garden*
Grow for
    food
*Plant
    garden*
Leaves
    make shade
Have to
    mow and
    weed
*Compost
    pile*

VACATIONS
Beach
*Do a
Fieldtrip*
Hiking
Mountains
Driving in
    cars
Airplane trip
Guest pilot
Go new places
Visit
    grandparents
Sailing
*Make paper
    boats*
Ride trains
*Trip to
    aquarium*

Summertime

ACTIVITIES
Baseball
T–ball teams
Swim meets
Frisbees
Relay races
Sprinklers
*Five-headed
    hose in sandbox*
Fireworks
Water slides
*Try one on
    grassy area*

WEATHER
Hot
Humid
Sunny
*Melting ice in
    water table*
Foggy
Thunderstorms
*Make puddle
    prints*
No snow
Make snowcones
Stays light
    longer
Clouds
Rainbows
*Rainbow of my
    own*

PEOPLE
Wear shorts
Go swimming
*Swimming story &
    group poster*
Barbeques
Play outside
*Frog & Toad
    story*
Make gardens
*Collect garden
    books*
Go camping
*Do campout at
    end of summer
    camp*

F i g u r e 6 . 1 0 Sample Curriculum Web
When the kinder-camp staff members planned their curriculum, they began with a webbing activity for the children.

Note: The children's ideas are shown in regular type, with the staff members' planned activities in italics.

alive as you observe how children respond to learning and give you clues to the next challenges they need as noted in "Lessons from the field" at Chapter's end.

Planning for Groups

At various times of the day, teachers often gather children together in small and large groups. The purpose of each group differs according to the needs of the children, the program, and the number of staff members.

Large Groups. A gathering of the whole class for group time (or circle time or class meeting time) creates a sense of community and belonging, and gives children experience in listening and participating in a large group. Whereas the teacher has an agenda, children often want to share something important with everyone. Early morning group times include a discussion about the day's activities and plans. Group times at the end of the day help bring about closure as the children reflect on the day's activities and plan for tomorrow. Depending on the age of the children, group times may last as little as 5 to 10 minutes with a class of 3-year-olds to 30 minutes in a primary classroom. Group times usually include a combination of songs, fingerplays, stories, and movement activities. Reading one of the children's (or teacher's) favorite books is also a popular group-time activity.

Planning and leading group times is an important learning experience for the student teacher.

When you lead a large-group-time activity, keep in mind the following guidelines:

- Position yourself in a chair in front of the group and make sure there is an appropriate space for the children so that they can see you and be free of other distractions: "I'm going to sit right here so I can see everybody and you can see me."

- Open with the familiar: a song, chant, or fingerplay that captures their attention and invites their participation: "You will know the words to this song, so sing them with me—'If You're Happy and You Know It, Clap Your Hands.'"

- Be prepared with several songs or fingerplays until the whole group gathers: "Let's sing about the Eeensy Weensy Spider, and then we'll sing it in Spanish."

- Maintain eye contact with all the children in the group to ensure their continued interest: "I see Juanita's eyes, and Damion's eyes. Where are yours, Carla?"

- Be enthusiastic and keep the pace moving because children are influenced by your tone and actions: "This was one of my favorite books when I was little!"

- If you have a story or activity planned, move into it as soon as all the children are settled: "Good, you are all here. Look at the person next to you, and sit facing them for 'Row, Row, Row Your Boat.'"

- While reading a story or explaining the activity, ask the children questions, but don't get lost in them, as this helps maintain their involvement: "What do you think happens next to Curious George? I want three ideas. If you have one, put your hand in the air."

- Keep your focus and stay in charge, so that one or two children do not dominate the interactions or the group falls apart from lack of leadership: "I can hear two more ideas and then we will finish the story and find out what really happens."

- Use phrases that demonstrate what is to occur and how to proceed to maintain control and give directions: "I am walking around with a box of scarves; please take one when I get to you."

- Conclude group time with a clear message of what children are to do next: "Will all the children with blue socks get their jackets on to go outside?"

A minimum of two teachers is needed for a large-group gathering. One teacher usually takes the responsibility for planning and conducting group time and a second teacher acts as support, helps keep the children focused, and deals with any disruptions. With some groups, more adults may be needed to keep children's attention on the group leader, or to help individual children find a

At circle time, I led the activity. I was really nervous. I pulled out the surprise bag filled with five frogs, one blue sheet, and one log. I introduced the song "Five Little Speckled Frogs," which we all sang together. I asked three children to come and stand next to me. Teacher Jeannie was in tunc with my apprehensiveness and assisted when needed. We all sang the song again and the three children jumped and "swam" back to their seats (well, sometimes they did this). In all honesty, it went OK, but I wasn't happy with it and I'm not sure the kids really enjoyed it that much.—Isabella

Your Thoughts

1. How would I feel?

2. What would I do?

3. What might the result be?

seat, learn to take turns, or raise their hand to speak, along with other large-group skills. As you can see in the Reflective Incident, things do not always go well.

Small Groups. Many learning experiences are more successful with a small group of children. A smaller group encourages greater interaction between the teacher and each child, offers time for individual contributions, and allows teachers to observe more closely each child's growth and development.

There are many reasons why small groups are an important part of the daily schedule. Teachers can focus on certain skills, such as listening and taking turns; encourage children in their social interactions; explore a topic in greater depth; or introduce a new concept, game, or activity.

One teacher can manage a small number of children for this type of group. The groups can be created informally ("All children with red shirts can go with Mr. Chang") or the teachers may preselect the group in order to promote certain interactions, or to work on a specific task with children who need more assistance. In multiage settings, small-group times are scheduled for the individual age groups to offer appropriate-level activities.

The Teacher's Role. Successful group times come about through careful planning. One important rule to remember is that group times are for and about children. Sometimes inexperienced teachers have the impression that they have to carry all of

"The Value of Less"

by Stacey James

Mentor Teacher, Geo-Kids Menlo Park, CA

The curriculum that excites me the most is when I provide interesting, new, open-ended material and then stand back and watch. When working with open-ended materials, children are able to formulate for themselves the problems that most challenge them, and then they set about solving those problems. I have seen this occur with every age group with which I have worked, from infants to 4-year-olds. The idea that children create appropriate challenges for themselves and construct their own knowledge is basic to constructivist philosophy in early childhood education, but it is always astonishing to me when I see it happen. The diversity of problems and solutions within a group of children, the absorption with which they pursue them, and the intriguing tangents that they explore are always surprising, sometimes dazzling.

This probably happens much more often than I realize. But the challenge is to see it, to capture and understand and make visible the learning that occurs in these situations. It requires very close attention on my part, undistracted by other things in the classroom. This is what happens less frequently—not the learning but the witnessing of the learning. And, trickiest of all, it requires the least possible amount of interference from me: too much and the magic is lost.

the discussion and conversation. All group times, regardless of size, provide the occasion for teachers to encourage children's listening and speaking skills and help them gain the ability to share their thoughts and ideas. Younger children will interrupt the teacher and other children in their excitement or desire to talk. A part of working with a group is helping those children learn to take turns and listen when others are talking. As you observe other teachers conducting group times, you will see that it takes very little to get children involved and ready to talk. Look at how other teachers handle children who have difficulty waiting for their turn.

At some point in your student teaching you will be required to plan and conduct a group time. Start with the developmental level, interests, and skills of the group. When you begin planning, revisit the planning approach outlined in Figure 6.10. Group times can be one of the most enjoyable activities you have as a teacher once you get past your first few attempts. It is one of the areas of teaching that gives you an opportunity to put your personal stamp on an activity and demonstrate your abilities to be creative, think on your feet, and be in charge.

Practicum Activity

Design a lesson plan for the age level you teach. Indicate how each developmental area (physical/motor, cognitive/language, social-emotional and creative) is being addressed by this activity. Show how the lesson plan could be adapted for the age just above and just below. Bring the lesson plan to class and share with the group.

Journaling Assignment

What is developmentally appropriate curriculum to you and how does your teaching site measure up to DAP? What trouble spots do you see and what changes would you make in the curriculum to remedy these?

Resources

Bredekamp, S., & Rosegrant, T. (Eds.). (1995). *Reaching potentials: Transforming early childhood curriculum and assessment* (Vol. 2). Washington, DC: National Association for the Education of Young Children.

Chard, S. (1998). *The project approach.* New York: Scholastic.

Copple, C., & Bredekamp, S. (Eds.). (2006). *Basics of developmentally appropriate practice.* Washington, DC: National Association for the Education of Young Children.

Gardner, H. (1993). *Multiple intelligences.* New York: Basic Books.

Gronlund, G. (2006). *Make early learning standards come alive: Connecting your practice and curriculum to state guidelines.* St. Paul, MN: Redleaf Press.

Gordon, A. M., & Browne, K. W. (2007). *Beginning essentials in early childhood education.* Clifton Park, NY: Thomson Delmar Learning.

Gordon, A. M., & Browne, K. W. (2008). *Beginnings and beyond: Foundations in early childhood education* (7th ed.). Clifton Park, NY: Thomson Delmar Learning.

Jones, E., & Nimmo, J. (1994). *Emergent curriculum.* Washington, DC: National Association for the Education of Young Children.

Lam, M., & Wiggins-Dowler, K. (2005). "Project Blueprint: A construction project." Unpublished documentation board, College of San Mateo Child Development Center.

National Association for the Education of Young Children and National Association of Early Childhood Specialists in State Departments of Education. (2002). *Early learning standards: Creating the conditions for success.* Retrieved from http://www.naeyc.org/about/positions/pdf/position-statement.pdf

National Association for the Education of Young Children and National Association for Early Childhood Specialists in State Departments of Education. (2003). *Early childhood curriculum, assessment, and program evaluation—building an effective, accountable system in programs for children birth through age 8.* Retrieved from http://www.naeyc.org/resources/position-statements/pscape.pdf

Parten, M. (1932). Social participation among preschool children. *Journal of Abnormal and Social Psychology, 27,* 243–369.

Piaget, J. (1962). *Play, dreams, & imitation in childhood.* New York: Norton.

Web Sites

Association Montessori Internationale
www.montessori-ami.org

Bank Street
www.bankstreetcorner.com

Creative Curriculum
www.TeachingStrategies.com

High/Scope Educational Research Foundation
www.highscope.org

National Association for the Education of Young Children
www.naeyc.org

Project Approach
www.projectapproach.org

Reggio Emilia
www.reggiochildren.org
www.reggioalliance.org

Team Teaching in Early Childhood Settings

Team Teaching: Collaboration at Its Best

By virtue of your student practicum, you are a member of a team of people who work together for the children and their families who are enrolled in the center or school. The function of the teaching team is to help the many interested parties involved in children's education relate to each other through a mutually respectful and supportive system.

What Is Team Teaching?

There are always two parts of every educational endeavor, the nonteaching team and those who work directly with the children.

Definitions. The total team consists of everyone that has some role to play in the lives of the children and families. This includes the sponsoring organization (such as a church or synagogue and the board or council); the authorizing or licensing agency; the administration staff; the director of the program; and specialists such as nurses, social workers, nutritionists, doctors, and psychologists. Maintenance personnel, such as the cook and janitor, and the bus driver, fill out the remainder of the nonteaching part of the team. Each person plays a critical role in the effectiveness of the school organization.

Parents and families are an integral part of the team as well. Some families are able to participate in the classroom itself; others may help drive on fieldtrips or pull weeds on family work-days at the school. A growing number of centers encourage families to help set policy by serving on the decision-making committees and boards. Families in which both parents work outside the home do tasks that do not require their presence in the classroom, such as calling other parents to remind them of school events, participating in fund-raising, or contributing to the class newsletter. In any event, every family who is enrolled in the school is considered part of the team.

The classroom team is the day-to-day group of which you are a part. A teaching team is defined as two or more adults working together in one classroom with one group of children. As you have probably noted, the actual number may vary from one day to the next. At any given time, the team may consist of the supervising teacher, teacher's aides and assistants, student teachers, parent volunteer, early childhood specialist, and observers.

Team Size and Composition. The size of the teaching team is determined by the number of children in the classroom. This core group of teachers has the primary responsibility for the program. The number may be mandated by the licensing or accrediting agency, the state, or the school's philosophy. Organized groups for children's education and care may be family, center, or institution based, which will affect group sizes and age ranges. Taking into consideration these groups, we suggest adult–child ratios for different age groups such as the following:

- Infants and toddlers (birth to 30 months) should keep their group size to 12 or fewer children, with ratios ranging from 1:3 up to 1:6 with the oldest children.

- Preschoolers (30+ months to age 5) should keep group sizes to 20 or fewer children, with ratios ranging from 1:6 up to 1:10 with the oldest children.

- School-age children (ages 5 to 8) should keep their group size to 30 or fewer children, although some after-school programs have children up to age 12 and thus increase group size in the late-afternoon times, with ratios ranging from 1:10 to 1:12.

You can see that the younger the child, the greater the number of adults (teachers, teacher's aides and assistants, and other adults who are regular members of the teaching team) that are needed to support the program. Infants and toddlers require more intense care than do preschoolers who have learned to dress and feed themselves. Each team size reflects the developmental levels of the children in the class and requires less teaching staff as children mature and function more independently.

The composition of each team will vary. Each teacher is an individual with different experiences, interests, and abilities. Team members are chosen for the unique blend they add to the team, so that they can use their abilities and teach to their strengths. At the same time, each team member can learn from and teach others on the team.

Teaching teams usually consist of a head or lead teacher, one or more assistant teachers and/or teacher's aides, and sometimes a parent or other volunteer. Student teachers add to the mix in settings that serve as training grounds for early childhood teachers. For family-based programs, there may be a single caregiver. In laboratory schools, researchers and observers may be present, whereas in schools

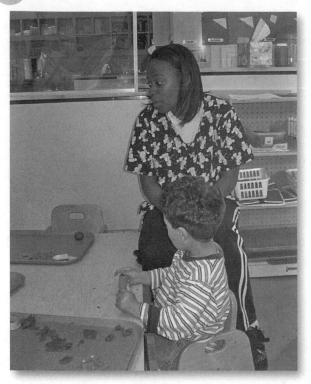

A teacher's job on a team takes many forms, always grounded in working with children.

that enroll a significant number of children with special needs, consultants and specialists will be part of the team. Special resource teachers in art, music, and physical development can also be part of the staff, meeting with children a few times a week. Substitute teachers and those who are hired to assist with a child with special needs may also be part of the team.

A teacher's position on the team generally depends on the level of education, training, and experience with young children. The head or lead teacher usually has the most education and experience in early childhood education and child development, preferably a bachelor's degree in early childhood education. Assistants and aides usually have less education or experience, and are often taking courses, working toward certification or degrees.

Benefits of Team Teaching

There are many reasons why a team of teachers is a standard practice in good early childhood programs. Team teaching not only fulfills the appropriate teacher–child ratios necessary for effective interactions with young children, but has other benefits as well. Teaching on a team makes it possible to:

- *Provide a wide range of adult role models* as well as diverse attitudes, cultural backgrounds, and social interactions.
- *Be supportive of children*. If staff changes occur, the rest of the team is intact and provides stability through the transition.
- *Share information* about children, families, curriculum, guidance strategies, and professional growth opportunities.
- *Contribute new ideas* on curriculum planning, behavior management, professional growth opportunities, and family–school relationships.
- *Solve problems* as they arise and make mutually acceptable decisions that reflects the best thinking of the team regarding class policy, behavior management, and parent or family issues.
- *Resolve conflicts* that may occur within the team involving differences in opinion, approach, personality, and style.
- *Support other team members* by sharing the workload and providing help and encouragement when needed.

It is easy to see how the program is enriched by a team of people working together, sharing their talents and resources for the benefit of the children and families in their class. Most of the disadvantages of team teaching stem from poor communication styles, issues of power and control, or unclear job descriptions. These issues will be addressed in the "Challenges of Team Teaching" section later in this chapter.

Role Set

Because early childhood programs are busy, people-filled places, teachers come in contact with a multitude of people, as discussed previously. Each person has a set of expectations about what the teacher should do and how to do it. Together, they compose what sociologists call a *role set* (Katz & Kahn, cited in Caruso & Fawcett, 1999). The members of a role set communicate their expectations to each other based on their understandings and beliefs about the role and their perceptions of how their messages are received. For instance, teachers may feel that the director should give them more help in working with difficult children, whereas the parents may want the teachers to call in a consultant, and the director may want the parents to do more at home. Members of the teacher's role set "push and pull" the teacher, competing for time and attention and creating multiple demands. This pressure is part of any job; those "with clear priorities, goals, and philosophy of education will be better able to formulate realistic expectations" (Caruso & Fawcett, 1999).

Unlike elementary classrooms, where there is usually just one teacher, early childhood teams include many partners. Teachers are usually supervised by a head or lead (or mentor) teacher, coordinator, or director. There are assistants (paid or volunteer), student teachers, and parent or adult family members. Figure 7.1 illustrates a role set of a head teacher.

Essentials of Team Teaching

How do a group of teachers become a productive and cohesive unit? If you have ever played on a sports team you know that teamwork does not just happen. It takes intention, organization, planning, and practice as well as coordination, communication, and cooperation. Team teaching is successful when each member understands the complexity and challenges, as outlined in Figure 7.2 (adapted from Gordon & Browne, 2004).

Professionalism

In Chapter 2 you learned some of the factors that influence a professional approach to teaching. Teacher preparation and experience, knowledge of ethical guidelines, and effective evaluations are important considerations. Professional attitudes and behaviors can make or break a successful teaching team.

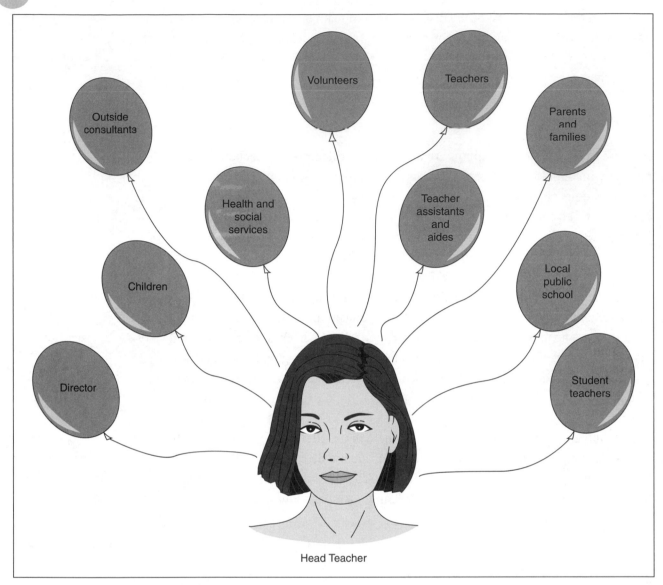

Head Teacher

Figure 7.1 Role Set of a Head Teacher

The role set of a head teacher includes all the major players in the professional life of classroom teaching.

Source: Reprinted by permission of the publisher. From Joseph J. Caruso with M. Temple Fawcett, *Supervision in Early Childhood Education. Third Edition: A Developmental Perspective.* New York: Teachers College Press. © 2006 by Teachers College, Columbia University. All rights reserved.

Figure 7.2
Top 10 Tips for Team Teaching

1. Professionalism
2. A satisfying role
3. Flexibility
4. Open and frequent communication
5. Self-awareness
6. Mutual respect and acceptance
7. Collegiality
8. Willingness to share the spotlight
9. Clearly defined roles and job description
10. Evaluation

In a team setting it is important to maintain confidentiality. You may be aware of matters within the personal lives of your team members that should remain in confidence and your knowledge of the intimate details of children and their families should not be discussed outside the professional team setting.

When differences arise with other team members, as they do, the professional teacher attempts to work out the issues with the other person(s) directly and in a timely fashion. Complaining about personal grievances and gossip (see the My Reaction feature later in the chapter) undermines the trust and cooperation necessary for a good team relationship.

A Satisfying Role

Each teacher is a unique resource, with individual talents, training, and interests, and likes to be appreciated for that special something he or she brings to the team. It is essential that the assignment for each team member be appropriate to his or her role and abilities. As a team member, you will want to have some understanding of your own talents and experiences and how they might be best used on a teaching team. Look again at your role set where you are student teaching, and think of the roles each person plays.

Flexibility

Effective teachers learn to change and adapt to children's interests and needs. As a team member, you will need to learn to be flexible with your adult colleagues as well. The daily give-and-take among staff members is key to team effort. A team functions well when its members change with the emerging needs of the staff. This is especially critical with a small team, such as in family child care. As a team member, you will want to keep an open mind to ideas presented by coworkers and be able to adapt to changing preset plans or filling in where needed.

Open and Frequent Communication

Interweaving the resources represented by each team is a dynamic process that requires good communication skills from the team members. Some of the techniques for working with other adults were discussed in Chapter 1. It is important to remember that adult relationships within the early childhood setting are as critical as relationships with the children.

Aside from informal communications among the team, there are other reasons for developing strong communication links: sharing information about children and their families or changes in the schedule; contributing new ideas, such as a recent article from *Young Children*, or resources from a recent workshop; and working through differences of opinion that may arise. Open and honest communication is an essential element in teamwork.

Self-Awareness

One of the fundamentals of teaching noted in Chapter 1 discussed the importance of self-reflective teaching. Throughout this text, you have been asked to reflect on various aspects of a student teacher's life within the context of each chapter. Self-awareness is obviously one of the most significant qualifications for a good teacher. This is especially true when you are a member of a teaching team. Student teachers may feel uncomfortable or uneasy in their relationship with other teachers. Once you know more about yourself as a teacher, however, you can apply this self-awareness to your connections with others on the staff.

It is useful to know what your teaching strengths and weaknesses are and how they might complement or conflict with others on the team. As you teach, you will come to understand yourself in new ways, discovering when and where you do—or do not—feel comfortable in certain teaching situations, and how you perceive yourself as a learner. Fortunately, evaluations are a part of the teaching–learning process. Feedback from master to student teacher provides opportunities to learn more about yourself and grow and change with experience.

Mutual Respect and Acceptance

One of the most important roles teachers model for others is the degree to which we accept and respect differences in our fellow humans. Appreciating the individuality of each team member is as important as appreciating the uniqueness of each child we teach.

All members of a teaching team should learn about the people with whom they work. Knowledge of your team's diverse personalities, experiences, strengths and challenges, values, culture, and background leads to greater understanding in the work environment. In the interest of developing a respect for, and acceptance of, the uniqueness of team members, you might look at what you have in common with your coworkers and appreciate what you can learn from your differences. Self-awareness helps you understand what you bring to the team; you will want to know what other team members believe to be their particular gifts. What is it you want the team to respect and accept about you? What is something you can learn from each team member?

Collegiality

Collegiality is the extent to which the team is friendly, supportive, and trusting of one another (Jorde-Bloom, 2005). A sense of collegiality or "teamness" is the result of a conscious effort to share and communicate openly and honestly, to value professional interactions, and to learn to be a cohesive group. When each team member promotes and sustains a high level of sharing and caring, a team spirit develops.

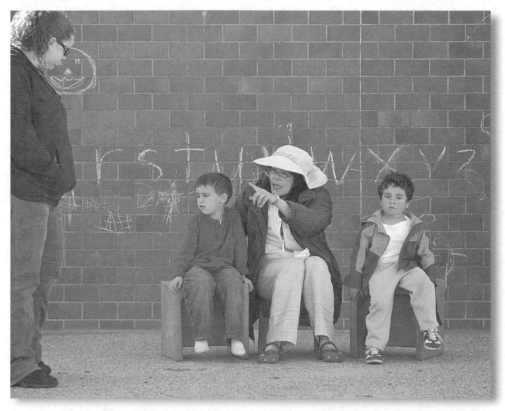

Student teachers learn the many roles of teaching by staying nearby and observing closely.

Opportunities for collaboration and teamwork abound in early childhood settings. Teachers can work together on projects for the classroom, share resources and curriculum ideas with the rest of the team, or plan a parent meeting together. Depending on the schedule, sharing lunch or break time together promotes team spirit, as do monthly birthday celebrations for the staff. A sense of community can be nurtured through structured and unstructured times when teachers are able to have frequent communication with one another. As they share problems and achievements, the team will grow in admiration and respect for one another.

Share the Spotlight

Being a good team member means sharing your strengths in ways that support the rest of the team but does not create a climate of competition. Everyone on the team is good at something, whether it is working with difficult children, creating outdoor curriculum, or relating to parents and families. We all like to be acknowledged for what we do well and hear from our colleagues that they agree. Differences notwithstanding, all team members are dedicated to their work and deserving of recognition. A supportive and collegial team shares the success when things work well, just as they share the responsibility when problems arise.

Clearly Defined Roles and Job Descriptions

A clear understanding of the roles and unique responsibilities of each team member is essential. Teamwork is more efficient when each teacher's role is outlined and understood by all. Clearly articulated responsibilities also serve as a guard against legal and ethical problems, particularly if a child is injured at school. Knowing the extent of and limits on your role and responsibilities give you the confidence to act with authority in areas you supervise.

For further in-depth discussion of role definition, see the following section titled "Challenges of Team Teaching."

Evaluation

In Chapter 2 you read about the importance of a regular evaluation process. As members of the staff of the center or school, you will probably participate in an annual evaluation. The goals you set and the feedback you receive influence your role as a member of the teaching team. More than likely, the head or lead teacher participated in your evaluation process and will, with the help of the teaching team, support and encourage you in your progress.

These 10 essentials of team teaching apply to the individual teacher as well as the group. They are also attributes that provide good models for young children through positive adult relationships, embracing differences and sharing the responsibilities.

Challenges of Team Teaching

Team teaching involves those many cooperative efforts that are best done when everyone knows his or her function. "I consider that everybody in my site is on the same side," writes Patricia in her student teaching journal. "We are all there because we love our work, we understand the importance of making a difference in the life of each child enrolled at Wu Yee Center, and we all try to support the families to the best of our abilities, and support each other to make the work less stressful."

Clarifying Roles

The roles and responsibilities of an early childhood teaching team are complex, and teams work best when all members have clear roles. As mentioned earlier in the chapter, the classroom team has the major responsibility for working with children, although role sets outline the secondary obligations of these jobs. Whitebrook (1989) found that head teachers and teacher-directors, teachers, and aides all have the same range of duties about curriculum planning and implementation, meal preparation, and maintenance. Head teachers often have more family communication and administrative work; all classroom teachers plan and carry out the program for children.

The jobs of aide or assistant and student teacher are important. These positions are usually jobs with few qualifications or education requirements. Assisting the teacher may involve performing housekeeping duties as well as teaching children directly, and can include supervising areas when a teacher is called away, or overseeing naptime while others meet. Attending staff meetings, training sessions, and meetings with consultants or parents may be included. Preparing curriculum materials or participating in child assessment might be part of these jobs.

However, there is a wide range of expectations for these positions, and the jobs can be misused and misunderstood. Clarifying what is—and what is not—in the job is crucial. For instance, a student teacher can be expected to make snacks, mix paint, or set up cots part of the time, but should also get experience assisting in activities, supervising free-play areas, and running planned small or large groups. If student teachers are unclear about what to do, problems occur. This note came from a classroom teacher:

> At my school, there are two Practicum student teachers who are not as willing to put in effort to help regular teachers in the classroom. These students sit by themselves away from the children. One even made a comment putting down a teacher's discipline. The situation needed to be resolved; fortunately, the master teacher spoke with them about how one could shadow a difficult child and the other could get busy involving herself without being invited. So far, the two of them have assisted more in the classroom and we appreciate the efforts and help.

If you are unclear or uncertain about your job, be sure to talk with your supervising teacher right away. Inquire if your fieldwork site uses any of the following items to clarify roles and responsibilities.

Job Descriptions

Specific job descriptions define roles: In some centers, job cards are given to each participating parent, the student teacher, and the head teacher. These cards outline the team member's responsibilities throughout the session (see Figure 7.3 for a sample). "As my mentor says, 'The higher the organizational component, the less stress on both children and staff,'" student teacher Gordon reports. "Teachers and staff are individually responsible for a small group of children; this responsibility includes doing observations, collecting work samples, providing developmentally appropriate small group activities, and managing the children. Then, at staff meetings, everyone is to relate that information—and get advice—back to the rest of the staff."

Figure 7.3
Sample Team Teaching Job Card

A job card can clarify what is expected to successfully fulfill the teacher's responsibilities.

Teacher 1: Art, Snack, and Sand Areas

8:30–9:00 a.m. *Set up art area:* Set up easels, help-yourself table, and structured art project. Set up sand area: Open shed; put out sample toys.

9:00–10:00 a.m. *Supervise all art areas:* Invite children; help them put on smocks; help write names on and pin up work; keep areas more or less organized.

10:00 a.m. *Assist children in cleaning up areas:* Put caps on paint jars; set brushes in sink; put materials on shelves; spray and wipe tables.

10:15 a.m. Set up snack trays for each small group during circle time; place near tables.

10:30 a.m. *Sit at table for snack:* Help children settle from handwashing and prepare their own snack space; supervise their passing and serving; read a story or converse; ensure they clean up their own space and stay at table until you can go outside together.

10:45–11:45 a.m. *Supervise sand area:* Get out a sample of toys; decide if using water and assist; start cleanup by 11:40 and get children to help.

11:50 a.m. *Assist at story time:* Help children settle; sit with wiggly ones.

Noon *Move to art counter:* Help children pick up their projects; say goodbye.

12:10–12:30 p.m. Clean up art and sand areas after everyone has left.

Team Roles. On a typical team, people will have different roles depending on their position, similar to a family or athletic team. Having clearly defined responsibilities helps all team members understand their designated roles; having fuzzy roles or vague tasks causes confusion, conflict, and dysfunction. Leaders might think of themselves like coaches (who guide but don't actually play the game) or team captains (who give directions while on the floor in the action). Team members may have different talents, even roles to play, yet always, everyone contributes and stays focused on the same goals. The scorekeeper role may be given to one or more members, but keeping track of time, goals, and accountability is important.

Basic team roles help all members address challenges that arise. One such team role might be responsibility for handling what is decided during a meeting, who would be best suited to create teacher job cards, and what member would be involved in finding the money to buy a new rug for the classroom. In addition to the official team roles, there are usually informal ones that can be either helpful or harmful. Helpful roles promote communication and smooth achievement of goals; harmful ones keep the team from being successful. We all appreciate someone on the lookout for who needs help, or attempts to help when people are in conflict because this helps keep the team headed in the right direction. If your team seems to have someone who always points out what is wrong with something or labels behaviors without being asked, the morale of the team is at risk. Think about your team and how it operates.

Surveying Your Team. Staff surveys can be used to measure teamwork effectiveness and identify areas for improvement. Although student teachers are not likely to be assessing organizational climate, they may find such work enlightening.

Consider your own fieldwork site as you read these aspects of overall staff relations from Jorde-Bloom (2005):

- cooperative and friendly
- competitive
- people are reluctant to express their feelings
- teachers are very helpful to new staff
- good team spirit
- staff are generally frank and candid
- morale is low
- people socialize outside work
- people feel isolated
- people complain a lot

When responsibilities are clear and roles feel equitable, the interpersonal climate of the team is more likely to be positive, and student teachers will integrate easily into the teaching environment. "I have felt very welcomed and accepted here as a member of this team," comments Gordon. "The teachers/assistants are all responsible for individual areas; those are rotated every 3 weeks. Staff works hard to coordinate their efforts to help ensure smooth transitions, maintain proper ratio at all times, and deal with safety issues. Everyone is very supportive of one another and I have been encouraged to become fully integrated and engaged in the team effort. Gonna be hard to say goodbye."

Team Leadership: Power and Hierarchy

Team structure varies from setting to setting. Each school or center has its own hierarchical structure that differentiates the multiple roles of the team. The team leader has a significant role to play in creating a healthy work climate where the staff members are valued and involved. Good leaders provide clear expectations, support, and encouragement to the team, giving honest and open feedback that is respectful and fair (Jorde-Bloom, 2005).

The decision-making process indicates how the power is distributed throughout the team and how much influence each team member has in the program. Team morale is high in programs where the teachers feel the decision-making process is fair; high morale leads to deeper commitment to fulfilling the program goals and greater satisfaction from the job.

In a classic study, Baumrind (1971) gathered information about parents' child-rearing patterns, which you will read about in Chapter 8 about families. It is also useful to adapt this to team leadership styles (Berk, 2003):

1. *Authoritative style:* characterized by acceptance, interaction, patience, warmth, and sensitivity to teacher's needs. Leaders have reasonable

expectations of their staff, place a premium on communication, engage in joint decision making, and encourage teachers to express their thoughts and feelings.

2. *Authoritarian style:* characterized by the need for control and by demands through criticism and command. Leaders rarely listen to another's point of view and make all the decisions for the team.

3. *Permissive style:* characterized by warmth and acceptance yet also inattention or overindulgence. Clear standards and rules are not set and those that exist are not reinforced consistently. Leaders appear not to be in control, make few demands on the staff, and allow teachers to make their own decisions, appropriate or not.

Teachers take on different roles in response to the leader's style. As in parenting, each leadership style can work, but has distinct strengths and weaknesses. With *authoritative* leaders, teachers participate in much of the decision making even though this adds to their workload. Teams often feel involved but sometimes overextended in their commitment. Teachers on the team feel good about expressing themselves to each other and the leader. In contrast, an *authoritarian* style is a top-down approach in which teams are not involved in making decisions, but told what to do. Teachers like the clarity of expectations, but sometimes resent being left out. In a *permissive* team, it is sometimes difficult to understand priorities and rules (see "Reflective Incident"). Although allowed to make decisions on their own, teachers are sometimes confused and feel ignored, though others like the more nebulous boundaries.

Which style do you think your supervising teacher has? How does it affect you? How does it affect the team? As you observe your team leader in action, you can form your own understanding of good team styles.

Team Dynamics

Team relationships and the dynamics among teachers are the "good the bad and the ugly," as Roseline's supervising teacher put it. "With every job and situation you have to expect the unexpected, but compromising and problem solving is necessary." As the student teacher, you are coming into an ongoing team. As mentioned in Chapter 1, this is a challenge. "It's a strain having to start new," notes Ichun's mentor teacher. "With time, one does learn to work in a team. As we mature, we learn to accommodate, to let go, becoming less critical, more reflective." Many early childhood programs have regular turnover; others use a "continuity of care" philosophy or Waldorf-type system that moves teachers with children so that teaching teams change.

Reflective Incident "When It Isn't Working"

I've been working at my site for 6 months now, but I still feel like I am new. As I expressed in class, sometimes I still feel like we don't work as a team on some days. We never have enough time to plan together and so a lot of times it depends on someone to take the initiative to plan the lesson for the week. Right now, lesson planning is done by me and another teacher, but we don't really sit down together because our prep/lunch schedules are one after the other. Then, when another teacher doesn't follow it, I get discouraged. I also feel that some of the teachers who have been working at the center longer are spending a lot of time talking with each other. Overall, I feel that the staff is not very organized and me being the "newbie," I don't know what to do.—Barbara

Your Thoughts

1. How would I feel?

2. What would I do?

3. What might the results be?

Taking into account one another's personal and professional characteristics, each person's stage of development and of teaching, and everyone's learning style and preferences are a challenge.

> When we talk about staff relationships, we really are talking about how harmoniously we as individuals get along with members of a group—how well we interact with one another; how well we communicate, support, and accept each other's differences, strengths, weaknesses, and points of view. (Zavitkovsky, 1992, p. 14)

"Team relationships at our site are important, and they make an effort to have meetings and share the responsibilities," note student teachers Michelle and Theo. "It seems that they are direct with each other, and the nicest thing we've observed and felt from them is their warmth. They hug each other when one comes into work, and are diverse both culturally and personality-wise."

As a student teacher, you concentrate your efforts on working with children. However, because early childhood teaching is usually in team settings, knowing something about stages of development in adults and for teachers is helpful in dealing with team dynamics and conflicts.

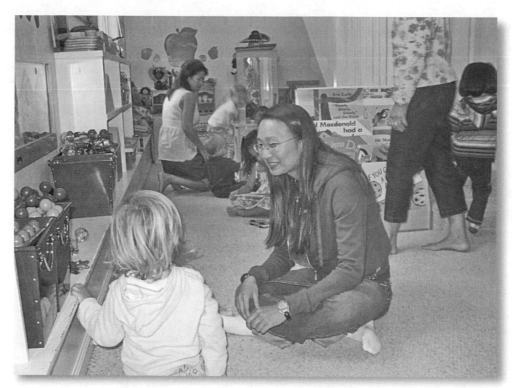

Team dynamics involve keeping other adults in mind while still teaching in the classroom.

Stages of Adult Development. Knowledge of self is fundamental to effective classroom teaching, and it contributes to positive team teaching as well. "By understanding ourselves and the impact of our early life experiences and cultural backgrounds, we increase the control we have over our own behavior and can more easily modify it when necessary" (Caruso & Fawcett, 1999). Understanding adult development increases this level of self-knowledge. Moreover, it will help us understand our coworkers, because teaching teams are usually comprised of adults of all age groups.

Each stage of adult development has certain characteristics and key concerns that affect our work as team members. "At 61, I have many life experiences," states student teacher Pat. "Yet in some ways I have led a sheltered life—I haven't traveled much, and haven't been in school (well, college) for 25 years. I could use some broader experiences. Still, I have a stable self-concept and am responsible and productive in my life. I am good at abstract thinking, but not at expressing it verbally." We have an accumulated set of experiences and beliefs that shape our work as team members, from childhood to the present (Arin-Krupp, 1981). Think about where you and your teammates are in terms of your stage of adult development:

- Young adults invested in identity and becoming independent?
- Middle adulthood with family obligations, trying to demonstrate stability and competence?
- Later adulthood with increased individuation, modification of dreams, either integrating or regretting accomplishments?

Table 7.1 Stages of Teacher Development

Stage	Developmental Task	Training Needs
Survival (usually year 1)	"Can I get through the day in one piece? Can I really do this work day after day?" Reality is *not* like theory! Looking for patterns.	Support, understanding, encouragement, reassurance, guidance. Instruction in specific tasks and skills; needs onsite assistance.
Consolidation (often years 2–3)	"I can survive!" Concern with individual children; can identify problem situations; can see variations in patterns.	Mutual exploration of a problem onsite; extensive give-and-take conversation; has information about specific children or problems; ready for access to specialists and consultants; chances to share feelings with others in this stage.
Renewal (may be years 3–5)	"What are new techniques, ways to do things?" Sees self as a teacher; ready for innovations, new ideas.	Meet colleagues from different programs, conferences, and workshops; may be ready to look closer at own teaching.
Maturity (years 5-plus)	"What is the nature of growth and learning?" Meaningful search for answers.	Participate in conferences; lead workshops; become mentor teacher.

Source: Compiled from *Talks with Teachers: Reflections on Early Childhood Education.* By L. Katz, 1977, Washington, DC: National Association for the Education of Young Children.

Stages of Teacher Development. Teachers have a developmental sequence in their professional growth patterns (Katz, 1977). Four stages have been outlined, and there are tasks and training needs that are associated with each one. Individual teachers may vary greatly in the length of time spent in each of the stages (see Table 7.1 to ascertain where you and your supervising teacher may be). You may be able to determine the kind of help you need to grow into the next stage. How might this affect the way a team works together?

Conflicts. Whenever there is contact between two or more people, there is likely to be both cooperation and conflict. Conflict can be seen as a predicament or opportunity, although most people see it as problematic rather than as a vehicle for greater understanding or intimacy. Many teachers, even those who handle problems among children with ease, prefer to smooth over conflicts with adults. However, it is a challenge of team teaching that we cannot avoid.

When a disagreement of principle or practice arises, teams must devise ways to resolve their differences. As you read the five common approaches that follow, think about how you—and the teacher on your team—address conflicts.

Approach	Description
No-nonsense or command	I don't give in. I try to be fair and honest. I know what's best. Confronting the issue head on is the way to go.
Problem-solving	If there's a conflict, there's a problem, and we all share it. We need to solve it together. This produces creative ideas and stronger relationships.
Compromising	I listen to everyone and support them in listening to me. Then I help each one give in a little. Half a loaf is better than none.
Smoothing	I like things to stay calm and peaceful whenever possible. Most teacher concerns aren't life threatening, so I just direct attention to other things.
Ignoring	I am uneasy dealing with conflict. There is not a whole lot I can do about these situations, so I avoid it.

At one time or another, each of these approaches is appropriate. For example, if a teacher sees children pushing one another off the slide, she must move in swiftly; the *no-nonsense approach* is best, even though the team member at the slide may feel upset at being chastised or taken over. If, however, a teacher is unhappy that a coworker interrupted his circle time, he can use a *problem-solving approach* later, at break time or during the next staff meeting. When student teacher Ellen began to tell Nathan's mother new ways to calm him, her mentor teacher observed the interaction, then took a *compromising approach* when she saw the parent's discomfort, offering a way that both parties could feel heard and satisfied with their viewpoints.

Communicating your thoughts is important; how to do so is challenging. Although you are probably not a supervisor, the "Director's Golden Rule" will still work: "Do Unto Teachers As You Would Have Teachers Do Unto Children" (Beals, 1996). In other words, be a good listener, showing that you are concentrating and asking open-ended questions. Student teacher Yuji keeps his "eyes on the prize" in the midst of conflict.

I see sometimes the teachers do not get along with some issues, so I (or another teacher) volunteer to be a bridge between teachers to find a solution. I believe that all humans are different, so it is just a normal thing that some people will disagree. I don't think it is a bad thing that someone makes me upset. When there is a conflict with teachers, I first think that I am here for the children, and what choice should I make with the person to provide a better environment for the children? That way I avoid mixing my own personal feelings in the action. It is sometimes difficult, but I have managed to adjust my personal feelings aside.

Others get discouraged. For example, frequent interaction and an exchange of information and ideas is an important part of good teamwork, but sometimes difficult. Sau-Kuen faces a different substitute frequently, and there is a language

My Reaction

"Gossip in the Workplace"

I think most teachers at ECE centers are generally really busy and have to stay focused on everything that is going on with the children. They don't have a lot of time to talk to each other—at my place, we don't even have overlapping lunch schedules. It's ironic, then, that the teachers seem to find a way to talk a lot about "things" but not about the program. I get so sick of all the gossiping at the center. If you have an issue with another teacher, then you should go talk to her, right? What's the point of talking *about* her to another teacher? Nothing gets solved and the person just keeps on behaving the same way because no one talks to her. I know that straight communication doesn't come easy to some people (like me, too ☺), but if your goal is to provide the best education for the children then you should do anything to accomplish that goal.

—GITEL

barrier between her and one of the teaching team members. And Paula finds that "there are so many cooks but we are all cooking up something completely different!" Gossip is another issue (see the My Reaction feature) that often occurs at the workplace.

Many factors contribute to positive conflict resolution. Everyone needs help learning positive approaches to solving interpersonal problems. Refer back to the six steps to problem solving in Chapter 3 (Figure 3.6). At the same time, clear roles and responsibilities, frequent ongoing communication, and an organized framework for discussion helps a team bring up important matters. One of the best ways to do this is through staff meetings.

Staff Meetings

Staff meetings offer a place and time for teams to get together "off the floor" of a program. Regular meetings, although often difficult to schedule, provide the best opportunity for team members to talk together, listen, and broaden their own views as they make decisions affecting themselves and the children they teach. In family child care settings, student teachers may be able to talk with their supervising teacher easier than in a larger center. School-age programs are often spread thin, and student teachers may find themselves at the far end of a playground, out of earshot of their supervisor. Meetings can serve many purposes, and clarity of goals helps any meeting run better.

Curriculum is a common focus of staff meetings; student teacher Ming Hong notes that "the teachers always plan together for the weekly theme, and they like to prepare the materials and share their ideas while they do it. I really like their practice because it saves time and they can talk over conflicts while they are doing something together for the program." Meetings also target children; in Tiana's program, weekly staff meetings are a productive means of discussing each child's development, planning for the required assessments, and discussing children before family conferences.

Whereas organizing the agenda often falls to the team leader, items may be suggested by all members. Formats vary, as do the frequency of meetings. Agenda items include plans for activities, discussion of children, issues from families, strategies for managing behavior and schedules, conflict resolution, as well as more formal training such as CPR or first aid or consultations with specialists. "The more formal ways my team communicates/plans together are through a monthly shared calendar, and a daily list of each teacher's responsibilities," notes Fontana. In addition, many early childhood programs try to include celebrations, fun activities, conference or workshop attendance or site visits together, even an annual retreat to build a sense of teamwork as well as provide staff training and education.

Some programs do not have regular staff meetings. Without them, creating a shared vision and ensuring smooth operations are difficult. Weekly meetings are preferable, with more informal check-ins and debriefings throughout the day. Half-day programs usually meet after the class session, and school-age programs can meet before the children arrive. In full-day programs, and those with staggered staff, meetings for everyone are more challenging to schedule. A center that operates from 7 a.m. to 6 p.m. may meet bimonthly in the evening, or alternate the meeting times so that an early staff meeting has a team member from the morning staff and the afternoon meeting can get an afternoon teacher during naptime.

My room 4 teachers get together once a week, for 1 to 1–1/2 hours; they e-mail and communicate in class. They have an in-service day, and quarterly staff meetings for all the school. Then they know what the teachers in the other rooms are doing, and also the children in the other rooms. I think these are some of the reasons that they are very supportive toward each other, not just about children, but taking into account one another's personal well-being.

—JANE

Find out about staff meetings at your fieldwork site, and see if you can attend at least one during your practicum. You will find it interesting to observe and participate in this important part of team teaching.

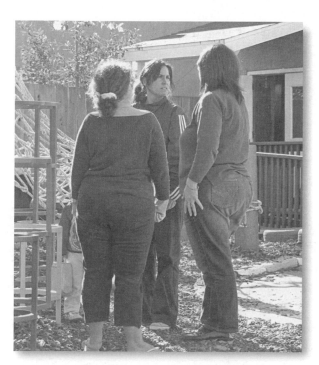

Communicating frequently with each other is an important part of participating on a team.

Betwixt and Between: Student Teachers on an ECE Team

What is the role of the student teacher in a team teaching situation? Ideally, your fieldwork site is ready for you, looking forward to your participation with a clear plan, and has a supervising teacher who will shepherd you through your practicum experience. There is so much to learn—classroom environments and schedules to understand, team roles and responsibilities to learn, systems to follow, and an organizational culture to understand. One's self-esteem is fragile, and teachers' remarks or looks, even well-intended, can seem critical. Sylvette's comments echo this feeling: "I'm afraid that I am in a new situation where I do not feel I am part of the team. I have been there less than a month, but I only have a semester here. Initially I felt a cool reception and a lack of communication. Sometimes I feel like I am pretty much on my own." Anxiety is common, and uncertainty brings low initiative. In one study, "92% of beginning teachers did not seek help directly from colleagues. They admitted being afraid of acknowledging uncertainty of problems in their classrooms. At best new teachers swapped stories about problems informally and attempted to hide weaknesses from colleagues" (Berl, 2004).

To feel part of a teaching team, new and student teachers must focus on getting to know the teachers as well as the children. As mentioned earlier in the chapter (see Figure 7.2), having a clear and meaningful role is important. Observing and taking notes about children and a program should expand to other significant duties. Augusto comments:

> The teachers help student teachers and volunteers feel at home by placing a lot of trust in us to help with activities, interact with the children (including handling their behavior), prepare meals and snacks, etc. The head teacher is kind enough to check in with me to see if there are any practicum assignments that I have to do, or if I have anything for her to fill out. All in all, I think the outlook of the teachers is that we are part of their family.

As you learn the names of teachers as well as the children, you can greet and speak to each of them, finding out their expertise and educated opinions. It is more likely that you will get included as things happen. Joan notes:

> The other teachers at my site let me try to handle whatever happens at my table. They will help me out if I have trouble, but I think it's a good way to learn by trying to deal with it myself first. If there is a big conflict, they will step in so there are two teachers. They will also call me over and then I'm that second person.

One way to bring you closer to the team is to be open to feedback to your work. Notice how this student's teaching practice is shaped as her supervisor "catches her at being good":

> When my head teacher is at the table when I am doing a project, he might say to the children "When Teacher Grace shares with me, it makes me feel good, isn't

that right?" I agree, and it feels like he is putting me on the same level in front of the children.

Another point to remember is that we learn first by doing, by trying things concretely. Only later do we learn the same things conceptually. So, ask for specifics when you are to do something, and offer to help alongside a more experienced teammate. As Marc points out, there are strategies for putting you into the team:

> Because the center gets new student teachers every semester, the teachers try their best to make the transition as easy as possible and make us feel part of the team. One way of doing this is having job cards, and these include step-by-step directions of how to fulfill the duties. Also, student teachers are invited to staff meetings and take part in the discussions.

Figure 7.4 offers ideas for getting involved in teaching teams.

A final note: Team teaching may be challenging, but it is an integral part of teaching in early childhood programs and is an excellent way to find out a lot about yourself (see "Lessons from the Field"). In response to his practicum instructor's assignment to discuss team relationships, student teacher Yuji offers this quote from Joseph Campbell (1988): "If you follow your bliss . . . . you begin to meet people who are in your field of bliss, and they open doors for you."

Figure 7.4
Getting Yourself In: Teamwork as a Student Teacher

Getting yourself into a teaching team requires some key strategies so you feel part of the team.

- Focus discussions on how to understand situations—describe an incident and ask for team members' ideas, their assumptions about how children learn, what works and what doesn't, what they expect of themselves, and what you could have done (or do next time).
- Look for opportunities to offer another teacher what you observed about the children, and how you wonder what it means, or how to help children express ideas and feelings.
- While respecting each team member's privacy, try to relate to each person on a more personal level as well as on a professional level. Teaching teams are made of individuals, and knowing each person will help you understand the dynamics of each unique member.
- Make a list each week of what you have learned, and then practice those skills to refine them the next time you go to your site.
- Nurture your own curiosity, enthusiasm, and eagerness. Try to balance your anxiety with these more positive feelings. Feel free to model the children in this regard.
- Ask for and be open to suggestions from other teachers regarding changes in your approach or behavior.
- Cultivate a habit of suspending judgment of yourself, both when others step in and also if you do not get help in tricky situations.
- Avoid the temptation to find *the one and only right way.* There are many appropriate practices. You will need to develop your own style, but also need to align your work with that of your team.

"Team Teaching"

by Jill Watkins

Mentor Teacher

I've often been asked why I didn't pursue a career in elementary education. Primarily, it's because I so value the experience of team teaching that is typical of the preschool environment.

As a teacher for nearly twenty years, I have benefited immensely from working with some amazing women. I was told early on—and continue to pass on the wisdom to teachers mentoring with me—to be a sponge. These senior teachers genuinely desired to see me succeed and were eager to assist me in acquiring more tools for my belt. I had built in resources to observe, bounce things off of, and model myself after. I still utilize some of the strategies gleaned from the teachers I first worked with.

A definite advantage of the team teaching approach is that we each bring a slightly different set of interests and skills to the table. For instance, while I have a real love for literacy but science doesn't appeal to me too much, one of my co-teachers can compensate. Or, 1 may respond more easily to the "slow to warm" child whereas my co-teacher connects fabulously with a child who is gregarious and/or creative.

Similarly, we all have those days when our patience reserves run a little lower. In those times we can rely on our co-teachers to take over in a given negotiation with a child. Ultimately, having this balance serves the children most effectively.

However, the reality is that these aforementioned differences can present challenges in the team dynamic. The most helpful thing I have learned— and this applies to any healthy relationship, really—is communicate, communicate, communicate. It is much better to be able to be open and honest with each other, in an atmosphere of respect. And while you don't always have to see eye-to-eye, the bottom line is a foundation of mutual caring and support.

Practicum Activity

Using the model in Figure 7.1, sketch a role set for yourself as a student teacher. List the expectations you have for each member of your role set, and their expectations of you. Next, go through each list, marking which are reasonable and what are not. What adjustments can be made for more sensible targets?

Journaling Assignment

Discuss team relationships at your practicum site. How do teachers work together? Resolve conflicts? Build a team?

Resources

Arin-Krupp, J. (1981). *Adult development: Implications for staff development.* Manchester, CT: Adult Development and Learning.

Team Teaching in Early Childhood Settings

Baumrind, D. (1971). Current patterns of parental authority. *Developmental Psychology Monograph, 4*(1, Pt.2).

Beals, C. (1996, September). Do unto teachers as you would have teachers do unto children. *Child Care Information Exchange.*

Berk. L. (2003). *Child development.* Boston: Allyn & Bacon.

Berl, P. (2004, January/February). Insights into teacher development: Part 1. The emergent teacher. *Child Care Information Exchange.*

Caruso, J. J., & Fawcett, M. T. (1999). *Supervision in early childhood education: A developmental perspective* (2nd ed.). New York: Teachers College Press.

Gordon, A. M., & Browne, K. W. (2008). *Beginnings and beyond: Foundations in early childhood education.* Clifton Park, NY: Thomson Delmar Learning.

Gordon, A. M. & Browne, K. W. (2004). *Beginnings and Beyond: Foundations in early childhood education.* (6th edition). Clifton Park, NY: Thomson Delmar Learning.

Gordon, A. M. & Browne, K. W. (1989). *Beginnings and Beyond: Foundations in early childhood education.* (2nd edition). Albany, NY: Delmar Publishers.

Gordon, A. M. & Browne, K. W. (1985). *Beginnings and Beyond: Foundations in early childhood education.* (lst edition). Albany, NY: Delmar Publishers.

Jorde-Bloom, P. (2005). *Blueprint for action: Achieving center-based change through staff development* (2nd ed.). Lake Forest, IL: New Horizons.

Katz, L. (1977) *Talks with teachers: Reflections on early childhood education.* Washington, DC: National Association for the Education of Young Children.

Whitebrook, M.(1989). *Who cares? Child care teachers and the quality of child care in America.* (Final Report, National Child Care Staffing Study.) Oakland, CA: Center for the Child Care Workforce.

Zavitkovsky, D. (1992, January). Docia shares a story about staff relationships. *Child Care Information Exchange.*

Web Sites

Association for Supervision and Curriculum Development
www.ascd.org

Center for Child Care Workforce
www.ccw.org

Child Care Information Exchange
www.childcareexchange.org

Early Childhood Research and Practice
www.ecrp.uiuc.edu

National Teaching and Learning Forum
www.ntlf.com

chapter 8

Collaborating with Families

Who Is the Family?

Today's families are widely defined, reflecting the sociological changes over the past 50 years, when the "nuclear family" consisting of a mother, father, and two children was the prevailing model. A family unit today may consist of parents (who may or may not be married to one another or who may be adoptive or foster parents); and other family members, such as grandparents, aunts, and uncles, as well as step- or half-brothers and sisters. Two people can consider themselves a family, as can a collective or commune of greater numbers of people. These characteristics of families may be very different from the way your parents and grandparents were raised, or they may be similar to your next-door neighbors. These are the kinds of families you meet as you enter the field of early childhood education. A student teacher reflects on her own family of origin in the following "Reflective Incident."

In your student teaching experience, you may have noticed that the teachers often refer to families, rather than just "parents." Increasingly, we have become more aware of the influence of not only the child's immediate family, but the extended family and community as well. In today's world there are a significant number of people who take care of children and we want them all to feel included, for through these family networks we gain greater knowledge and understanding of the child.

Parent is a word that has expanded to fit a variety of situations, not just people who have the legal status of the mother or father. The definition of a parent has broadened to include not only those individuals who are raising their own biological children, but also those who are raising foster children, adopted children, and children of other family members or friends. The complexity and number of varying lifestyles today causes us to continue to look at how we define the parents and families of the children we teach.

Reflective Incident *"The Family I Grew Up In"*

I have the best memories of my childhood. Being the second of eight children gave me the opportunity of having lots of experiences in all areas that helped me grow not only in a wonderful but also safe environment. I grew up in a small town in Mexico. I would say that was a gift to have my infancy in Teocaltiche, Jalisco, where there weren't neighborhoods for different social levels. We knew and trusted each other. Everybody had the doors on their houses open during the day because delinquency was not an issue for us. We were very respectful about others' property. All the children had the fortune of playing on the streets every afternoon until our parents called us in (in summer we used to play all kinds of games until 9 or 10 P.M.).

Adults were persons who deserved respect and obedience. Adults were the persons who had all the authority to suggest (or order) children what to do, what not to do, and/or how to do it. For this reason, trying to solve a problem, fight, or conflict was not easy. The most natural thing for me was that my mother, my teacher, a relative, or any adult would come and solve it.

Even though those adults around my childhood could be considered rigid and strict, it somehow helped me learn very important values in life. The role that my parents played encouraging me to grow in different aspects was decisive. For many things they gave us specific rules, but for other things, they gave us freedom for choosing and making our own mistakes.—Patricia

Your Thoughts

1. How would I feel?

2. What would I do?

3. What might the results be?

The Diversity of American Families

Changing sociological patterns have given rise to a number of families with unique needs. Economics, immigration, medical technology, divorce rates, career commitments, lifestyle changes, demographics, and gender issues are some of the influences that are reshaping family structure. Some family situations are more challenging for parents and teachers and the early childhood educator must be prepared to work with the diversity that is typical today. This includes:

- Families with children with developmental delays and disabilities
- Adoptive and foster parent families
- Single-parent families

- Blended families
- Families where both parents work outside the home
- Multiracial families
- Families raising children in a culture not their own and where English is not their primary language
- Grandparents who are raising grandchildren
- First-time older-parent families
- Gay and lesbian families
- Homeless families
- Teenage-parent families

As you read through the list you might think about some of the families you are meeting through your student teaching. How many of them fit one or more of these categories? What are some of the difficulties these families face? In what ways do the teachers and the school support these families?

Valuing Home Culture

Child-rearing practices are culturally based, so it follows that understanding a family's culture is an essential element in building strong family–school relationships. Children's growth and development can be understood only within their cultural context. Each culture has its own values and attitudes that must be recognized and respected by the teaching staff as they share their strengths with families for the benefit of each child.

Together, teachers and families build strong communication links to foster trust and understanding.

To be successful, teachers must first reflect on their own cultural heritage, experience, and attitudes. Teachers must examine any prejudice and bias they may have toward cultural groups different from their own that would prevent them from connecting with families in the school. Different perspectives on eating, sleeping, toileting, disciplining, and showing respect, for instance, could be barriers to working together in a child's best interest. When viewed in a cultural context, these differences can become understood and respected as the teacher and the family work toward mutually acceptable resolutions.

Children learn best in a setting that reflects and supports their families. Families are more comfortable in school settings where they and their cultural influences are acknowledged and understood (see the section titled "Family Involvement" later in this chapter). Children gain when there is some similarity between their home and their school. Hyun (1998) refers to this as "cultural congruency," and suggests that becoming sensitive to diversity is not the only issue, but that understanding individual histories, families of origin, and ethnic family cultures is what makes us similar rather than different from one another.

Bradley and Kibera (2007) cite four important characteristics of culture to consider when working with families of diverse backgrounds (see Table 8.1). Each of

Table 8.1 Cultural Characteristics and Diversity

The questions that are posed may help you reflect on how powerful culture is in shaping children's development and our teaching.

Cultural Dimensions of Families	Questions for Reflection
Values and beliefs	How is *family* defined? What roles do adults and children play? How does the family make sense of the child's behavioral difficulties? How does culture inform the family's view of appropriate and inappropriate ways of dealing with problem behavior and child guidance? What is most important to the family?
Historical and social influences	What strengths and stressors does the family identify? What barriers does it experience?
Communication	What is the family's primary language? What support is required to enable communication? How are needs and wants expressed? How are unhappiness, dissatisfaction, or distress experienced and expressed?
Attitudes toward seeking help	How does the family seek help and from whom? How do members view professionals, and how do professionals view them?

Source: From "Closing the Gap: Culture and the Promotion of Inclusion in Child Care," by J. Bradley and P. Kibera, 2007, in D. Koralek (Ed.) *Spotlight on Young Children and Families.* Washington, DC: National Association for the Education of Young Children. Adapted with permission from the National Association for the Education of Young Children.

the questions concerning a cultural characteristic encourages further exploration of the cultures you find in your classroom.

Understanding Parenthood

As families and teachers work together, the assumption is that we are all working for what is best for the child, yet there is often a difference of opinion about what "best" is and whose "best" will prevail. Parents and teachers come together with different viewpoints, different needs, and different experiences. Each has a point of view that enlightens the other; in this spirit we look at two areas of parenting with implications for working with parents: stages of parent development and patterns of child-rearing.

Stages of Parent Development. The parents you meet are in various stages of development, just like their children. A first-time parent has different experiences and feelings than a parent with three older children, or older parents of an only child. Galinsky (1987) noted six stages of parenthood and found that the role of the parent changes in various ways as the parents and children grow old together.

In the earliest stages, beginning with pregnancy, parents fantasize about what kind of parents they would like to be and prepare for the inclusion of a child in their lives. During the first two years, attachment is a primary concern as is matching their fantasy of child-rearing with the actual experience.

From toddlerhood to adolescence, family rules are clarified and the parent's authority style is established. During the same time period parents interpret themselves and the world to their children through the values, knowledge and skills they pass on.

The teen-age years are a time for renegotiating family rules and authority and creating new relationships between parents and child. As the child matures and leaves home, the parents examine their sense of accomplishment and again redefine the relationship with their now adult child.

The six stages demonstrate how parents change and grow in relation to having children and how they alter their own behavior and attitudes to the reality of child-rearing. In larger families, many parents go through several stages at once. With a single or the oldest child, parental feelings may be intensified. Just as we look at the developmental needs and stages of children, we can also be aware that parents have unique developmental tasks, too. Do you recognize if any of the parents you know are going through these stages?

Patterns of Child-Rearing. In Chapter 7, Baumrind's (1972) authority patterns were discussed under the topic of team leadership. Now we will look at the study as it relates to parental styles of behavior because children are affected by the way their parents treat them. Teachers find their role with each family becomes clear as

Table 8.2 Parental Child-Rearing Styles

These have a powerful effect on how children behave.

Parental Style	Characteristics	Effect on Children
Authoritative	Warm, responsive, attentive to child's needs; consistent in enforcing rules; permits child to make reasonable decisions when ready	High self-esteem, self-control; upbeat; persistent with tasks; cooperative
Authoritarian	Focuses on control, demanding, critical, makes all the decisions for the child; rarely listens to child's point of view	Hostile when frustrated, anxious, withdrawn, unhappy; resort to force when they do not get their way
Permissive	Warm, but overindulgent; makes few or no demands; accepting, but often inattentive; does not impose limits; lets children make inappropriate decisions	Impulsive, disobedient, rebellious; overly demanding and dependent on adults; poor task persistence

Source: From Laura Berk, *Infants, Children, and Adolescents,* 5e. Published by Allyn & Bacon, Boston, MA. Copyright © 2004 by Pearson Education. Adapted by permission of the publisher.

they learn more about parental styles of behavior. The three parental styles and their effect on children are shown in Table 8.2.

Research has continued to support Baumrind's findings that there are more positive outcomes for children when parents use an authoritative style. The findings suggest that there are more positive interactions with peers and with siblings (Hamner & Turner, 1996). How does this study help you relate to the families in your student teaching setting? What does the study tell you about your own childhood?

When teachers understand the parental styles of child-rearing they are better able to help families learn more appropriate and effective ways to raise their children. Because child-rearing is culture-bound, teachers must always be sensitive to each family's cultural values when discussing child-rearing issues.

The Importance of Family–School Connections

> The caregiver maintains an open, friendly, and cooperative relationship with each child's family, encourages the family's involvement in the program, and supports the child's relationship with the family. (Lane & Signer, 1996, p. 2)

In creating a guide for infant–toddler caregiving for the Child Development Division of California's Department of Education, Lane and Signer crafted this vision statement to highlight how to create partnerships with families. From the first contact with a prospective family, early childhood teachers are developing a relationship.

Why Relationships Matter

Whether the young child is an infant entering child care for the first time, a preschooler ready to try nursery school, or a third grader coming to the after-school club, he or she is faced with the challenge of adapting to a strange environment, different routines, and new relationships. Families must make adjustments, too, because they are sharing the care of their child with someone outside the family. The changes are more likely to be positive and happen smoothly if teachers can develop a cooperative relationship on the child's behalf.

"Working with families gives me a better understanding of the children," notes student teacher Sylvette. "I then have better insights on how to deal with them that I might not know otherwise." Life for young children is shaped by many experiences, and having caring and attentive relationships is crucial to their growth. "Adults really count in a young child's life. . . . Research only confirms what we know from experience: children thrive when they are surrounded by people who are crazy about them" (Baker & Manfredi-Petitt, 2004, p. 2).

Creating a Caring Community

All national standards of excellence recognize the importance of the parent–caregiver relationship. Creating a caring community is a key indicator of quality early education, as identified by the National Association for the Education of Young Children (Leading Edge, 1999). The quality of a caregiver's approach to families is emphasized in the accreditation process of the National Association for Family Child Care. Head Start involves families as partners by providing a family advocate, having home visits, and involving parents in reviewing program effectiveness. The environmental rating scales for all age groups (see Chapter 5) include family involvement.

This community should include everyone who is fulfilling the role of parent. Regardless of family structure (see the previous section "Who Is the Family?"), the one unifying theme is that all adult family members are stressed by their obligations in the workplace, wishes for healthy relationships with significant people in their lives, and dreams of raising their children well. As we address the challenges of meeting our mutual obligations for children, we must create a community of members who care for one another.

Common Goals, Different Perspectives

At first glance, teachers and families have similar goals. They both want the child to be safe, to learn, and to thrive. Both school and home are "seats of learning" for the young child, so both sets of adults have the goal of educating young children in common. Still, families and teachers have different perspectives on the child and on the enterprise. Katz (1980) discussed these distinctions between the two parties on several dimensions, adapted in Table 8.3.

Table 8.3 Families and Teachers: Different Perspectives

Key Dimension	Families	Teachers
On connection to child	Optimum attachment: emotionally intense, even unrealistically optimistic	Detached concern: emotionally warm but more objective
In viewing the classroom	Individual, from my child's perspective, partial	Whole group, from the group or team's perspective, impartial
With a rational role	Optimally irrational: "in the service of the heart," "crazy about that kid"	Optimally rational: careful analysis, use research and knowledge
On spontaneity	More impulsive, responsive, casual	More intentional, rational

Source: From "Mothering and Teaching—Some Significant Distinctions," by L. G. Katz, in *Current Topics in Early Childhood Education* (Vol. 3), by L. G. Katz (Ed.), 1980, Norwood, NJ: Ablex. Used with permission.

Families and teachers should have different perspectives; after all, their relationship to the child, their function in the educational setting, and their areas of expertise do differ. Parents are experts on one child (or a few) in an intimate, primary way, whereas teacher expertise lies in experience with many children and more studied knowledge. As student teacher Grace puts it:

Working with families provides rich information about the child's background, culture, etc. . . . basically everything that's been going on in the child's life since birth. Despite our knowledge in early childhood development, as educators we must remember that nobody knows a child like his family. If you just put yourself in the parents' shoes, working with them becomes easier.

Katz (1995) sees the roles of parents and teachers as complementary but distinctive. If it seems that parents expect you to teach only *their* child, it may be an expression of the perspective of "optimal attachment." You can help by acknowledging how important their child is while still asserting your more detached, but warm, concern— "You're right; she *is* a pistol and does need help getting on her shoes. At the same time, when she needs to wait while I help someone else first, she learns about the give-and-take in a group that sometimes includes waiting."

No one knows a child better than his or her own family members.

Family Involvement

Both families and teachers indicate they think family involvement in their children's education is beneficial (Diffily, 2004). Families usually start their involvement because of a specific request or at the invitation of a teacher.

Involvement takes many forms, as seen in Figure 8.1. When parents have a positive experience the first time they attend an event or volunteer at school, they are likely to repeat those experiences. Beginnings are critical: Many families feel tentative in school settings with teachers who they fear may be critical, and teachers must work gently and carefully to nurture the relationship in order to get involvement.

A single negative experience may decrease the family's interest in staying involved, so teachers—and their students—must be sensitive and alert to how to be welcoming and clear. Family feelings and attitudes can undermine their involvement with teachers or a center. Parents may have conflicted feelings about leaving children in care. Moreover, time with their children can feel rushed or restricted because of the demands of school or the workplace, which cause cranky or resentful feelings. Some families worry that they will be displaced by teachers in the eyes of their children; indeed, often children seem more cooperative, even happier, in child care. A parent with a balky child at pickup time may wonder what's happening to the family. Occasionally families and schools seem to vie for authority over a child; Brazelton and Sparrow (2002) call this "gatekeeping"—competitive urges among adults to protect and care for children. Finally, families often feel exposed and uncomfortable sharing private information. This reluctance has complex cultural and personal roots.

For example, student teacher Raquel noted that families often get defensive when being told about their children's misbehavior. She gets nervous herself, and ends up avoiding talking to those families at pickup time. To encourage a stronger bond and thus deeper family involvement, Raquel needs to initiate informal conversations with exactly those families. At arrival time, she can communicate in positive ways by greeting the child and family and inviting them to her table. Then, she can offer an explanation about the activity, and ask the family what they do at home that is similar. The joint focus on the child's learning builds camaraderie and common purpose, and makes a later conversation about a child's difficulties in other areas a bit easier to have.

Establishing frequent, ongoing interactions helps families and teachers become comfortable with each other. Phone calls, e-mails, notes, home visits, conferences, and the daily connection at the beginning or end of school are some of the ways to keep in contact. With the vast array of possibilities and family configurations, cultures, and styles, cultivating family involvement is a complex and time-consuming task.

Some teachers are reluctant to involve families, and student teachers often feel ill-equipped to work with parents. Some think their job is to teach children, not

Figure 8.1
Kinds of family Involvement

From low to high levels of involvement, teachers [*in italics*] support families' involvement [in regular type] by scaffolding their participation.

Low--Moderate--High

Take leadership position
Support parent leaders

Participate weekly in classroom
Prepare, observe, and *support*

Create class newsletter
Jointly publish newsletter

Work in the office or library
Visit when parent is there

Help with school events
Send appreciation notes, assist parent

Collect or make materials for class
Have "helping hands" meetings

Participate in parent–teacher conferences
Plan conferences carefully, send follow-up note

Attend class or school events
Plan welcoming, send home appreciation notes

Visit the class or help with an activity
Invite to work alongside you; offer feasible tasks

Stay to observe on arrival or before departure
Be available and talk with them

parents. Many feel uncomfortable with someone watching them teach, fearing the same criticism families may feel when entering a classroom. Teachers who are not parents themselves worry that parents will dismiss them as inexperienced. Others are uncertain how to involve family members, seeing the class as the teacher's territory.

Overcoming these barriers is essential, because families are often hesitant and will withdraw if feeling unwelcome. Teachers are responsible for reaching out to families. If you are uncomfortable with parents and other family members, talk with your supervising teacher. Find out what teachers do to establish a relaxed rapport, and if you can, observe or participate in some of the activities that include families. Figure 8.2 describes 10 steps to creating positive family relationships.

The same skills for creating an inviting environment for children can be applied to families. Student teacher Ellen noticed this:

> In our room I feel that the "open-door policy" is fully operational and there is a sense of partnership between the parents and staff. Teachers are so warm and inviting that "the moms" feel both welcome and at ease, so they spend time in the place where their babies spend so much of *their* day, to get a feel for the surroundings. Moms also introduce themselves to each other, learn about the other babies, and frequently greet other babies by name. And I feel at the end of the day that this positive experience has rubbed off on me, too. I am starting to talk with them and add some things I've been seeing with their babies.

Strategies for Collaboration

All families are interested in the education and well-being of their children. Good family–school relationships encourage a strong partnership that benefits everyone. Student teachers are to follow the lead of their supervising teacher and the program's policies. Although there are many strategies for family–school collaboration, what follows are those that affect the student teacher.

- Respect families' religious, cultural, social, and ethnic backgrounds. Respect their right to disagree, and respect their privacy.
- Listen without judging. Accept parents as they are.
- Enhance the family's perception of their child by telling them something positive about their child's day.

See the top 10 tips for positive family–school relationships in Figure 8.2.

---

1. Treat each family with dignity and respect.
2. Listen and learn.
3. Have clear expectations of one another.
4. Share the responsibility and the power.
5. Understand each family's culture and values.
6. Encourage participation at any level.
7. Teach families what they need to know.
8. Keep informed: it works both ways.
9. Provide families with support.
10. Promote interactions between families.

Figure 8.2
Top 10 Tips for Positive Family–School Relationships

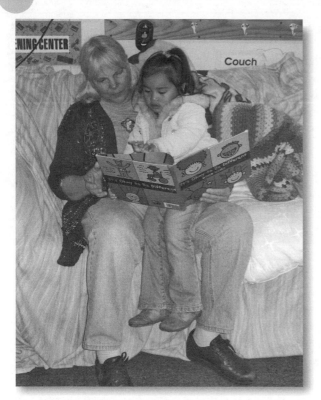

There are many ways for parents to be involved in their children's education.

Person-to-Person Communications

Some of the many informal ways that the school and the family maintain contact with each other were discussed in the previous section. More formal contacts are made through meetings, events, and conferences that allow for greater personal interaction between the teaching staff and the family. Student teacher involvement with families varies widely; ask your lead teacher how you should interact.

Meetings and Events

Parent meetings can have any number of functions. The teaching staff may develop workshop topics designed to teach parenting skills or introduce a home literacy program. These meetings are scheduled at times when working parents can participate and child care is often provided. Some meetings are social events, just for enjoyment, such as a potluck dinner at the school where parents can mingle with teachers and other families and take time to look through the classroom where their children spend so much time. Parent workdays are scheduled on weekends so that parents can share in the upkeep of the school and grounds. In some school settings, the parents are in charge of the fund-raising activities and plan festivals, auctions, and other activities to support the school's budget (see Figure 8.1). Ask your supervising teacher if you are expected to attend any of these events.

Conferences

Family–teacher conferences are the backbone of any good family–school relationship (Gordon & Browne, 2008) and one of the most important links for a successful partnership. They should be a regular part of the communication process in all early childhood programs. In some settings, a conference is scheduled soon after the child begins for the purpose of getting to know the child and family. Important information such as health issues and family concerns may be discussed. Later on, the family–teacher conferences focus on communicating teachers' observations and assessments of children, building mutual goals for them, and creating mutual trust and respect. Individual conferences, called by the family or the teacher, are used to share knowledge and information, resolve conflicts and problem solve together, and set goals for the child that can be reinforced at home and at school.

As a practicum student, you will probably not have to conduct a family–teacher conference on your own. It would be to your advantage if you ask to participate in

1. Be prepared, organized, and have a clear purpose. Use a written format to maintain focus. Ask for staff input and up-to-date examples. Ask parents to think about what they might want to talk about.
2. Put the family at ease with a warm welcome and thanks for attending. Help them relax by stating some of their child's strengths, citing examples. Complement them on something you have noticed, either with their own child or when in the classroom with other children. Be sensitive to any cultural differences that may arise.
3. Ask—don't tell. Begin with open-ended questions ("How is that new schedule working?" Or "Can you tell me more?"). Learn how to listen carefully to what family members say.
4. Keep the focus on the child. Keep the conversation based on mutual concerns and how to help each other. Make a plan of action together and discuss ways to follow through and stay in touch.
5. Write a brief report after the conference. Make a special note of the important issues that were discussed, solutions that were agreed on, and dates for checking progress.
6. Student and beginning teachers should find a good role model in a more experienced teacher who will act as a mentor. Ask a respected colleague to sit in on a conference with you and them critique with you afterward. Learn from experience.

Figure 8.3
Six Tips to Successful Family–Teacher Conferences
Successful conferences are a result of good planning and clear communications.

Source: From Gordon/Browne, *Beginnings and Beyond*, 7e. © 2008 Wadsworth, a part of Cengage Learning, Inc. Reproduced by permission. www.cengage.com/permissions.

one to experience this important teaching responsibility. Your supervising teacher can share the preparation process with you and ask the family for permission for you to attend. You will see firsthand how sharing information and observations of the child help draw the teacher and family into deeper discussion and dialogue.

To ensure a successful family–teacher conference, a quiet space, sufficient time, comfortable seating, and adequate planning are necessary. Figure 8.3 highlights some of the ways to make sure the family–teacher conference works well.

Conferencing with a family can be challenging, yet it offers some of the most personal insights into the life of the child. Following are ways to handle some of the difficult situations that may arise during a family–teacher conference.

When Difficulties Arise

When asked what was difficult about working with families, the group of student teachers clamored to respond:

"Parents are often so busy."

"They are so picky."

"Sometimes they aren't interested in what we tell them."

"They get defensive when you have to tell them about misbehavior."

"It seems like they're always two steps behind the child's development."

"Some are not open to teachers' views."

"They are uncomfortable with us."

"The teachers don't [speak] the same language as the parents."

"They expect you to teach just *their* child."

"They smother their child."

"Parents . . . gossip or complain to each other and don't tell us teachers."

"The teachers and families [may] come from different cultures."

"There just isn't enough time each day to really talk to each one individually."

When families withdraw, disagree, or have issues that we don't know about or understand, problems arise. As student teacher Denise puts it:

When working with parents it is important to remember where the person is coming from—not only on a daily basis, such as a rough day at work, but also from a cultural, personality, and family life standpoint. This takes time and patience and can be difficult at times.

We will discuss these difficulties in two areas: problems between the program and the child, and conflicts between the family and the program.

Problems Between the Program and the Child

Dealing with children's behavior is challenging (see Chapter 3)!

Even when it is typical, situations in the classroom can be problematic for teachers and families. "This week we had a serious situation in my room due to a bite," writes student teacher Ani.

One of our children bit another, and it left a big mark on the back of his "victim." It was very tense when I was giving the bitee's mother the report. Of course she was upset, but she asked me to promise that her child will never get another bite. I needed to tell her that I am unable to make that promise, although I can do many things to try to prevent it. Both parents came the next day and talked to the master teacher. The father asked to exclude the biter from the program. They even went to the director!

The student teacher made the appropriate response, yet because the family was still upset, they took their concerns to other authorities. It is important to realize that parents need to have a clear chain of command to use when dealing with problems about their child. After hearing for the third time the same response, the family came to understand that a bite did not constitute expulsion, but also that the program would offer a parent workshop about biting, and would work to shadow both children. "For a few weeks, the parents still looked upset, and they did not talk much with the staff," continues Ani. "But their child did not get bitten again; we treated the family with the same friendliness as before the incident, and slowly things warmed up."

A parent may walk into a situation, not understand the whole picture, and form a negative opinion. Tobi mentioned one child at her fieldwork site who hit other children and pulled hair. Teachers needed firm intervention, often putting themselves between the child and others, using a strong tone of voice in telling the child to stop. An arriving father was alarmed at the teacher's behavior, and told parents in the parking lot that the teachers were picking on the child. What could Tobi do when the next three parents came to her about the situation?

Parents may hear about a conflict from their child and want to be reassured that it was handled ethically and with respect for the child's self-worth.

For ethical reasons (see Chapter 2 and NAEYC's Code of Ethical Conduct) Tobi needed to respect the dignity of each individual and keep professional confidentiality by not talking about the child in question. At the same time, she could explain to those concerned parents that each child develops and learns social skills in unique ways. Children whose home language differs from what is used in the classroom need clear nonverbal communication. Ani can also show them the picture cards she keeps with her that help all children understand and start to communicate their wishes in nonviolent ways.

Delivering complaints or bad news is one of the most difficult kinds of communication for most of us. Families are sensitive to how teachers tell them about their children. "If a professional says, 'in my professional opinion,' a parent hears 'This is what I'm telling you to do, and I have the power to say so.'" (Tomko, 2005). When you deliver information that is hard to receive, try to think through what you want to say and not have the conversation occur in an intense or public manner. "Gunther had some problems at group time today," student teacher Fadwa tells his uncle before he greets the child. "I know you two need to get home, but do you have a few minutes now, or would you rather talk on the telephone this evening?" The message is clear and complete, but does allow Uncle Dioli to decide on the time and place for the conversation. He decides to step outside and hear Fadwa describe how Gunther kept playing with Jessica's braids and had to be moved. Her calm and honest description helps both adults discuss the situation.

Making professional referrals is one of the toughest issues. Student teachers new to their practicum setting or in an assistant position are unlikely to be in this position. However, it is important to note that this is an especially delicate situation. As with any conflict, a systematic problem-solving approach is called for (see Chapter 7). In addition, it is critical that teachers have specific anecdotes and evidence and do not pass judgment on what they hear. It is likely that parents will feel upset; try to accept how they feel and what they say without getting defensive. Every so often, notes Stone (2001), a teacher faces a child

> so troubled, so embattled by circumstance that he cannot find a way to live with others in the classroom. If, after an enormous effort along with ongoing consulta-tion with his family, this child is unable to make progress, the teacher may have to suggest referral not only for special help but for placement in a different setting. The hope is that the child and family will find the help that is so urgently needed. This can be a difficult and sad time for everyone. However, the concern for the health and safety of all the children in the class must be first above all. (p. 51)

Conflicts Between the Family and the Program

Families sometimes have a disagreement about the program, feel uncomfortable about differences with the staff, or do not follow policy and procedures. "No matter how nice a teacher is or how much she reaches out to families, there will inevitably be time when she misunderstands a parent or a parent misunderstands her" (Diffily, 2004). Two common areas of conflict are cultural differences and policy disagreements.

Cultural differences occur frequently in early childhood programs. "Culture includes ethnicity, racial identity, economic level, family structure, language, and religious and political beliefs" (NAEYC, 2005); with that complexity, it is likely that there will differences between the teaching staff and families. It is not possible to describe here all the many cultural values and habits of every family or of each teacher. However, teachers need to be aware of their own cultures, gain an under-standing of other cultures, and learn about the particular constellation of the life habits, traditions, and beliefs of the particular families in their current center.

> **Student teacher Ping:** Gina is almost 3 years old, and I don't know what to do. She gets into a power struggle every day when her father comes to pick her up. It is so disrespectful, but he does nothing. It looks like he lets her walk all over him, but won't take any suggestions or offers of help from me.
>
> **Parent Gil:** I am tired of Gina's teacher. She hovers over Gina and me when-ever I come to pick her up, which isn't that often because I get her only every other weekend. I wish she'd just back off and give us some space; eventually Gina will get tired of running around and then I'll just sweep her up and get out of there.

Family structure and different cultural expectations make this conflict uncomfortable for both teacher and parent. If Ping thinks further about her own upbringing (see the first section of this chapter), she may see that there are many ways to interact and raise children. Finding out more about joint custody challenges may also help her understand Gina's father.

Differences in school culture also occur. Gordon found himself in a conflict with a parent when she decided to stay for his small-group activity:

> The mom came in and started directing her child, trying to help her get the "right answers." It really changed the dynamic of the activity and threw me off course. She began to ask me exactly what we were doing—in this case, identifying the letter names of musical notes on the scale. She then turned to the small group of five kids and showed one of them "the mistakes" on her little wipe-off board. I casually explained to her that they didn't have to get it right, and that the idea was not to get all (or any!) of the notes correctly identified, but rather to get the kids familiar with what notes look like and that the sounds have names like letters of the alphabet. She got real quiet, and I was wondering if I was out of place telling her that. When I asked my mentor teacher, she told me it was all right to let the mom know what I was and wasn't trying to do, but also that the mom has three kids in elementary school. Oh, she's kind of into that study-test-grade mindset!

Early childhood educators should remember that they, too, have a school culture that not all families know, understand, or even agree with.

Policy disagreement is another area of conflict between families and programs. Figure 8.4 shows a handbook introduction that outlines the center's philosophy and approach to families. The handbook also lists guidelines for how to handle arrival and departure, clothing, health and safety, billing, and complaints. It is important for families to have this information; still, it is unrealistic to assume that the handbook is as well known to families as it should be to teachers.

As you read the My Reaction feature think about what your center policy is and how you might handle the situation.

Our policies and practices are designed to:

Create a place where everyone feels welcome anytime and is respected.

Have classrooms that reflect and celebrate the life of every child's family.

Respect the cultural, racial, and linguistic diversity of the children and their families.

Understand, respect, and support the values and goals of each family.

Communicate with parents in positive ways and with confidentiality.

Help parents understand and appreciate the value of developmentally appropriate programs.

Encourage parent participation in the classroom.

Invite parent involvement in the development of policies and curriculum that are culturally sensitive.

Help strengthen the bond between child and parents.

Provide community resources and/or professional services that support families.

Figure 8.4
A Family Handbook: Our Commitment to You

A family handbook is a helpful guide to a center's policies and procedures, and student teachers should be familiar with its contents.

My Reaction

"Megan's Blanket"

For over a week, the teachers at our child care center were having trouble getting 2½-year-old Megan to take a nap. Megan was usually good about finding a book to look at and getting on her cot and falling asleep quickly. But that all stopped and nothing the teachers did seemed to make a difference. Megan was told she could "just rest" and not sleep. That didn't work. She was told she could keep the book with her during her rest and that didn't work either. One of the teachers sat by Megan's cot, rubbing her back to help her relax and go to sleep. That didn't work either.

The head teacher told Megan's father when he picked up Megan about their difficulty with napping. The next day, he came back and asked if it would be okay for Megan to bring a favorite blanket to school with her to use at naptime. He was concerned about the school policy of not bringing special things from home. The teacher told him it would be fine, so he went out to the car and brought in her blanket. Megan put it in her cubby and ran off to play. Megan sleeps well at naptime again.

—ANDY

Working with families is a complicated and essential part of being an early childhood professional. Whether you are working in a family child care home, providing center-based care, or working with school-age children, you are teaching both the child and the family. In the following "Lessons from the Field," the director of a parent co-op nursery school offers her suggestions for successful parent-school relations.

lessons from the field

"Working with Families: The More, the Better"

by Jeanne Lindberg

Director-Teacher, United Methodist Co-op Nursery School, Burlingame, CA

Children and Parents. Our school is a parent co-operative. That means the parents participate both in the classroom and in the operation of the school. Because the parents are often on-site, it is easy to get to know them. If you only see the parents at drop-off and pick-up times, it is no doubt more difficult to establish a relationship. Still, it is well worth the extra effort. One of the most important things you can do for the success of your program is to work with children in the context of their families.

Communication. Informal, in-person interchanges are probably the best ways to communicate, but time is limited for that. Drop-off and pick-up are busy times. Be sure to make some contact—a few words about the day, what is happening in their lives, or even just warm eye contact and a wave from across the room are valuable bits of communication.

Written communication is also important. We put out a monthly school-wide newsletter and each teacher writes a monthly class bulletin. E-mail makes communication a lot easier. The information gets to everyone and e-mail allows private communication with individual parents. Of course, phone calls are still sometimes necessary and appreciated. Remember to communicate positive things as well as negative. You don't want parents cringing when they get a call from you!

Parent conferences are a good way to ensure that each family has set time aside to talk with you about their child. A little advance planning is important. You want to make sure the time is well-spent. The most important thing is to establish an atmosphere of partnership with the parents—you are working together for the good of their child.

Families need to be able to trust you, not only with the care of their child, but also with information about their families that they may not want others to know. If a parent confides in you, remember that information is confidential. Be careful how and why you share it with other staff members.

Attitude. The regard you have for children—the respect and appreciation of each child's unique qualities—is the same regard you should have for parents. Sometimes this can be harder with parents because adults are usually not as open as children. Some people are slow-to-warm by nature. Be patient. You are the one who will have to be open. Guard against being defensive. Assume that they will like you. The most valuable tool you have is your own attitude.

Train yourself to put aside the all-too-human tendency to judge others. After all, we cannot know what each person's life is really like. We can try to see things from what we imagine is their perspective, but we can never really know. I have learned that, despite appearances, no one's life is trouble-free. Try to truly appreciate the good you see in each person. It will be reflected back to you.

Dealing with Problems. If you have a problem with a parent, or they have a problem with you, first of all examine your own attitude and then try to see things from their perspective. People need to be heard, especially if they are upset; so be sure to look in their eyes and listen carefully for their feelings as well as their words. While you are listening, reflect on something positive about that person. Acknowledge their feelings and take the time to think carefully before responding. You may be amazed by the creative solutions and the increased understanding that can result from such conversations. There is very seldom just one right way to do things—we do not need to be rigid in our expectations regarding families.

Appreciation. A mutual appreciation for the talents and contributions of all the members is what makes a community strong. Each person truly does have something important to contribute. You need to be on the lookout for it. Once you get to know the families in your program, you will be delighted by what they have to offer.

Practicum Activity

How is your center family-friendly? Ask your supervising teacher to list the ways that the program encourages family involvement. Add your own ideas to that list, and bring it to your college class.

Journaling Assignment

What are my feelings about working with families? What parent(s) am I most comfortable with and why? What families do I have difficulties with and why? What do I hope to learn that will help me feel more comfortable and more effective?

Resources

Baker, A. C., and Manfredi-Petitt, L. A. (2004). *Relationships, the heart of quality care*. Washington, DC: National Association for the Education of Young Children.

Baumrind, D. (1971). Current patterns of parental authority. *Developmental Psychology Monograph*, 4(1, Pt. 2).

Berk, L. (2003). *Child development*. Boston: Allyn & Bacon.

Bradley, J., & Kibera, P. (2007). Closing the gap: Culture and the promotion of inclusion in child care. In D. Koralek (Ed.), *Spotlight on young children and families*. Washington, DC: National Association for the Education of Young Children.

Brazelton, T. B., & Sparrow, J. D. (2001). Touchpoints: Three to six. Cambridge, MA: Perseus Books Group.

Diffily, D. (2004). *Teachers and families working together*. Boston: Allyn & Bacon/Pearson.

Galinsky, E. (1987). *Between generations*. Reading, MA: Addison-Wesley.

Gordon, A., & Browne, K.(2008). *Beginnings and beyond: Foundations in early childhood education* (7th ed.). Clifton Park, NY: Thomson Delmar Learning.

Hamner, T., & Turner, P. (1996). *Parenting in a contemporary society*. Boston: Allyn & Bacon.

Hyun, E. (1998). *Making sense of developmentally and culturally appropriate practice (DCAP) in early childhood education*. New York: Peter Lang.

Katz, L.G. (1980). Mothering and teaching—Some significant distinctions. In L. G. Katz (Ed.), *Current topics in early childhood education*. (Vol. 3). Norwood, NJ: Ablex.

Katz, L. G. (1995). *Talks with teachers of young children: A collection*. Norwood, NJ: Ablex.

Lane, M. B., & Signer, S. (1996). *Infant/toddler caregiving: A guide to creating partnerships with parents*. Sacramento: California Department of Education.

Leading Edge. (1999, December). *National TeleConference*, 1999.

National Association for the Education of Young Children. (2005). *Code of ethical conduct*. Washington, DC: Author.

Stone, J. G. (2001). *Building classroom community: The early childhood teacher's role*. Washington, DC: National Association for the Education of Young Children.

Tomko, C. T. (2005). *When a professional says* . . . Retrieved from http://www.kidstogether.org

Web Sites

Families and Work Institute
www.familiesandwork.org

National Coalition for Parent Involvement in Education
www.ncpie.org

National Parent–Teacher Association
www.pta.org

Parents without Partners
www.parentswithoutpartners.org

Partnership for Family Involvement in Education
www.pfie.ed.gov

Partnership for Learning
www.partnershipforlearning.org

chapter 9

The Dynamics of Diversity

Reflections on Diversity

The middle-aged White woman with a bachelor's degree and teaching certificate is no longer the prototype for today's early childhood teacher. Although it is true that women make up most of the workforce in early education, their race and ethnicity, age, and educational level have changed dramatically. The same is true for the children you teach. Classrooms are filled with a "salad bowl" of children (Gonzalez-Mena, 2005), each a wonderfully diverse flavor which, when added to the whole, creates something unique.

Today's Context

Twenty-first-century teachers are working across cultures with children, their families, and teammates in an early childhood setting. No matter what culture you were raised in, you will need to adapt to others with diverse backgrounds. Census reports (U.S. Census Bureau, 2006) indicate that 13% of people living in the United States were foreign born and that 20% of the population spoke a language other than English at home. Other changes in the American scene bring greater diversity to the population as well. Parents who are gay or lesbian, the mandated inclusion of children with a variety of disabilities, and the influx of world religions add to the classroom "salad bowl."

This chapter focuses on many facets of diversity to help student teachers achieve a level of competence in working with children and families whose backgrounds and culture may be different from their own. Our intention is to shift the focus from just cultural diversity to that of *human* diversity. To do so requires responding to differences with a broad viewpoint, incorporating what we know about the wide range of human experience as it is expressed in children and in families.

To reflect on diversity means making a second paradigm shift, this time in our identity as teachers. Teachers are often considered "experts" in education, but to

Teachers, like children, come in a variety of sizes, shapes, colors, genders, and ages.

work in today's diverse classrooms, teachers must become learners, a concept stressed throughout this text. We have to redefine the nature of teaching and learn to say "I don't know." Our sources of information will be the children, their families, colleagues, the media, and the Internet. All information will need to be screened for bias and stereotypes.

The aim of this chapter is to explore the many aspects of diversity—culture, race and ethnicity, gender, religion, age, ability, language, social class and income, and temperament—as components that influence children's behavior and identity. As a teacher, you will be able to go forward in your own learning as you work with diverse children. A working knowledge of the issues facing the families you teach is an important element in creating a responsive and inclusive environment.

Culture

The blueprint for human development is the culture in which a person is raised. Gonzales-Mena (2005) suggests looking at culture as a framework that is influenced by race, gender, ability, social class, status, income, sexual orientation, religion, and age. Like growth and development in the whole child, cultures are integrated systems that must be viewed in their entirety, not discrete and isolated parts. Change in

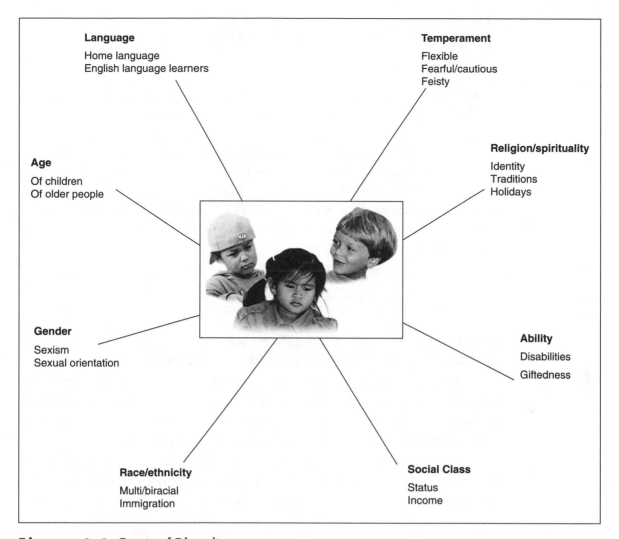

F i g u r e 9.1 Facets of Diversity
The components of human diversity interact and influence children's well-being, behavior, attitudes, and growth.

one component will affect the rest of the system (Banks, 2001). Figure 9.1 illustrates the components that interact to influence who we are. In the following sections, each of these elements will be discussed individually.

Culture is a set of rules we learn from birth that tell us how to behave in ways that are similar to our family and larger community. Phillips (1995) has defined culture and its influence on development extensively, and the following segment reflects her work. Cultural rules dictate our behavior—for instance, whether we bow or shake hands when greeting someone, or what we feed our children. The rules are sometimes articulated ("Don't put your elbows on the table when you eat") and often demonstrated (men holding doors open for women).

Depending on the family in which you grew up, you may behave according to rules from more than one culture. A Japanese mother and African American father each bring their own cultural rules to their family. If they raise their children in London or Los Angeles, a third set of cultural rules may be added. Often cultures

---

My Reaction

"A First Impression"

My first impression of the school was that there were different cultures which I love greatly! The staff were all so kind. I noticed that all the teachers were either Latin descent or Caucasian but the supervisor was African American. I thought, "How am I going to fit in?" I would be the only African/Filipino teacher there; will the children be scared? But then I said to myself, I am going to be a beautiful addition to the preschool because of my love for children and my hardworking ability. My main focus is to be the best observer, learner, and teacher I could be! I look forward now to start working with the children at the site and experience new teaching skills!

—RAQUEL

---

share the same rules yet exhibit different practices. People may speak the same language, for instance, but have widely different child-rearing views.

The rules governing our behavior are culture-bound, but not everyone maintains the rules to the same degree. Some people are immersed in their culture and others have a lesser degree of involvement. This may explain why a friend of yours who is Italian may not know anything about cooking a good pasta sauce.

Culture is shaped by the group and is passed down from one generation to another. We all develop within a cultural context, exhibiting behaviors appropriate to that cultural group. What cultural experiences do you remember that are important to your family? In "My Reaction" above, a student teacher reflects on her cultural contributions to her teaching.

The Many Facets of Diversity

As humans, we are deeply influenced by the cultural socialization we experienced and our attitudes and behavior reflect the values we were taught. As educators, we work in institutions that are dedicated to educating each individual child and also helping all children learn to live together.

As a developing professional, you know that children are best understood in the context of their families, and that you pledge to adhere to a code of ethical conduct (see Chapter 2) to respect the dignity and worth of each family. The following components of culture challenge teachers in their relationships with children and families.

Race and Ethnicity

Race and ethnicity, as used in this text, refer to a shared common ancestry, history, traditions, behavioral characteristics, culture, and a sense of identification. Some social scientists say that race is designated by genetic heritage (Banks, 2001), whereas some have other views (Phillips, 1995).

The ethnic/racial diversity in the United States has changed dramatically over the past decade. Between 2000 and 2005, the Hispanic population increased 21%, the Asian population grew by 20%, Pacific Islanders by 12%, and the Black population by 6%, while the White population decreased. Those who claim two or more races increased by 17% (U.S. Census Bureau, 2005) Unlike the great European immigration pattern of 100 years ago, most of the recent immigrants are from Asia and South and Central America.

For America's teachers these demographic changes have several implications. There will be more cultures to learn about in order to gain a sense of a family's cultural values. There are still problems of racial bias that impact children and families of color. We know that as early as 2 years of age children notice physical differences, by 4 years they may have a sense of their ethnic identity, and by primary school they begin to assess value to different cultural groups (Trawick-Smith, 2006). Teachers need to develop strategies for ensuring that all children receive an equal and bias-free education. Later in this chapter (as referred to in Chapter 6) you will learn about the antibias curriculum that will introduce you to some of the techniques you can use to fight bias.

Gender

The behavior of males and females is influenced by culture and every culture has its own gender stereotypes (Trawick-Smith, 2006). By the time children are in preschool, they begin to acquire and understand their gender identity and in the early elementary years children have a sense that certain behaviors and attitudes are expected of them because they are boys or girls. It is not uncommon to hear children say "You can't play ball—you're a girl" or "Boys don't cook." Erasing sexual stereotypes is not simply a matter of having books that show boys cooking or helping girls gain a place in the playground. You must also look at family patterns of gender roles and the cultural values that support the behavior.

Many educational settings continue to reflect gender stereotypes in their choice of books and literature, toys, displays of photographs and pictures, and their acceptance of rigid role definitions. Teachers can expand children's experiences in more equitable learning activities that help eliminate stereotypes. Group games, activities, and projects can break down gender barriers by encouraging mixed-gender play and positive interactions between boys and girls. It is a more complex task to work with families around gender stereotyping; ask your supervising teacher about what your program does to address gender bias.

For children of gay and lesbian parents, it is important to ensure a safe environment where family structure and sexual orientation is respected. Clay (2004) describes four areas of concern for gay and lesbian parents. They want (1) emotional safety from homophobia; (2) visible diversity throughout the school environment so that their child is not considered "unique"; (3) staff who are comfortable with and have experience with gay and lesbian people; and (4) to feel part of the whole community, not be treated as "outsiders." Gay and lesbian parents also feel that adoption issues are more critical to them than issues of sexual orientation. It is only through open, honest, and trusting relationships with families that teachers can learn what families need most from the school experience.

Language

Maintaining their home language is an important aspect of family culture and identity. Respecting home languages in the school setting enhances family pride in their unique heritage.

There are several communication challenges with a multilinguistic clientele. Some families may be fluent in both English and their native language, whereas others know little or no English. Building bridges to cross the language barrier will help families feel less isolated and establish a relationship of equality and respect. Using translators in communicating verbally and in print tells families that you want to involve them in their children's education.

For children whose first language is not English, the situation can be complicated. Families vary in their desire for how much home language and English they want their children to hear and use. Find out the home languages of the children in your care, and learn some key words and phrases (see the "Putting Diversity into Action" section). This way you can offer children reassurance that they will be understood, and demonstrate your appreciation of what they already know well.

The NAEYC (1995) position statement *Responding to Linguistic and Cultural Diversity—Recommendations for Effective Early Childhood Education* states that for optimal development, "educators must accept the legitimacy of children's home language," and further recommends that early childhood programs recruit teachers who are trained in languages other than English.

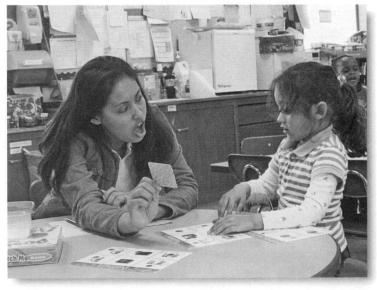
Preserving a child's home language is important.

Abilities

Children with special needs come in all sizes, colors, and shapes, and their disabilities cover a wide range of characteristics. There are two types of children with special needs: those who have some sort of disability and those who are gifted. Allen and Cowdery (2005) suggest that children are considered disabled if their normal growth and development is delayed, abnormal, or severely affected in

Speech and language: hearing impairment, stuttering, articulation difficulty, cleft palate, chronic voice disorders, learning disabilities

Physical-motor: visual impairment, blindness, perceptual motor deficits, cerebral palsy, spina bifida, loss of limbs, muscular dystrophy

Intellectual: cognitive delays, brain injury or dysfunction, dyslexia, autism, Asperger syndrome, learning disabilities

Social-emotional: self-destructive behavior, severe withdrawal, dangerous aggression toward self and others, moodiness, lack of communication, tantrums, attention-deficit hyperactivity disorder (ADHD), severe anxiety, depression, phobias

Health impairments: severe asthma, epilepsy, congenital heart defects, severe anemia, malnutrition, diabetes, tuberculosis, cystic fibrosis, Down syndrome, sickle-cell amenia, Tay-Sachs disease, AIDS

Specific learning disabilities: difficulty with language use and acquisition, perceptual handicaps, brain injury, minimal brain dysfunction, dyslexia, developmental aphasia

Figure 9.2
Disabilities That Teachers May Encounter
These disabilities may range from mild to severe and vary widely with individual children.

Source: From Gordon/Browne. *Beginnings and Beyond,* 7e. © 2008 Wadsworth, a part of Cengage Learning, Inc. Reproduced by permission. www.cengage.com/permissions.

their mental, social, emotional, physical, and social developmental domains. A gifted student is one who has an exceptional ability in one or more areas of development.

The number of programs that enroll children with disabilities has risen dramatically due to federal legislation that mandates equal educational opportunities for children with disabilities (P.L. 94-142 and P.L. 99-457; www.ideapractices.org). From infancy through age 21 people with disabilities are included in regular classrooms whenever possible, in the least restrictive environment, and with an individualized plan (see the following text).

As an early childhood educator you will meet and teach children with a variety of disabilities. Figure 9.2 lists some of the conditions you may experience.

Hopefully, you have had a course about children with special needs as you prepare to teach in the early childhood field. Your primary concern as a teacher is to plan programs that are adaptable to a wide range of developmental differences of the children in the class. In Chapter 6, Figure 6.6 is an example of how to adapt an art project for children with special needs.

There are two important aspects about working with children with special needs. The first is about language: *Put children first.* As you speak or write about a child with a disability, you mention the child, followed by the specific disorder. For example, you say "Tito, a *child with* Down syndrome, is in my class," not "Tito is a Down syndrome child." It will take practice to speak of a *child who is blind* rather than a blind child. The difference may be subtle but critical to enhancing a child's self-respect. Putting the child first helps you remember that children are defined by an abundance of adjectives, not by their abilities.

The second key factor is to remember the phrase *more alike than different.* The children are more like normally developing children than they are different from them. You will want to look at the similarities children with special needs have with other children, not just at their specific disability. In the Lessons from

The Dynamics of Diversity

the Field article at the end of the chapter, mentor teacher Elaine Francisco describes this factor in personal terms.

Working with families whose children have special needs can be challenging. Your initial role may be to help identify areas of concern through observations and assessments (see Chapter 4). In many cases, the family will have an individualized family service plan (IFSP) if their child is less than 3 years of age, or an individualized education plan (IEP) if their child is older than 3. The two plans are mandated by law to help families and specialists work together to identify priorities, resources, and concerns, and to become the guidelines for providing appropriate intervention services (Allen & Cowdery, 2005). You may also be part of a team of teachers who implement the plan and are links between classroom practice and treatment recommendations.

Religion or Spirituality

Along with other cultural values, it is important for teachers to respect the religious heritage and customs of children and their families. Immigration patterns have brought increasingly diverse models of religious expression into communities and classrooms today.

Saxton (2004) notes that some people may feel a sense of identification within a community of faith more than their membership in a racial or ethnic group. We know that children are spiritual beings and will talk about God, a brother's bar mitzvah, or their grandmother's hijab anytime with their teachers. Student teachers often wonder how to respond to children's comments and questions. For example, what should student teacher Sylvia do when Joseph tells her, "If you don't go to church, you can't go to heaven." Her response should be twofold: First, she is mindful of her school's policy about the separation of church and state, so she refrains from speaking about church doctrine. Second, she is respectful, so she shows interest in what he is sharing by asking him some questions, such as when do you go there and who goes with you.

Holidays often bring religious differences to light because there is great diversity in what holidays and celebrations are important to different religious groups. If these are celebrated in the classroom, the question becomes one of excluding children because of their families' religious beliefs or not celebrating holidays at all. How is this handled in the setting where you practice teach?

Age

Issues around ageism primarily relate to older people. The media often stereotypes older people as physically and mentally inferior, useless, and unwanted (Wolpert, 2005). This picture of our aging population is unfortunate, especially at a time when many senior citizens are enjoying full and useful lives for a very long time. Older people do face issues of fixed incomes and declining health, but that should not prevent a more equitable portrayal of their strengths and level of activity. Many seniors find new careers after retirement and are involved in extensive volunteer work within their communities.

Wolpert (2005) notes that social injustice is the real cause of discrimination of older individuals. Poverty is a factor, as are discrimination policies such as enforced retirement at a certain age. The same type of bias surrounding people with disabilities also applies to older people who use wheelchairs, canes, or walkers. Children need models of older citizens who display the whole range of human abilities and who delight in sharing their lives with people of all ages.

Social Class, Status, or Income

A family's socioeconomic status is determined by level of education, income, place of residence, and the occupation of the primary wage earners (Trawick-Smith, 2006). Families of wealth and families of poverty come to school with different perspectives, needs, and resources. For children raised in poverty, issues of health and nutrition are of concern. Working with families of privilege raises different issues. For example, these children may be developing a sense of superiority and entitlement, or have a strong focus on material things.

Derman-Sparks, Ramsey, and Olsen Edwards (2006) suggest some ways teachers can address the inequalities of class distinctions:

- Make frequent observations about how children are identifying themselves; use self-portraits to stimulate conversation.

- Note which activities children prefer and/or avoid to discover more about their self-image.

- Listen to children's conversations as they play to ascertain any feelings they may have about race and ethnicity of themselves or others; pay close attention to any sense of superiority or entitlement.

- Check to see if the social or racial/ethnic differences influence children's choice of friends.

- Identify the overall tone of the classroom to see if children are sensitive, empathetic, inclusive, negative, or full of conflict.

Through these and other strategies you will uncover a lot of information about how children see themselves and others. The judicious use of curriculum, materials, and activities will help them understand their own identities and appreciate the differences in other people.

Temperament

From birth, a child's temperamental characteristics are observable through their attention span, general mood and activity level, and the regularity of their routines such as eating, sleeping, and digestion. Researchers Thomas and Chess (1977) identified nine characteristics of temperaments and noted that many children have one of three types: easy, slow-to-warm, and difficult. Today they are often referred to as follows:

1. The *flexible* child (about 40% of all children) is adaptable, optimistic, cheerful, and easily trained in eating, sleeping, and toileting; has mild reactions to frustration.

2. The *fearful* child (about 15%) seems shy and although uncomfortable with new situations, adapts slowly if allowed to observe and watch; needs to go at own pace and expresses negative mood slowly.

3. The *feisty* child (about 10%) is the opposite of the flexible child with irregular sleeping and eating habits; is fussy about new situations; is often disagreeable, prone to temper tantrums, and adapts slowly.

As you come to know and understand the diverse reactions of the children you teach, you will gain insights into their behavior and find strategies that suit their innate temperament.

Putting Diversity into Action

To help children develop a solid sense of self, teachers need to incorporate the kaleidoscope of identities they bring into the classroom. Putting diversity into action can be done, and done well (see Figure 9.3).

Becoming Competent

Many of us grew up with the contradictions of race, gender, and class. We may have been segregated from people with differing abilities, or raised with biases about differing languages or religious practices. Many of us grew up hearing statements that stereotyped people by their age or even temperament, often in negative tones.

Looking Within. To become sensitive to issues of diversity, student teachers start by looking within. You are developing a teaching style and need to understand your own roots and habits first. At the same time, your style evolves over many

Figure 9.3
Top 10 Strategies for Addressing Diversity

1. It begins with me.
2. Realize that there is not only one best or right way.
3. Move from an "either/or" to a "both/and" perspective.
4. Foster a climate of acceptance.
5. Recognize bias in yourself, others, and institutions.
6. Become competent in issues of diversity.
7. Create inclusive classrooms and programs.
8. Expand your teaching strategies.
9. Promote equity in teaching teams.
10. Invite families into the process.

1. What is your ethnic group or cultural identity? What has it meant to belong to your ethnic group?
2. What are your earliest images of color and race?
3. Have you ever had the experience of feeling different? If so, what was your first experience?
4. Have you ever experienced a feeling of powerlessness in relation to your ethnic, class, gender, or sexual identity? What was it like?
5. What values, history, or traditions of your group identities have been sources of strength?

Figure 9.4
Uncover Your Beliefs
When putting diversity into action, start with yourself.

years; As you gain experience, you will form your own unique personal and professional approach (Gordon & Browne, 1996). Build on solid ground by examining your own attitudes; only then can you proceed. You can add your experience to new knowledge and apply what you are learning. Start by asking yourself the questions shown in Figure 9.4.

Moreover, self-awareness begins with an exploration of your own background and beginnings. "Issues such as place of origin, time of immigration, reasons for immigration, languages(s) spoken, and the place of the family's first settlement in the United States all help define one's own cultural heritage" (Lynch & Hanson, 1995, p. 37). The second step is to examine some of the values, behaviors, beliefs, and customs in your own cultural heritage. As student teacher Ellyn relates:

I was thinking about my own English and Danish background when I was reading to the children in the center from a book of nursery rhymes. Cutting off the three blind mice's tails with a carving knife! How horridly cruel—what were my relatives thinking? What kind of life did they live that mice were so threatening? I start to catch myself, when I sing a song to one of the babies, "Are these lyrics OK? What exactly is a "Knick-knack" or "Paddy-whack"? Is this a slam against the Irish? And how does this connect to giving a dog a bone?

Moreover, remember that you bring so much to your program in yourself. Mentor teacher Venecia offered this example:

Charlene was different than anyone I'd known, with a Filipino and Chinese cultural background. Her relationships with the other staff and children fit in right away. Maybe this was because the children and staff had diverse cultural backgrounds as well. As a Venezuelan and a seasoned teacher, I had certain ideas about things. My relationship with Charlene helped me learn to step back and observe more closely how Charlene spoke to and played with children and how she re-directed any negative behaviors that might have occurred. I learned new ways for myself!

Gaining Knowledge. Student teaching and becoming culturally competent go hand-in-hand. Through your own cultural exploration you are finding out the impact that culture has on the individual. Look for cultural information about others; there is an abundance of material about diversity and difference in our field (see the Resources at the end of the chapter). There is not only one right way to do things. The world in which you were born is only one model of reality: Rather than seeing things as "either my way *or* not," think about adding another way so that your thinking becomes both yours and another's. Lynch and Hanson (1995) outline four effective ways to learn about other cultures:

1. Learning through studying and reading about the culture

2. Talking and working with individuals from the culture who can act as cultural guides or mediators

3. Participating in the daily life of another culture

4. Learning the language of the other culture

Applying What I Learn. Communicating across cultures is challenging. We interpret the meaning of behavior based on our own culture. Each of us has a set of familiar body language, facial expressions, and voice tone that convey a variety of messages to us. Others, however, may see things differently:

> I once sat by a window looking out across the street at a man who was acting very strange. . . . He was making extraordinary gestures and facial expressions. . . . The words coming out of his mouth were in a language I didn't understand. . . . I had decided he was crazy and had begun to feel afraid when finally I stood up and saw the whole picture. There at the man's heels was a dog. Immediately everything made sense. Aha, he's training a dog. (Gonzalez-Mena, 2005, p. 31)

Applying what we learn can be difficult; learning the meaning of behavior from other perspectives will help keep biases in check and expand our own view of the world.

For example, nonverbal communication is important to observe and act on with very young children, who are not yet fluent in verbal language. What about immigrant families in your care? "Nonverbal communication is culturally based, so what is admirable by U.S. standards may be considered rude in your first culture"(Rusch, 2001). Some examples of nonverbal behavior that is culturally accepted elsewhere are burping, not making eye contact, and bowing instead of handshaking. How can you become more "fluent" yourself in the nonverbal ways of your children and connect to them? Student teacher Monica describes what it takes to apply what you learn:

> How I wish I could communicate in other languages! I find that I try to be aware of the limitations when "talking" with English learners and I use lots of gestures and lots of full sentences. Somehow that is working; I get kids nodding their heads that they understand. Today I had the greatest experience when a young boy who speaks only Cambodian made it a point to run to the fence as I walked by to a college class. He was waving and smiling and gesturing and saying goodbye in English. It has been 4 weeks of being there for him, and smiling and gesturing and talking with his parents and getting him included in activities with others. I felt so high from his running across the playground and waving and speaking to me. I wish I had a photo to match the mental picture I will always carry!

Using what you have learned helps you become culturally competent. Be aware, however, that culture is only one aspect of personal identity. Proceed with caution as you learn new ways of cross-cultural communication. Acknowledging and respecting differences rather than minimizing them will go a long way.

Learning to REACH. It is likely that today's children in the world of child care are learning diversity firsthand, differently than many of their teachers did. So it is important that their teachers see diversity in its many forms and develop cross-cultural competence. Figure 9.5 offers a way student teachers can reach for answers.

R	**React/*Reaccionar***	Recognize your initial feelings and thoughts about the situation.
E	**Examine/*Examinar***	Think about your reactions. Identify any beliefs you hold that may be affecting your response. Are there any biases that might be shaping your feelings and thoughts?
A	**Ask/*Preguntar***	Look for multiple perspectives. Look for other perspectives to expand and deepen your own understanding.
C	**Consider/*Considerar***	Generate multiple strategies. Look deeply into the situation and explore those strategies that help address the situation in ways that are culturally and linguistically respectful of others and have the best potential for positive results.
H	**Handle/*Manejar***	Look at the situation with respect and honor. Implement the strategies that you select, being vigilant of the reactions of others in order to make adjustments to your approach when warranted.

Figure 9.5
Reach/Alcanzar

Follow a process for creating dialogue, reflection, and action, and for addressing the many challenges we face in diversity work.

Source: From *Reaching for Answers: Forum on Diversity in Early Childhood Education,* by BANDTEC (Bay Area Network for Diversity Training: Building Equity and Social Justice for Children and Families), 2006, San Mateo, CA: San Mateo County Office of Education. Used with permission.

Recognizing Bias

A second step in cultural competence is recognizing bias in ourselves and others, and taking appropriate action. This is a crucial aspect of the *antibias curriculum* (described in Chapter 6) and is essential to the process of becoming a competent educator.

> The goal of anti-bias work is inclusion, not exclusion, self-esteem for all, empathy, and activism in the face of injustice. These goals were developed because there is ample evidence of the early formation of bias in young children. We think these goals are also needed to address the inequities that still exist in our field. Early childhood educators can't always walk our talk. (Carter & Curtis, 1994, p. 93)

If we start seeing the meaning of diversity, we need to examination our own biases. We can then see bias in others, listen to voices traditionally silenced, and incorporate what we learn into our teaching.

Personal Biases. Sometimes we surprise ourselves. Teaching young children brings us face-to-face with new experiences and feelings. Kate writes:

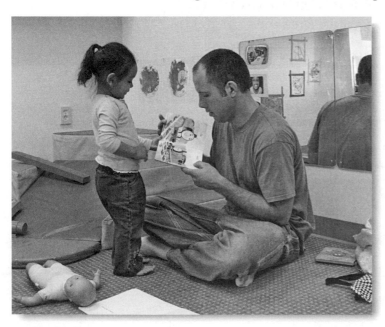

Understanding diversity means getting to know the child.

As a new teacher in a university lab school, I was nervous but excited about teaching there. This school incorporated children with special needs, which was new for me, but I was looking forward to being in a place that welcomed everyone. One day Jonathan—one of the youngest in our room—was toddling into the bathroom; 6-year-old Dawn, with Down syndrome, came barreling behind him and pushed him down. Running over to Dawn, I took her by the arm and made her help me pick up Jonathan and get him a tissue. I was shaking inside: "They shouldn't let these kids be here!" I seethed. Later, I was embarrassed to even write those words. How could I be so prejudiced?

Over time in the learning process, we come to see how bias can shape our lives without our awareness. As we identify our own feelings, we can work to find our own voices.

Biases of Others. It is often easier to spot bias or prejudice in others than it is in to see it in ourselves. Use your observation skills well: First, you can see yourself in a different light and, second, you can develop strategies for addressing the biases you may encounter. For example, Jimenez (1999) recounts an experience in a teacher support group:

> I was frightened and intimidated by some of the participants. Later, I would find out they felt the same way. When Rosa, another Chicana in the group, would question Louise, I would think to myself, "What a troublemaker." Now, as I look back, I realize I wouldn't have labeled her a troublemaker if she had been white. (p. 36)

Over time, the process of incorporating a broader perspective can help educators become more honest about who they are, and allow them to grow. Discovering messages of inferiority or superiority you internalized growing up can help you "nurture the construction of a knowledgeable, confident identity" (Wolpert, 2005, p. 2). Again, Jimenez (1999) states: "Shutting people out just keeps you from being able to peel back through all the layers of bias and misunderstanding" (p. 36).

As a student teacher, your work in the program and with the children is your first priority. Having a strategy to respond to biased behavior will support your efforts. Figure 9.6 lists questions you should ask yourself when you encounter bias.

Notice how student teacher Ellina tries to process a typical situation she encounters. In her journal she writes:

> One of my worst moments was with a child who is hard of hearing, so he has trouble speaking. During lunch time, one of the teachers said to the boy, "Say 'Teacher.'" When he couldn't, the rest of the table starting saying "Say Teacher, Say Teacher." I was waiting for the teacher to tell the children to stop, and then explain to them. But nothing happened, and the boy didn't talk for the rest of the day.

1. *What happened:* The bias was the teacher's assumption that exposing the child was OK. Mine is that you should never embarrass a child, and it reminds me of how people treated me with my polio since I couldn't walk or run as well as everyone else.

2. *Why it happened:* That teacher probably has never been in that position. She doesn't see people with hearing impairment as any different or sensitive to being pointed out.

3. *The impact of what happened:* The child stopped talking—it affected him all day and who knows how long. The kids who overheard behaved badly, teasing and practicing how to be bullies, not how to have empathy.

Figure 9.6
When You Encounter
Bias: Feel-Think-
Respond
Practice responding to
incidents involving bias
using these feel-think-
respond questions.

1. What happened?
   a. What issues of bias are involved?
   b. What is your bias in this situation?
   c. How does the situation make you feel?
   d. Is there a conflict between your own beliefs and those of other adults involved or those of the families of the children involved?
2. Why did it happen?
   a. Why do the people involved have the ideas they have?
   b. What societal images and messages are influencing them?
3. What is the impact of what happened?
   a. What is the impact on people directly involved?
   b. What is the impact on others who overhear?
4. What intervention can change what happened?
   a. What do you want to accomplish?
   b. If there is a conflict between your own beliefs and those of other adults or the families of children involved, how will you be respectful of those beliefs?
   c. What developmental issues will influence your response?
   d. What can be said to affirm the feelings and identity of each person?
   e. What questions will model investigation and encourage critical thinking rather than interrogation that will embarrass or shame?

Source: From *Start Seeing Diversity: The Basic Guide to an Anti-Bias Classroom,* by Ellen Wolpert for the committee for Boston Public Housing. Copyright © 2005 by Ellen Wolpert for the Committee for Boston Public Housing. Reprinted by permission of Redleaf Press, St. Paul, MN, www.redleafpress.org.

4. *Intervention that could change what happened:* I want the child to be protected from meanness; maybe that's not realistic. I want the kids to understand how their teasing hurt him—how do I do that with preschoolers? "Did that hurt your feelings?"—then what? "When you tease people about something they can't help, it's not OK"—what else? Maybe I need to ask the children individually. Stop the teasing; then ask "How did that make you feel?" of all the kids.

Taking Action. The biases we find in society are reflected early in school life. Student teachers who choose to address these inequalities when they arise in their programs are taking an active stance in promoting tolerance. This is not always comfortable, as evidenced by the following Reflective Incident. Yet by understanding the complexity of our diverse society, you come closer to providing an equitable educational experience for all children. As Tatum (1999) states:

> We all have a sphere of influence. Each of us needs to find our own sources of courage so that we will begin to speak. There are many problems to address, and we cannot avoid them indefinitely. . . . I have seen that meaningful dialogue can lead to effective action. Change is possible. (p. xii)

Reflective Incident "Gordon and the Pumpkin Eater"

I had an interesting experience around Halloween at the center. I downloaded an activity that included the Peter Piper poem and a cut-out project. When I read the classic poem, I realized I needed to change it. I still started it "Peter, Peter, Pumpkin Eater," but then changed the rest of it.

Instead of . . .	I changed it to . . .
"Had a wife and couldn't keep her"	"Had a wife but couldn't see her"
"Put her in a pumpkin shell and"	"Looked into a pumpkin shell and"
"There he kept her very well."	"There he saw her very well."

I was proud of myself for keeping the rhythm but getting rid of the sexist tone. I thought I had covered all the bases, but I had not. The Peter and Wife cut outs were dressed as Pilgrims. I did not see that very well, but several parents did and were vocal in their complaints to the director and my head teacher. They informed me that the school policy, formed in cooperation with parental input, was to not use anything "pilgrim" because of the barbaric practices pilgrims and missionaries perpetuated against Native Americans. I was aghast at my gaffe. I should have recognized Peter as a Pilgrim rather than a Pumpkin Eater with bad fashion sense.—Gordon

Your Thoughts

1. How would I feel?

2. What would I do?

3. What might the results be?

Creating a Climate of Acceptance

There are several concrete actions student teachers can take to create a climate of acceptance in their fieldwork sites. Several of these focus on aspects of student teaching already introduced in this book, such as the environment (Chapter 5), the curriculum (Chapter 6), teaching strategies (Chapter 3), your site or team (Chapter 7), and families (Chapter 8). We weave these ideas into all we do; at the same time, using diversity as the focal point underscores both a multicultural focus and an antibias perspective.

Preparing a Diverse Environment. As a student teacher, you know that a key part of teaching is to prepare an appropriate environment for children (see Chapter 5). How do we provide for diversity? Derman-Sparks (1989), the primary author of *Anti-Bias Curriculum,* defines the task:

A diversity-rich, stereotype-free visual and auditory environment provides the sights and sounds that young children use to begin developing positive self-awareness and comfortable relationships with others. All child care environments must reflect the rich variety between and within cultural and ethnic groups. Every adult has the responsibility to ensure that:

1. Every child in the program is represented visually.
2. The diversity in the United States is represented.
3. No stereotypical or insulting images exist. (p. 11)

Environments that are developmentally appropriate will be rich in a variety of materials; those that are also diversity-responsive will ensure that materials and activities successfully address the previous list.

Of course, no one is perfect, but it is important to be vigilant about what is used in the learning environment (refer back to the Reflective Incident). Be sure to look at the total environment; learning through outdoor play, for instance, is important for all children, and may need individual adaptations to include those with special needs. A child with autism may need a physical boundary around a garden area or a specific area to dig and plant, whereas one who is blind might need an adapted ball with a beeper noise inside (Flynn & Kieff, 2002).

Integrating Diversity into the Curriculum. Once space and materials are organized, teachers prepare the curriculum (see Chapter 6). Planned activities require following the goals of multicultural education (Kendall, 1983), and might look like Table 9.1. "The natural curiosity of young children triggers questions about differences they see among peers such as language use, behavior, skin, hair texture, and body size or weight (Klein & Chen, 2001), so curriculum can emerge from these interests.

Student teacher Miho was at a loss about what to do when Diaz's grandfather died unexpectedly in the fall. Supervising teacher Karen asked her to research how to talk to children about death, then conferred with Diaz's mother Maria about the family's plans. The next month, Maria offered to speak with the children about El Dia de los Muertos, and Diaz brought in photos of the altar they had at home. The children were fascinated, and wanted to build boxes for their loved ones (including pets). An

Student teachers experience hands-on learning when families share their interests and culture with the class.

Table 9.1 Multicultural Goals Transformed into Curriculum for Diversity
The goals of multicultural education can aid in developing a curriculum for diversity.

Goal	Curriculum Example
Teach children to respect others' cultures and values as well as their own.	With the children, cook a dish from each child's culture and serve it for snack.
Help all children function successfully in a multicultural, multiracial society.	Make people-colored fans with skin-colored paint on index cards that get fastened together with brads.
Develop a positive self-concept in those children most affected by racism, such as children of color.	Using persona dolls, do storytelling about someone being teased about their hair texture or style.
Help all children experience their differences as culturally diverse people and their similarities as human beings in positive ways.	In developing a unit on "heroes and sheroes," introduce children to the concepts of personal shields and have each make a powerful and safe one to use and share.
Encourage children to experience people of diverse cultures working together as unique parts of a whole community.	Make sequence cards to illustrate food chains in their community. Then visit those places or invite people in to "show and tell" what they do as part of the food chain.

Source: From Big as Life: The Everyday Inclusive Curriculum, by S. York, 1998, St. Paul, MN: Redleaf Press.

informational meeting was held and a packet was prepared for the families, and Miho learned how to make calaveras (sugar skulls) and to cook chayotes (a type of Mexican squash), while Karen worked with the children to make a "special place" for the boxes. Each step was documented in the entry hall, and the culminating event was a "Sharing Celebration" in which several families and teachers offered flowers, photos, and memories of their beloved dead. This example is integrated curriculum at its best, starting with individual need, emerging into cultural diversity, involving many families, and concluding with a project of great interest and meaning to all.

Developing Teaching Strategies for Diversity. The strategies around teaching diversity parallel what good teachers use with children every day. Observing, guiding, facilitating, and intervening carefully are all techniques that the effective teacher uses in developing relationships and handling children's behavior (see Chapter 3). Student teachers often feel overwhelmed by the daily interactions with young children, and the thought of adding more "tools to the kit" seems impossible. Fortunately, you will not need to master a completely new set of skills; rather, you will need to focus your efforts in some special ways.

"Can I p'ay wif you?" Nieta asks Lourdes and Sarah who are in the playhouse. "No, it's already full here," Lourdes replies. "Yeah, and we don't need anyone else," adds Sarah, while they both turn their backs on her. Student teacher Fiona has seen this happen before with Nieta, and is concerned she is being excluded because of her language skills. In fact, she notices that all the English language learners are isolated from the "power players," more so on the playground than during indoor activity time.

What can Fiona do? She is wise to attend to this issue; in an English-language classroom, the child who does not yet understand or speak English may find it difficult to interact appropriately with children and may be treated as invisible or marginalized by others. The same can be said about any child who is not of the dominant language, culture, gender, religion, or ability of the group as a whole. Several strategies may help (Derman-Sparks et al., 2006):

- *Help children develop authentic identities based on personal abilities and interests, family history, and culture rather than on notions of inferiority or superiority.* If it is OK for Nieta to be left out, then all three girls experience the results of exclusion, and may come to accept it as a reasonable, common strategy for play. Fiona intervenes by saying, "It looks like you need some shoppers in your store, Lourdes. Nieta and I have some money; do you have anything for us to buy today?" Nieta becomes a powerful figure in the play without needing words, while Lourdes and Sarah get the experience of inclusion.

- *Know, respect, and value the range of diversity of physical and social attributes among people.* By tracking what activities interest Nieta, Fiona can help her learn some vocabulary that would help her be more successful and see how she can contribute. Fiona modifies the environment by adding several tools and clothing familiar to Nieta (and not to the others). Later, she invites Nieta to start the play with her. When Lourdes and Sarah approach as newcomers, Nieta can show *them* how to play.

- *Build the capacity for caring, cooperative, and equitable interactions with others.* By observing the overall social tone of the classroom, Fiona sees that the White children seem to have a sense of entitlement that emphasizes children outdoing each other. For circle time she starts a discussion about what activities the children like to do with family and friends that show caring ("I help Mom wash the car"), then organizes a game to act out those activities with partners chosen from names in a hat. Lourdes and Nieta are partners "helping Dad give the baby a bath," and everyone laughs when Nieta splashes Lourdes!

As you work and play with the children at your site, you will find that the observing and interacting you started with (see Chapter 1) will help you develop teaching strategies for diversity, as in the My Reaction feature that follows.

My Reaction

"Me and the Shu"

I was so happy Thursday that the little boy who speaks Cantonese has started speaking and laughing with me. It was so heartwarming! The center just hired a teaching assistant who speaks Cantonese so I asked her to teach me some words. We were having broccoli for lunch and the boy said "Shu," which I knew is the word for "tree." I pantomimed getting under the "shu" and everyone at the table thought it was a riot. We all did it, saying "tree-shu." We had so much fun!

—TIANA

Promoting Equity with the Team. As mentioned in Chapter 1, placements in a practicum vary widely, particularly in the role the student teacher may play in the teaching team. Many of you will be new to your site, and so your primary connection may be to your supervising teacher, rather than to the whole team. Some of you may already be working at the fieldwork site. In that case, you may have a larger role to play on your team. In any case, do what you can to build a sense of community among the teaching team (see Chapter 7). This increases the level of communication and trust, which helps create a dialogue about diversity.

Working with Families. The first component in working with families around issues of diversity is convincing them that their home's cultural values and norms are honored (NAEYC, 2005). Involving families in the program in many ways (see Chapter 8) helps you incorporate a range of activities and ways of doing things into the life of the center. "My fellow teachers and myself always talk to the parents and find out what's going on at the home life," offers student teacher Lenoir. "I use their food sometimes because at lunch they send food I haven't seen. So at the end of the day I will ask them, 'What was the food you sent? Is it from your culture or just something you like?' It really is a conversation-starter, and I have learned a lot about families, where they are from, and what they do at home."

You do not need to know everything beforehand about every child or his or her culture. Rather, you need to learn how to *find out* what you need to know to be sensitive and responsive to every child.

Each of us is a unique manifestation of the human spirit; teaching with diversity as a cornerstone allows each child to express this spirit while also bringing everyone together in community. (See Lessons from the Field.)

"Opportunities for Every Ability"

by Elaine Francisco

Mentor/Preschool Special Needs Teacher

During my classroom's free-choice period, I observe John walk straight to the sandbox, scoop up a handful of sand, and throw it on the floor. At the same time, Erica picks up the broom and dustpan, and randomly sweeps the grains of sand as they fall to the ground. These two students have been doing this same activity for over a month. It heartens me that John, who was diagnosed with autism, and Erica, a child who has a severe language impairment, are engaging in near cooperative play. It was not long ago that both students started in my class as mere onlookers who were not interested in any type of play interaction.

Although I was an early childhood teacher for 10 years when I began to teach special education, I thought that I needed to implement a different approach in my teaching methods. Knowing that a special education environment is supposedly a "restrictive" environment, I decided I must restrict many of the hands-on, child-initiated, and discovery learning strategies that I had always believed in. I started shelving many of my classroom toys and took to designing specific goal-focused play activities for my students without considering the choices they could have made independently. This implementation deprived the children of the opportunity to engage in spontaneous play at their own pace, since I literally "dictated" what they could and could not do.

As my classroom began to look like a highly structured, well-defined environment that encouraged teacher-initiated activities, I often had moments of guilt, but always reminded myself that my class dealt with special education and should therefore be different from general education. Despite my own doubts, student teachers in early childhood special education who spent entire semesters with me observed that I did implement "best practices" in special education. They mentioned that I effectively connected with parents, addressed individual goals, was able to collaborate effectively with the IEP team, and had implemented activity-based interventions, the majority of which, unfortunately, were strictly teacher-directed.

By my third year of teaching special education, I unknowingly became a focused "interventionist," and began to emphasize my student's disabilities rather than viewing each as a "whole" child. With this newly adapted mindset, I had a true restrictive environment. I focused on planned work between an adult and child rather than promoting spontaneous child play as I aimed to promote language and social cognition.

Then I was invited to apply to an ECE mentor teacher program. Part of the application process was a self-assessment and classroom environmental rating, after which evaluators would visit my classroom. I was fortunate to be given honest feedback by the evaluators as they used the tool to assess my classroom. I passed many areas of the rating, but the findings were a wake-up call for me. I did not have enough toys out, my classroom materials did not represent the diversity of my student population, and my outdoor play activities failed to provide choices for my students. Even my sandbox was not part of everyday play!

To make it short and simple, I had lost sight of my own early childhood "roots" in the quest to be a competent teacher in special education. I had forgotten how promoting spontaneous child's play is crucial to the development of *every* child. In my focus on planned adult–child interactions, I had moved toward an idea of isolated play with such limited choices that the children's "diversity" of special needs was overriding their "universality" of being children. I mistakenly judged their abilities prior to giving them opportunities.

Now, as I observe John and Erica play in the sandbox area, I am inspired by the conviction that someday, both will advance their play as I consistently give them multiple opportunities to interact with materials and with their peers throughout the day. I feel relieved that once again, I regard spontaneous play as a fundamental element in an early childhood classroom without which learning becomes an adult's prescription rather than a child's personal discovery. They can do more, I can do better, and we all can grow together.

Practicum Activity

Examine the toys and interest areas in your program: Are there any forms of bias present? Which materials would you eliminate (and why) and what might you want to add?

Journaling Assignment

How aware are you of your own identity (culture, race/ethnicity, gender, language, ability, religion, age, social class, temperament)? What experiences have you had with feeling excluded because of your background?

Resources

Allen, K. E., Cowdery, G. E. (2005). *The exceptional child: Inclusion in early childhood education.* Clifton Park, NY: Thomson Delmar Learning.

BANDTEC (Bay Area Network for Diversity Training: Building Equity and Social Justice for Children and Families. (2006). *Reaching for Answers: Forum on Diversity in Early Childhood Education.* San Mateo, CA: San Mateo County Office of Education.

Banks, J. A. (2001). *Cultural diversity and education: Foundations, curriculum, and teaching.* Boston: Allyn & Bacon.

Carter, M., Curtis, D. (1994). *Training teachers: A harvest of theory and practice.* St. Paul, MN: Redleaf Press.

Clay, J. W. (2004, November). Creating safe, just places to learn for children of lesbian and gay parents: The NAEYC code of ethics in action. *Young Children, 59*(6), 34–38.

Derman-Sparks, L. and the A.B.C. Task Force. (1989). Anti-bias curriculum: Tools for empowering young children. Washington, DC: National Association for the Education of Young Children.

Derman-Sparks, L., Ramsey, P. G., & Olsen Edwards, J. (2006). *What if all the kids are white?* New York: Teachers College Press.

Flynn, L. L., & Kieff, J. (2002). Including everyone in outdoor play. *Young Children, 57*(3), 20–26.

Gonzalez-Mena, J. (2005). *Diversity in early care and education: Honoring differences* (4th ed.). Boston: McGraw-Hill.

Gorden, A. M., & Browne, K. W. (2008). *Beginnings and beyond: Foundations in early childhood education* (7th ed.). Clifton Park, NY: Thomson Delmar Learning.

Gordon, A. M., & Browne, K. W. (1996). *Guiding young children in a diverse society.* Boston: Allyn & Bacon.

Jimenez, L. I. (1999). Finding a voice. In C. Alvarado, et al. (Eds.), *In our own way: How anti-bias work shapes our lives.* St. Paul, MN: Redleaf Press.

Kendall, F. E. (1983). *Diversity in the classroom: A multicultural approach to the education of young children.* New York: Teachers College Press.

Klein, M. D., & Chen, D. (2001). *Working with children from culturally diverse backgrounds.* Albany, NY: Delmar.

Lynch, E. W., & Hanson, M. J. (1995). *Developing cross-cultural competence: A guide for working with young children and their families* (4th ed.). Baltimore: Paul H. Brookes.

National Association for the Education of Young Children. (1995). *Responding to linguistic and cultural diversity: Recommendations for effective early childhood education.* Retrieved from http://www.naeyc.org/about/positions/pdf/PSDIV98.pdf

National Association for the Education of Young Children. (2005). *Many languages, many cultures: Respecting and responding to diversity.* Washington, DC: Author.

Phillips, C. (1995). Culture: A process that empowers. In P. Mangione (Ed.), *Infant/toddler caregiving: A guide to culturally sensitive care.* Sacramento, CA: California Department of Education Press.

Rusch, K. (2001, August 22). Nonverbal communication can be vital for immigrants. *San Francisco Sunday Examiner & Chronicle,* p. C2.

Saxton, R. (2004). A place for faith. In A. M. Gordon & K. W. Browne, *Beginnings and beyond: Foundations in early childhood education* (6th ed.). Clifton Park, NY: Thomson Delmar Learning.

Tatum, B. D. (1999). *Why are all the Black kids sitting together in the cafeteria? and other conversations about race.* New York: Basic Books.

Thomas, A., & Chess, S. (1977). *Temperament and development.* New York: Brunner/Mazel.

Trawick-Smith, J. (2006). *Early childhood development: A multi-cultural perspective.* Upper Saddle River, NJ: Merrill/Pearson.

U.S. Census Bureau. (2005, February). *Foreign born population tops 34 million, Census Bureau estimates.* Retrieved November 19, 2007, from www.census.gov/population/www/socdemo/foreign.html

U.S. Census Bureau. (2006). American Community Survey. Washington, DC: United States Census Bureau. Retrieved October 29, 2007, from http://www.factfinder.census.gov/serviet

Wolpert, E. (2005). *Start seeing diversity: The basic guide to an anti-bias classroom.* St. Paul, MN: Redleaf Press.

York, S. (1998). *Big as life: The everyday inclusive curriculum.* St. Paul, MN: Redleaf Press.

Web Sites

Early Childhood Research Institute on Culturally and Linguistically Appropriate Services
http:// clas.uiuc.edu

Individuals with Disabilities Education Act
www.ideapractices.org

National Association for Bilingual Education
www.nabe.org

National Association for Multicultural Education
www.nameorg.org

National Association for the Education of Young Children
www.naeyc.org

National Black Child Development Institute
www.nbcdi.org

Teaching in Various Settings: My Reflections

The purpose of Chapters 1 to 9 of this text was to introduce you to the key components of student teaching. The features in the chapters offered a context for the feelings, reactions, and behaviors both you and others might have in difficult situations. You now have some experience in how self-inventory and evaluation leads to growth and more effective teaching.

The reflective process is both internal and external and helps you

- examine your *self* (thoughts, feelings, reactions);
- use the *experiences* you have had (teaching, babysitting, parenting, coaching); and
- look at the *standards* for professional behavior (Code of Ethical Conduct, developmentally appropriate practices).

How It Works

This chapter includes forms for eight types of early childhood programs to help you personalize your teaching experience in greater depth and to stretch your reflective abilities. The workbook format encourages you to start with divergent thinking by looking at your own feelings and actions, and then engage in convergent thinking as you identify resources, strategies, and likely results.

The forms incorporate the following content:

1. A *description* of each of the types of early childhood programs, with key characteristics and challenges appropriate to that setting. You will use the form for the specific type of program in which you are doing your student teaching.

2. A space for you to describe *your experience* with this program, and identify a challenge you are having.

3. A section called *My Reflections,* where you will reflect on the challenge you face by responding to these questions:

How do I feel?

What can I do?

Whom can I talk to?

What do I bring to the current situation?

How does my experience in ECE so far help me?

What professional standards can I use as resources?

Reflecting on what is happening to you while you teach helps you act, not react. "How quickly we go to a solution," commented student teacher Jamie. "Since the children move so fast and everything seems so urgent, I don't think things through—even afterward." If you go through this process, you will be able to discern patterns not obvious in the moment, and thus be able to make a broader, deeper impact. Moreover, you will be able to consider your own biases and insights in ways that will help you incorporate what you are experiencing in the classroom into learning that will last. "If you talk and write about it, it is like magic," concluded Jamie. "It will get better, and you will become a teacher!"

"From the types available, to the numbers of children who attend . . . the name of the game in early childhood programs is diversity" (Gordon & Browne, 2007, p. 49). Because the age range in early childhood is birth to age 8, and programs for children run from once a week to full days (and beyond), group care arrangements serve many needs and have varied features. Programs in early childhood settings are defined by these elements:

- Age of children
- Philosophical or theoretical approach
- Program goals
- Sponsoring agency
- Teaching staff—number, composition, training
- Environment—size, shape, location
- Community makeup—culture, economic, linguistic, geographic
- Resources structure and stability

Because of this diversity—as well as the uniqueness of each student teacher—what you encounter in your practicum will also vary. Use this section to find the type of program that best matches your fieldwork site and to reflect and articulate your experience there. You can also use this section to compare similarities and differences in the group settings of other student teachers.

We have listed the major kinds of programs you are likely to come across in student teaching, organized roughly by age of the children served. Consider photocopying the appropriate forms and using them as situations arise over the course of your student teaching.

The Programs

Family Child Care

Type and Description

Key Characteristics: A family home setting, small and personalized, often in the neighborhood, which allows a caregiver (alone or with a helper) to work at home while caring for other children; homes often reflect the cultural and ethnic background of their clients, and provide continuity and emotional support over a period of time; child care provider is administrator and manager of a small business.

Age Range: Infancy through elementary school age.

Group Size: Anywhere between 2 and 12; usually around 6 children.

Setting or Environment: Private home.

Curriculum: May or may not have a formal curriculum; provides age-appropriate activities.

Challenges: Wide variety of age levels; isolation from other child care providers; effects on family life of the caregiver; space and storage issues for family and for program; individualized age-appropriate activities across a wide age span; long hours for child care provider; direct contact with parents; need to follow standard business practices and collect fees; regulation requirements for licensing, health, and safety; maintain environment; and time needed for professional development and early childhood education.

My Experience with This Program:

_____

_____

_____

_____

A Challenge I Face:

_____

_____

_____

_____

My Reflections:

How do I feel?

_____

_____

What can I do?

_____

_____

Whom can I talk to?

_____

_____

What do I bring to the current situation?

_____

_____

How does my experience in ECE so far help me?

_____

_____

What professional standards can I use as resources?

_____

_____

Infant–Toddler Care

Type and Description

Key Characteristics: May be full- or part-time care; combines physical care and emotional attachment with intellectual stimulation; relationships with families is most important; one-to-one physical care and routines used as learning opportunities; caregivers need sensitivity to interpret needs of babies and toddlers; gentle, extensively personal involvement of the caregiver is required; for infants, caregiving routines are the heart of the program; with toddlers, routines are opportunities for self-expression and language-rich interactions are key; low child–staff ratio and small group sizes; primary caregiving method of staffing is common.

Age Range: Infancy through 2 years of age; may be organized in narrow age groupings.

Group Size: Generally small; guidelines suggest infant groups of fewer than 6 with a staff–child ratio of 1:3; for toddlers the group size is slightly larger, up to 12 2-year-olds with ratio of 1:4.

Setting or Environment: Often part of a larger child care center; church-housed; occasionally in private homes.

Curriculum: Includes feeding, diapering, playing, helping with napping (infants); fostering independence through routines (toddlers), strong prosocial and language-rich experiences.

Challenges: Need for caregivers to provide individual attention; caregiving routines may bore teachers; expensive due to staff–child ratio; quality and stability of staff; parent–child attachment and separation issues difficult.

My Experience with This Program:

_____

_____

_____

_____

A Challenge I Face:

_____

_____

_____

_____

My Reflections:

How do I feel?

_____

_____

_____

What can I do?

_____

_____

_____

Whom can I talk to?

_____

_____

_____

What do I bring to the current situation?

_____

_____

_____

How does my experience in ECE so far help me?

_____

_____

_____

What professional standards can I use as resources?

_____

_____

_____

Nursery Schools

Type and Description

Key Characteristics: Also called preschools; often part-day (2 1/2 to 4 hours) and variable weekdays (Monday, Wednesday, Friday or Tuesday, Thursday); focus is on social competence, emotional well-being and self-expression; often characterized as an enrichment program; the importance of play is underscored so that children are encouraged to make their own choices, select their own playmates, work at their own rate; teacher's role is to support children's learning through play, mediate social interactions, observe for informal assessment, and work in small groups.

Age Range: May be mixed ages (2 1/2 to 5 years) or single-year range.

Group Size: Often fewer than 20 children.

Setting or Environment: Churches or synagogues, community centers, elementary schools, customized buildings.

Curriculum: Provides age-appropriate activities; may reflect a specific philosophy (Montessori, High/Scope, Reggio Emilia, etc.); free play emphasized for children to initiate their own activities; a highlight is balance in scheduling and a wide variety of activities; curriculum may overemphasize beginning academics.

Challenges: Possible homogeneous groupings; widely varying teaching qualifications; costs can be high; families' high demands on teaching staff; may be open only during school year; can be fast-paced because of time constraints; intermittent days may cause adjustment problems.

My Experience with This Program:

_____

_____

_____

_____

A Challenge I Face:

_____

_____

_____

_____

My Reflections:

How do I feel?

_____

_____

_____

What can I do?

_____

_____

_____

Whom can I talk to?

_____

_____

_____

What do I bring to the current situation?

_____

_____

_____

How does my experience in ECE so far help me?

_____

_____

_____

What professional standards can I use as resources?

_____

_____

_____

Child Care

Type and Description

Key Characteristics: Also called preschools; provides full-day service, with some variable days (Monday, Wednesday, Friday or Tuesday, Thursday); cares for children while parents work; focus is on health and nutrition as well as cognitive stimulation and social-emotional development; the importance of play is underscored so that children are encouraged to make their own choices, select their own playmates, work at their own rate; provides a balanced day (indoor/outdoor, resting/nap; meals); teacher's role combines education and care (supports children's learning through play, and integrates routines into the program); work in small and large groups.

Age Range: May be mixed ages (21/2 to 5 years) or single-year range.

Group Size: Often fewer than 20 children.

Setting or Environment: Churches or synagogues, community centers, elementary schools, customized buildings, corporate on-site settings.

Curriculum: Provides age-appropriate activities; usually eclectic approach, less likely to reflect a specific philosophy (Montessori, High/Scope, Reggio Emilia, etc.); free play with a wide variety of activity choices is balanced with routines and daily care.

Challenges: Long hours for children and staff; high staff turnover and substitutes; mixed quality; informal connection with families; maintaining environment difficult; low-income families may require more comprehensive resources; high child–staff ratios; wide variations in teacher qualifications.

My Experience with This Program:

_____

_____

_____

_____

A Challenge I Face:

_____

_____

_____

_____

My Reflections:

How do I feel?

_____

_____

_____

What can I do?

_____

_____

_____

Whom can I talk to?

_____

_____

_____

What do I bring to the current situation?

_____

_____

_____

How does my experience in ECE so far help me?

_____

_____

_____

What professional standards can I use as resources?

_____

_____

_____

Head Start

Type and Description

Key Characteristics: Provided the model for early intervention and put early childhood education into the American public mindset; federally funded, comprehensive program providing health, education, and social services to children and families; requires parent participation and involvement; enlists community collaboration; provides half- or full-day service; a leader in multicultural education and inclusion of children with special needs; focus is on health and nutrition as well as cognitive stimulation and social-emotional development; the importance of family and community is underscored; provides a balanced day (indoor/outdoor, resting/nap; meals); teacher's role combines education and care (supports children's learning through play, and integrates routines into the program); work in small and large groups.

Age Range: Primarily for 3- to 4-year-olds; Early Head Start provides for children under 3.

Group Size: Often fewer than 20 children.

Setting or Environment: Churches or synagogues, community centers, elementary schools, customized buildings; government office buildings.

Curriculum: Provides age-appropriate activities; uses prescribed Head Start guidelines for all aspects of program development; free play is balanced with daily health routines and focused small-group work.

Challenges: Sufficient federal funding; work with low-income families with significant disadvantages; political interference; controversial assessment policies; staff quality and retention; high level of English language learners.

My Experience with This Program:

_____

_____

_____

_____

A Challenge I Face:

_____

_____

_____

_____

My Reflections:

How do I feel?

_____

_____

_____

What can I do?

_____

_____

_____

Whom can I talk to?

_____

_____

_____

What do I bring to the current situation?

_____

_____

_____

How does my experience in ECE so far help me?

_____

_____

_____

What professional standards can I use as resources?

_____

_____

_____

Parent Cooperatives

Type and Description

Key Characteristics: Usually referred to as co-ops, often part-day (2 1/2 to 4 hours) and variable week-days (Monday, Wednesday, Friday or Tuesday, Thursday); organized and managed by parents, including working in the classroom on a scheduled basis and teacher hiring; may be half- or full-day; often nonprofit; monthly parent meetings are common and usually deal with child-rearing practices as well as program issues; focus is on child learning and parent education; often characterized as an enrichment program; parents raise funds, influence school philosophy, and manage the budget; role of the teacher is to provide sound educational experience for children and guidance for parent education.

Age Range: May be mixed ages (2 1/2 to 5 years) or single-year range.

Group Size: Ranges from 15 to 30 children.

Setting or Environment: Churches or synagogues, or in customized buildings, as part of adult education schools.

Curriculum: Varies widely and depends on parental influence.

Challenges: Need to work well with adults and conduct parent education meetings; if only one hired teacher, isolation from other professionals; time-consuming; may exclude working families; organize maintenance for parent work.

My Experience with This Program:

_____

_____

_____

_____

A Challenge I Face:

_____

_____

_____

_____

My Reflections:

How do I feel?

_____

_____

_____

What can I do?

_____

_____

_____

Whom can I talk to?

_____

_____

_____

What do I bring to the current situation?

_____

_____

_____

How does my experience in ECE so far help me?

_____

_____

_____

What professional standards can I use as resources?

_____

_____

_____

Kindergarten

Type and Description

Key Characteristics: A transition year from early childhood to a more formal school setting; more focused on academic skills; half- or full-day; children's independence is critical to success; teacher's role is to prepare children for first grade, make assessments, and work with children in both small and large groupings; play is often not valued as a tool for learning, but rather standards for performance are emphasized.

Age Range: Generally 5-year-olds; entrance age is an arbitrary date established by individual states.

Group Size: Typically 20 or more children.

Setting or Environment: Elementary public and private schools, religious institutions, some preschool or child care centers.

Curriculum: Ranges from relatively unstructured, free play settings to highly structured teacher-directed academics; subjects are often taught as separate skills, such as beginning reading; small groups may be organized around skill areas; emphasis on content over process.

Challenges: Diverse needs of children; need to welcome family involvement; incorporate diversity; inappropriate use of testing and use of retention; pressure on teachers to focus on academics rather than on children and DAP; teachers often not familiar with child development principles.

My Experience with This Program:

_____

_____

_____

_____

A Challenge I Face:

_____

_____

_____

_____

My Reflections

How do I feel?

_____

_____

_____

What can I do?

_____

_____

_____

Whom can I talk to?

_____

_____

_____

What do I bring to the current situation?

_____

_____

_____

How does my experience in ECE so far help me?

_____

_____

_____

What professional standards can I use as resources?

_____

_____

_____

School-Age Care

Type and Description

Key Characteristics: Also called out-of-school-time or after-school care; provides wraparound service, before and after the regular elementary school day; provides a safe environment for supervising children; flexible hours, reasonable tuition; encourages self-directed and self-paced activities; teacher's role is to supervise and provide after-school activities for creative expression and cooperation.

Age Range: Mixed ages, typically kindergarten through either third to fifth grade.

Group Size: Large; often greater than 30 children, with staff–child ratios of up to 1:12.

Setting or Environment: Child care center, public and private schools, churches or synagogues, family child care homes, community centers, worksites, and recreation and youth facilities.

Curriculum: Provides age-appropriate activities; usually eclectic approach, creative activities and projects, and informal "clubs" or "teams"; free play with a wide variety of activity choices balanced with time for homework; supplements and supports the regular school program; may include library visits, swim lessons, music time, and so on.

Challenges: Long day for children; high staff turnover and substitutes; mixed quality; informal and infrequent connection with families; maintaining environment difficult; high child–staff ratios; wide variations in teacher qualifications; sparse collaboration with elementary teachers.

My Experience with This Program:

_____

_____

_____

_____

A Challenge I Face:

_____

_____

_____

_____

My Reflections:

How do I feel?

_____

_____

_____

What can I do?

_____

_____

_____

Whom can I talk to?

_____

_____

_____

What do I bring to the current situation?

_____

_____

_____

How does my experience in ECE so far help me?

_____

_____

_____

What professional standards can I use as resources?

_____

_____

_____

Resource

Gordon, A. M. & Browne, K. W. (2007). *Beginning essentials in early childhood education*. Clifton Park, NY: Thomson Delmar Learning.

index

....

The letter *f* or *t* following a page number denotes a figure or table respectively.